ISBN 978-1-333-70787-3
PIBN 10515786

1 MONTH OF
FREE
READING

at

www.ForgottenBooks.com

By purchasing this book you are eligible for one month membership to ForgottenBooks.com, giving you unlimited access to our entire collection of over 700,000 titles via our web site and mobile apps.

To claim your free month visit: www.forgottenbooks.com/free515786

English
Français
Deutsche
Italiano
Español
Português

www.forgottenbooks.com

Mythology Photography **Fiction**
Fishing Christianity **Art** Cooking
Essays Buddhism Freemasonry
Medicine **Biology** Music **Ancient
Egypt** Evolution Carpentry Physics
Dance Geology **Mathematics** Fitness
Shakespeare **Folklore** Yoga Marketing
Confidence Immortality Biographies
Poetry **Psychology** Witchcraft
Electronics Chemistry History **Law**
Accounting **Philosophy** Anthropology
Alchemy Drama Quantum Mechanics
Atheism Sexual Health **Ancient History**
Entrepreneurship Languages Sport
Paleontology Needlework Islam
Metaphysics Investment Archaeology
Parenting Statistics Criminology
Motivational

FIJI AND THE FIJIANS.

VOL. I.

THE ISLANDS AND THEIR INHABITANTS.

BY

THOMAS WILLIAMS,

LATE MISSIONARY IN FIJI.

EDITED BY

GEORGE STRINGER ROWE.

LONDON:

ALEXANDER HEYLIN, 28, PATERNOSTER ROW.

1858.

LONDON :

PRINTED BY WILLIAM NICHOLS,

82, IONDON WALL.

PREFACE.

THE information contained in this volume is the result of the patient and intelligent research of the Rev. Thomas Williams, of Adelaide, during his thirteen years' residence as a Wesleyan Missionary in Fiji. Some additions have been made of facts which have transpired since Mr. Williams gathered and arranged the fruit of his own personal observations and inquiries.

As to the spelling and pronunciation of Fijian words, some few remarks are necessary. The general practice has hitherto been to represent—often very imperfectly —the sounds of the Fijian by English vowels. Captain Cook used this method with all Polynesian words; but, in his time, the Oceanic languages had not been reduced to a written form. Now that this has been effected in 'many instances, the practice just named must necessarily lead to misconception and confusion.

The Missionaries who have given to these languages a fixed orthography, have wisely adopted the Roman alphabet, and a system of vowels having the Italian power, which met the requirements of the case far better than the almost exceptional sounds of the English vowels.

As regards the consonants, the Missionaries found that the Fijian did not require all the characters used by ourselves : some of these were therefore rejected, while some were employed where we have recourse to a clumsy combination. Thus, for instance, they have taken the unnecessary *C* to express the soft dental *Th*.

There are no sounds in the Fijian peculiar to itself; but it has characteristic compound consonants. These are *Mb, Nd, Ng* and *Ng-g.* That is to say, the *b* is never pronounced without *m* preceding; the *d* never without *n*, and so on.

In this work, therefore,—

1. The vowels in Fijian words have the Italian pronunciation: *a,* as in *father; e,* like *a* in *mate; i,* as in *machine; o,* as in *pole; u,* as *oo* in *pool. All* the vowels are sounded.

2. The consonants have the same power as in English; except the following: *c* represents *th,* as in *that; B—mb; D—nd; G—ng; Q—ng-g.* Thus *Cama* is pronounced thama; *Bole—*mbole; *Dalo—*ndalo; *Gaga* —nganga; *Qia—*nggia.

3. In *proper names* only these peculiar combinations have, throughout the book, been represented by their English equivalents. Thus, Bau is spelt Mbau; and the name of its King, Cakobau, is written Thakombau.

For further information on these points, the reader is referred to the Chapter on Language, for which he is indebted to the Rev. John Dury Geden, of Didsbury.

This work also owes much to Miss Elizabeth Farmer, whose clever pencil has prepared most of the engravings which embellish its pages.

G. S. R.

London,
November, 1858.

CONTENTS.

LIST OF ILLUSTRATIONS.

VOL I.

Aiwa I.

Oneata I.

Observatory I.

O N E A T A   P A S S A G E
or Channel

Alailaka Reef

Matau Reef

Olorua

Vao Reef

Tavunuku R.
Chicki R.

Mothe I.

Komo I.

Koroni I.

Komaporu Reef

Talouno R

Tavunasithi.

Namuka I.

Levu Reef

Vuanggava I.

Kambara

Yangasa I.

Thikondua Reef
Kimaivo Reef
Revarreva Reef

Marambo I.

Ninukimiki Reef
Teteka Reef

Vulanga I.

Ongea I.

Nukusonga Reef

FIJI AND THE FIJIANS.

CHAPTER I.

FIJI.

THE Fiji group includes the islands lying between the latitudes of 15° 30' and 20° 30' S., and the longitudes of 177° E. and 178° W., comprising, among others, what were named by Tasman, " Prince William's Islands," and " Heeniskirk's Shoals," extending over about 40,000 square miles of the South Pacific, and forming a connecting link between the abodes of the Malayan and Papuan races which inhabit the widely-spread Polynesia.

The way of writing the name of this group is so remarkably varied as to deserve notice. Beetee, Fegee, Fejee, Feegee, Feejee, Feeje, Fidjee, Fidje, Fidgee, Fidschi, Fiji, Feigee, Vihi, Viji, and Viti, are forms that have come under my own observation. *Fiji* and *Viti* are correct; *Fiji* being the name in the windward, and *Viti* in the leeward, parts of the group.

More than two hundred years have elapsed since the discovery of these islands by Abel Jansen Tasman, the Dutch navigator, since whose voyage in 1643 they remained unvisited until Captain Cook lay-to off an island in the windward group, naming it "Turtle Island." In 1789 Captain Bligh, in the "Bounty's" launch, saw a portion of the group, and passed through other parts of it when commanding the "Providence" in 1792. In 1796 the "Duff," under the command of Captain Wilson, seems to have followed the same course as Tasman, and was nearly lost, just

B

touching the reef off Taviuni.   About the year 1806 Fiji began to be visited by traders for the purpose of procuring sandal-wood to burn before Chinese idols, or biche-de-mar to gratify the palate of Chinese epicures.   It was only from the men engaged in this traffic that anything was heard about the islands or their inhabitants; and, beyond the scanty information supplied by Captain Cook, neither standard geographies nor Admiralty charts deserve confidence.   Recent visits by British ships of war, added to the elaborate survey of the group by the United States Exploring Expedition, have resulted in more correct information.*

The early history of Fiji is necessarily obscure.   Whether the first stranger who gazed upon its extent and beauty was a Tongan or European, is doubtful.   If it can be admitted that up to the time of Captain Cook's visit to the Friendly Islanders, in 1772, they were unused to war, and were then only beginning to practise its horrors as learned by them in Fiji, the probability is in favour of the latter.   But whether these islanders, age after age, enjoyed the peace implied in the above supposition, is more than questionable.   The evil passions "whence come wars and fightings" are, in Tongan nature, of ruling power; and to suppose these at rest in a thousand heathen bosoms for a single year, is extremely difficult,—a difficulty which grows as we increase either the number of persons or the length of time.   Tongan inter-

* The following works contain reliable information concerning the islands and inhabitants of Fiji :—

Wilkes's Narrative of the U. S. Exploring Expedition, 1838–1842. New York.   (Two abridged editions have been published in England.)

Captain Erskine's Journal of a Cruise among the Islands of the Western Pacific. London. 1853.

Life in Feejee: or, Five Years among the Cannibals. By a Lady. Boston. 1851.

First and *Second Missionary Visits to the Friendly and Feejee Islands.* By the Rev. Walter Lawry. London.

Journal of a Deputation to the Southern World. By the Rev. Robert Young. London. 1855.

H. M. S. "Herald," under the command of Captain H. M. Denham, R.N., F.R.S., has now been engaged for some time in exploring and more accurately surveying the islands, from which expedition the most valuable results may be expected.

course with Fiji dates far back, and originated, undoubtedly, in their canoes being driven among the windward islands by strong easterly winds. More than a hundred years ago the recollection of the first of such voyages was lost, which seems to put back its occurrence even beyond Tasman's visit in 1643.

About the year 1804 a number of convicts escaped from New South Wales and settled among the islands. Most of these desperadoes lived either on Mbau or Rewa, the chiefs of which allowed them whatever they chose to demand, receiving, in return, their aid in carrying on war. The new settlers made themselves dreaded by the natives, who were awed by the murderous effect of their fire-arms. The hostile chiefs, seeing their bravest warriors fall in battle without an apparent cause, believed their enemies to be more than human, against whom no force of theirs availed, whose victory was always sure, while their progress invariably spread terror and death. No thought of improving and consolidating the power thus won seems to have been entertained by the whites. Had such a desire possessed them, the absolute government of the entire group lay within their reach; but their ambition never rose beyond a life of indolence, and an unrestrained gratification of the vilest passions. Some of them were men of the most desperate wickedness, being regarded as monsters even by the ferocious cannibals with whom they associated. These lawless men were twenty-seven in number on their arrival, but in a few years the greater part had ended their career, having fallen in the native wars, or in deadly quarrels among themselves. A Swede, named Savage, who had some redeeming traits in his character, and was acknowledged as head man by the whites, was drowned and eaten by the natives at Weilea, in 1813. In 1824 only two, and in 1840 but one, of his companions survived. This last was an Irishman named Connor, who stood in the same relation to the King of Rewa as Savage had done to the King of Mbau. His influence among the natives was so great, that all his desires, some of which were of the most inhuman kind, were gratified. The King of Rewa would always avenge, and often in the most cruel manner, the real or fancied wrongs of this man. If he desired the death of any native, the chief would send for the doomed man, and direct him to make and heat an oven, into which, when red-hot, the victim was cast, having been murdered by another man sent for the purpose.

Soon after the death of his patron, Paddy Connor left Rewa. He was thoroughly Fijianized, and of such depraved character that the white residents who had since settled in the islands drove him from among them, being afraid of so dangerous a neighbour. At the close of life his thoughts seemed only occupied about rearing pigs and fowls, and increasing the number of his children from forty-eight to fifty.

These men are thus mentioned because of their close connexion with the rise of Mbau and Rewa, which two places owe their present superiority to their influence, the former having long been the most powerful state in Fiji.

The entire group comprises not fewer than two hundred and twenty-five islands and islets, about eighty of which are inhabited. Among these, every variety of outline can be found, from the simple form of the coral isle to the rugged and often majestic grandeur of volcanic structure.

The islands in the eastern part of the Archipelago are small, and have a general resemblance to each other: towards the west they are large and diversified. The two largest are superior to any found in the vast ocean-field stretching thence to the Sandwich Islands; while the ever-changing beauties of scenery enable the voyager, as he threads the intricate navigation among reefs and islands, to share the feelings thus expressed by Commodore Wilkes: "So beautiful was their aspect, that I could scarcely bring my mind to the realizing sense of the well known fact, that they were the abode of a savage, ferocious, and treacherous race of cannibals." *

When each island of so large a group has a claim to be

* "U. S. Exploring Expedition," vol. iii., p. 46.

noticed, selection is difficult, and the temptation to detail strong. It must not, however, be yielded to, a few examples sufficing to give a general idea of the whole.

YATHATA and VATUVARA are placed by geologists in a class that has long been in high favour as the fairy-lands of the South Seas. They are composed of sand and coral *débris*, covered with a deep soil of vegetable mould. Yathata is hilly and fertile. Of this class there are few in Fiji. They are from two to six miles in circumference, having the usual belt of white sand, and the circlet of cocoa-nuts with their foliage of "pristine vigour and perennial green." Such islands have generally one village, inhabited by fifty or one hundred oppressed natives.

The other islands to windward are of volcanic formation, their shore only having a coral base. VULANGA is one of this class, and appears as though its centre had been blown out by violent explosions, leaving only a circumferent rim, which to the west and south is broad, and covered with rocks of black scoria rising to a height of nearly two hundred feet; but to the north-east is narrow and broken. This rim encircles an extensive sheet of water of a dark blue colour, studded with scoriaceous islets, enamelled with green, and worn away between the extremes of high and low water until they resemble huge trees of a mushroom form; thus giving a most picturesque effect to this sheltered haven of unbroken calm.

My first entrance to this lagoon was made at the risk of life; and the attempt would be vain to tell how welcome were its quiet waters after the stormy peril outside. A mountainous surf opposed the strong current which forced its way through the intricate passage, causing a most terrific whirl and commotion, in the midst of which the large canoe was tossed about like a splinter. The excitement of the time was intense, and the impressions then made were indelible. The manly voice of Tubou Toutai, issuing his commands amid the thunder of the breakers, and the shrieks of affrighted women; the labouring of the canoe in its heaving bed of foam; the strained exertions of the men

at the steer-oar; the anxiety which showed itself on every
face; were all in broad contrast with the felt security, the
easy progress, and undisturbed repose which were attained
the moment the interior of the basin was reached. Vulanga, although having its own beauty, is so barren that
little except hardy timber is found growing upon it. Its
gullies are bare of earth, so that neither the yam nor the
banana repays culture. Smaller roots, with fish, which
abound here, and *yavato*,—a large wood maggot,—give food
to the inhabitants of four villages.

MOTHE, lying to the N.E. of Vulanga, is very fruitful,
having an undulating surface much more free from wood
than the islands to the south. A fortress occupies its
highest elevation, in walking to which the traveller finds
himself surrounded by scenery of the richest loveliness. A
sandy beach of seven miles nearly surrounds it. There are
many islands of this size in the group, each containing
from 200 to 400 inhabitants.

LAKEMBA, the largest of the eastern islands, is nearly
round, having a diameter of five or six miles, and a
population of about 2,000 souls.

TOTOYA, MOALA, NAIRAI, KORO, NGAU, MBENGGA,
exhibit on a larger scale the beauties of those islands already
named, having, in addition, the imposing charms of volcanic
irregularities. Among their attractions are high mountains, abrupt precipices, conical hills, fantastic turrets and
crags of rock frowning down like olden battlements, vast
domes, peaks shattered into strange forms; native towns on
eyrie cliffs, apparently inaccessible; and deep ravines, down
which some mountain stream, after long murmuring in its
stony bed, falls headlong, glittering as a silver line on a
block of jet, or spreading, like a sheet of glass, over bare
rocks which refuse it a channel. Here also are found the
softer features of rich vales, cocoa-nut groves, clumps of
dark chestnuts, stately palms and bread-fruit, patches
of graceful bananas, or well tilled taro-beds, mingling
in unchecked luxuriance, and forming, with the wild
reef-scenery of the girdling shore, its beating surf, and

far-stretching ocean beyond, pictures of surpassing beauty.

MATUKU is eminent for loveliness where all are lovely. These islands are from fifteen to thirty miles in circumference, having populations of from 1,000 to 7,000 each.

MBAU is a small island, scarcely a mile long, joined to the main—Viti Levu—by a long flat of coral, which at low water is nearly dry, and at high water fordable. The town, bearing the same name as the island, is one of the most striking in appearance of any in Fiji, covering, as it does, a great part of the island with irregularly placed houses of all sizes, and tall temples with projecting ridge-poles, interspersed with unsightly canoe-sheds. Here is concentrated the chief political power of Fiji. Its inhabitants comprise natives of Mbau and the Lasakau and Soso tribes.

TAVIUNI—commonly called Somosomo, from its town of that name being the residence of the ruling chiefs—is too fine an island to be overlooked. It is about twenty-five miles long, with a coast of sixty miles, and consists of one vast mountain, gradually rising to a central ridge of 2,100 feet elevation. Fleecy clouds generally hide its summit, where stretches a considerable lake, pouring through an outlet to the west a stream which, after tumbling and dashing along its narrow bed, glides quietly through the chief town, furnishing it with a good supply of fresh water. A smaller outlet to the east discharges enough water to form a small but beautiful cascade. This lake is supposed to have as its bed the crater of an extinct volcano, an idea supported by the quantity of volcanic matter found on the island. However wild and terrible the appearance of the island once, it is now covered with luxuriance and beauty beyond the conception of the most glowing imagination. Perhaps every characteristic of Fijian scenery is found on Somosomo, while all the tropical vegetables are produced here in perfection. It has only a land-reef, which is often very narrow, and in many places entirely wanting, breaking, towards Tasman's Straits, into detached patches.

KANDAVU is another large and mountainous island, twenty-five miles long, by six or eight wide. It has a very irregular shore, abounds in valuable timber, and has a population of from 10,000 to 13,000.

A good idea of the general appearance of these islands is obtained by regarding them as the elevated portions of submerged continents. The interior is, in many instances, a single hill or mountain, and, in many others, a range, the slopes of which, with the plains mostly found at their feet, constitute the island.

There yet remain to be noticed the two large islands, which, when compared with those stretching away to the east, assume the importance of continents.

VANUA LEVU (Great Land) is more than one hundred miles long, having an average breadth of twenty-five miles. Its western extremity is notable as being the only part of Fiji in which sandal-wood can be produced. The opposite point of the island is deeply indented by the Natawa Bay, which is forty miles long, and named by the natives, "the Dead Sea." The population of Vanua Levu is estimated at 31,000. Its scenery much resembles that of

NA VITI LEVU (the Great Fiji) which measures ninety miles from east to west, and fifty from north to south. A great variety of landscape is found in navigating the shores of Great Fiji. To the S.E. there is tolerably level ground for thirty-six miles inland, edged, in places, by cliffs of sandstone five hundred feet high. The luxuriant and cheerful beauty of the lowland then gives place to the gloomy grandeur and unbroken solitude of the mountains. To the S.W. are low shores with patches of brown, barren land; then succeed narrow vales, beyond which rise hills, whose wooded tops are in fine contrast with the bold bare front at their base. Behind these are the highest mountains in the group, bleak and sterile, with an altitude of 4,000 or 5,000 feet. Westward and to the east, high land is close to the shore, with only narrow strips of level ground separating it from the sea. Proceeding northward, some of the finest scenery in Fiji is opened out. The lower level, skirted by a velvety border of mangrove bushes, and enriched with tropical shrubs, is backed, to the depth of four or five miles, by hilly ground, gradually reaching an elevation of from 400 to 700 feet, with the lofty blue mountains seen, through deep ravines, in the distance. Great Fiji has a continuous land or shore-reef, with a broken sea-reef extending from the west to the north. The Great Land also has in most parts a shore-reef, with a barrier-reef stretching from its N.E. point the whole length of the island, and beyond it in a westerly direction. Great Fiji is supposed to contain at least 50,000 inhabitants.

Scanty and imperfect as is this notice of some of its chief islands, enough has been said to show the superiority of Fiji over most other groups in the Pacific, both in extent of surface, and amount of population. This superiority will be made clearer by the following statement of their relative importance :—

The islands composing Viti-i-loma (Middle Fiji) are equal to the fine and populous island of Tongatabu together with the Hervey Islands.

The Yasawas are equal to Vavau.

The eastern group is equal to the Hapai Islands.

The Somosomo group equals the Dangerous Archipelago and the Austral Islands.

The Great Land is equal to the Marquesas, Tahiti, and Society Islands.

Great Fiji alone surpasses the Samoan group; while there still remains over, the Kandavu group, with a population of about 12,000.

Without pretending to write the natural geography of Fiji, occasional notices of its geology, botany, and zoology will be introduced, where such notices are likely to prove peculiarly interesting or instructive.

The volcanic formation of these islands has already been intimated, and the indications of craters alluded to; but as no lava in a stream has been found, the very remote construction of the group seems almost certain. Volcanic action has not, however, entirely ceased; violent shocks of earthquakes are at times felt, and at Wainunu and Na Savusavu, on Vanua Levu, and also on the island of Ngau, there is enough volcanic heat to produce warm and boiling springs. The high peaks and needles on the large islands are mostly basaltic. Volcanic conglomerate, tufaceous stones, porous and compact basalts, are found of every texture, of many colours, and in various stages of decomposition. In several places I have seen very perfect and distinct columns of basalt some feet in length.

The soil is in some places gravelly and barren; occasionally a stratum of reddish clay and sandstone is found; but a dark red or yellowish loam is most common: this is often deep and very rich, containing, as it does, much decayed vegetable matter. Decomposed volcanic matter forms a very productive soil, especially in those vales where such *débris* mingles with deposits of vegetable mould. Portions of the large flats, covered with rank grass, treacherously hiding the soft, adhesive mud beneath, would baffle the skill of the British husbandman, although much prized by the natives, who find in them just the soil and moisture needed for the cultivation of their most valued esculent, the *taro* (*Arum esculentum*). These swamps would perhaps answer well, under efficient management, for the cultivation of rice.

The lee side of a mountain generally presents a barren contrast to that which is to windward, receiving as this does on summit and slopes the intercepted clouds, thus securing regular showers and abundant fertility, while to leeward the unwatered vegetation is dying down to the grey hues of the boulders among which it struggles for life. To this, however, there are some marked exceptions.

In some places a surface of loose rubble is found. I have heard on good authority that, about thirty years since, a town within a few miles of Mbua was buried by a land-slip, when so much of the mountain face slid down as to overwhelm the whole town and several of its inhabitants.

From the shore we step to the reefs. These are grey

barriers of rock, either continuous or broken, and of all
varieties of outline, their upper surface ranging from a few
yards to miles in width. The seaward edge, over which
the breakers curve, while worn smoother, stands higher
than the surface a few feet within, where the waves pitch
with a ceaseless and heavy fall. Enclosed by the reef is
the lagoon, like a calm lake, underneath the waters of
which spread those beautiful subaqueous gardens which fill
the beholder with delighted wonder.

Shore or attached reefs, sea or barrier reefs, beds,
patches, or knolls of reef, with sunken rocks and sand-
banks, so abound in Fiji and its neighbourhood as to make
it an ocean labyrinth of unusual intricacy, and difficult of
navigation.

The coral formation found here to so vast an extent has
long furnished an interesting subject for scientific research,
and proved a plentiful source of ingenious conjecture;
while the notion has found general favour, that these vast
reefs and islands owe their structure chiefly to a micro-
scopic zoophyte,—the coral insect. Whether by the accumulated deposit of their exuviæ, or by the lime-secretion of
their gelatinous bodies, or the decomposition of those
bodies when dead, these minute polypes, we are told, are
the actual builders of islands and reefs; the lapse of ages
being required to raise the edifice to the level of the
highest tide; after which, the formation of a soil by drifting
substances, the planting of the island with seeds borne by
birds or washed up by the waves, and, lastly, the arrival of
inhabitants, are all set forth in due order with the exact-
ness of a formula based upon the simplest observation. A
theory so pretty as this could not fail to become popular,
while men of note have strengthened it by the authority of
their names. Close and constant inspection, however, on
the part of those who have had the fullest opportunity for
research, is altogether opposed to this pleasingly interesting
and plausible scheme. Wasting and not growth, ruin and
not building up, characterize the lands and rock-beds of
the southern seas. Neither does the ingenious hypothesis

of Darwin, that equal gain and loss—rising in one part, and depression in another—are taking place, seem to be supported by the best ascertained facts; for the annular configuration of reef which this theory pre-supposes, is by no means the most general. " In all the reefs and islands of coral that I have examined," writes Commodore Wilkes, " there are unequivocal signs that they are undergoing dissolution;"* a conclusion in which my own observation leads me entirely to concur.

The operation of the polyps is undoubtedly seen in the beautiful madrepores, brain-corals, and other similar structures which, still living, cover and adorn the surface; " but a few inches beneath, the reef is invariably a collection of loose materials, and shows no regular coralline structure, as would have been the case if it had been the work of the lithophyte." † These corals rarely reach the height of three feet, while many never exceed so many inches. The theory stated above assumes that the polyps work up to the height of a full tide. Such is not the case. I am myself acquainted with reefs to the extent of several thousands of miles, all of which are regularly overflowed by the tide twice in twenty-four hours, and, at high water, are from four to six feet below the surface; all being a few inches above low-water mark, but none reaching to the high-tide level.

But whatever may be the origin of the reefs, their great utility is certain. The danger caused by their existence will diminish in proportion as their position and outline become better known by more accurate and minute survey than has yet been made. To the navigator possessing such exact information, these far-stretching ridges of rock become vast breakwaters, within the shelter of which he is sure to find a safe harbour, the calm of which is in strange, because so sudden, contrast with the stormy sea outside. In many cases a perfect dock is thus found; in some large enough to accommodate several vessels, with a depth of from three to twelve fathoms of water. Besides these, a number of

---

* "U. S. Exploring Expedition," vol. iv., chap. viii.   † *Ibid.*

bays, indenting the coast of the large islands, afford good anchorage, and vary in depth from two to thirty miles. Into these the mountain streams disembogue, depositing the mud flats found in some of them, and rendering the entrance to the river shallow. Still the rivers, furnishing a ready supply of fresh water, increase the value of the bays as harbours for shipping. By these Fiji invites commerce to her shores; and in these a beneficent Creator is seen providing for the prospective wants of the group, ready built ports for the shelter of those " who go down to the sea in ships, that do business in great waters." To such persons the winds are a subject of prime interest. During eight months—from April to November—the prevailing winds blow from the E.N.E. to the S.E., when there is often a fresh trade-wind for many successive days, mitigating to some extent the tropical heat. These winds, however, are not so uniform as elsewhere. During the rest of the year there is much variation, the wind often blowing from the north, from which quarter it is most unwelcome. This—the *tokalau*—is a hot wind, by which the air becomes so rarified as to render respiration difficult. The months most to be feared by seamen are February and March. Heavy gales sometimes blow in January; hence these three are often called " the hurricane months." The morning land breezes serve to modify the strong winds in the neighbourhood of the large islands.

Considering the nearness of these islands to the equator, their climate is neither so hot nor so sickly as might be expected, the fierceness of the sun's heat being tempered by the cool breezes from the wide surface of the ocean around. The swamps are too limited to produce much miasma; and fever, in its several forms, is scarcely known. Other diseases are not so numerous or malignant as in other climes, especially such as lie between the tropics. The air is generally clear, and in the spring and autumn months the climate is delightful. In December, January, and February, the heat is oppressive: the least exertion is followed by profuse perspiration, and no ordinary physical

energy can resist the enervating influence of the season,
begetting a fear lest Hamlet's wish should be realized,
that—

> " Solid flesh would melt—
> Thaw, and resolve itself into a dew."

The temperature is nearly uniform; the greatest extremes
of heat and cold being experienced inland. My meteor-
ological journal kept at Lakemba in 1841, and ten years
later at Vanua Levu, shows 62° as the lowest, and 121° as
the highest, temperature noted. The low temperature here
recorded I ascribe, in part, to a river running close by my
house. The mean temperature of the group throughout
may be stated at 80°. Very hot days are sometimes
preceded by very cold nights.

No resident in Fiji having ever possessed a rain-gauge,
it is impossible to speak with accuracy about the quantity
of water which falls. I find the following entry in my
journal: "1850, March 14th. We have had forty-five days
in succession rainy, more or less. These were preceded by
four or five dry days: before these again we had twenty-four
rainy ones. On many of these days only a single shower
fell, and that but slight; so that the real depth of rain
might not be unusual."

Against the number of rainy days here given, must be
placed the long duration of uninterrupted dry weather,
often extending over two or three months. At times the
burdened clouds discharge themselves in torrents. The
approach of a heavy shower, while yet far away, is
announced by its loud beating on the broad-leaved vegetation; and when arrived, it resembles the bursting of some
atmospheric lake.

This glance at the discovery and general aspect of the
Fiji Islands may be fitly closed by a few remarks on their
division and classification, as described on some maps and
globes of modern date.

The division of the group, as laid down in the account
of the U. S. Exploring Expedition, viz., into seven districts,

under as many principal chiefs, is objectionable, as disregarding the divisions made by nature, and those recognised by the natives, while it excludes Lakemba and its dependencies, which form a district very much more important than either Mathuata or Mbua.

The peculiar character and relative rank of the several authorities in Fiji, render an accurate political division impossible.

The natives use terms equivalent to Upper, Lower, and Central Fiji, excluding the two large islands; thus making five sections, which, though well enough for general use, are far from having fixed boundaries. More minute distinctions are therefore made by the people, to enable them to refer with precision to the several parts of the group. I would submit six divisions; or eight, if the eastward islands are viewed as composing three sections, which certainly ought to be the case. They are virtually thus divided by the United States surveyors, who give a distinct name to those forming the north end, (Ringgold's Isles,) but exclude Ono—the extreme south—from their chart of Fiji.*

A division of the group into eight compartments would —following the course of the sun—be as under :—

THE ONO GROUP; comprising Ono, Ndoi, Mana, Undui, Yanuya, Tuvana-i-tholo, and Tuvana-i-ra.

THE LAKEMBA GROUP; beginning with Vatoa, and ending with Tuvutha and Thithia: thirty-three islands and islets.

THE EXPLORING ISLES, with Mango, Kanathea, Naitaumba, Vatuvara, Yathata, and a number of islets, form the third group.

MIDDLE FIJI; containing Matuku, Totoya, Moala, Ngau, Nairai, Koro, Ovalau, and a few smaller islands.

VANUA LEVU and Taviuni, with their contiguous

* Native tradition speaks of Ono as being formerly near to Ongea, and ascribes its present position to a lady of Lakemba, who expatriated herself, selected Ono for her adopted land, and then pushed it with her foot thus far from Lakemba, in order to escape the pursuit of her friends.

islands—about fifty—form the fifth group in order, and the second in importance.

GREAT FIJI, with the fifty islands on its coasts, is the sixth and most important division.

THE KANDAVU GROUP numbers thirteen islands, several of them small.

THE YASAWAS form the eighth group, and include more than thirty small islands.

This mode of division embraces every island properly belonging to Fiji, while it facilitates a reference to each individually.

Modern geographers class Fiji with the Tonga group, entitling them all, "The Friendly Islands." There is no good reason for such a classification; but there are several which show it to be erroneous, and demand its discontinuance. Geologically considered, the groups are different. The inhabitants also belong to two distinct types, having between them as much difference as between a Red Indian and an Englishman. Their mythologies and languages are also widely diverse. These facts protest against the confounding of the two groups in one.

CHAPTER II.

ORIGIN AND POLITY.

In considering the origin of the present inhabitants of Fiji, we seek in vain for a single ray of tradition or historical record to guide us through the darkness of a remote antiquity. The native songs are silent in the matter, and no hint of a former immigration is to be heard : the people have had no intercourse with other nations, except as visited by them; and the popular belief is, that they never occupied any country but that on which they now dwell. Hence can only be inferred that the period of the Fijians' residence in their islands is to be placed far back at a very early date, probably as remote as the peopling of the American continent. Uniformity of customs and habits, resemblance of religious belief and practice, and, still more, philological affinities, together with physical analogies, supply the data whence may be argued with some degree of precision the branch of the human race to which the Fijian belongs, and perhaps conjecture may be supplied with a surer footing in endeavouring to track the path by which he came to his present home.

Differences of colour, physical conformation, and language, combine to form a separating line between the East and West Polynesians sufficiently clear, until we reach Fiji, where the distinguishing peculiarities seem to meet, and many of them to blend, thus betokening a confluence of the two races. At the east end of the group the Asiatic peculiarities are found marked, but die away as we go westward, giving place to such as are decidedly African, but not Negro. Excepting the Tongans, the Fijian is equal in physical development to the islanders eastward, yet distinct from them in colour, in which particular he

c

approaches the pure Papuan Negro; to whom, in form and feature, he is, however, vastly superior. Many of his customs distinguish him from his neighbours, although he is by language united to them all.

Directed by such facts, there can be little doubt of the Fijian's connexion with the darker races of Asia. His ancestors may be regarded as the original proprietors of his native soil; while the race has been preserved pure from the direct admixture of Malayan blood, by the hitherto strict observance of their custom to slaughter all shipwrecked or distressed foreigners, who may have been cast on their inhospitable coasts. The light mulatto skin and well-developed muscles seen to windward, are chiefly the result of long intercourse with the Tongan race. These evidences of mixture are, however, feeble, compared with those marks which indicate a long isolation from other varieties of mankind.

Murray, in his "Encyclopædia of Geography," speaks incorrectly of the invasion and subjugation of this people by the Friendly Islanders, and seems to have copied the mistake from the account of the voyage of the "Duff." * The Fijians have never acknowledged any power but such as exists among themselves.

The government of Fiji, before the last hundred years, was probably patriarchal, or consisted of many independent states, having little intercourse, and many of them no political connexion, with each other; mutual dread tending to detach the various tribes, and keep them asunder. The great variety of dialects spoken, the comparative ignorance of some of the present kingdoms about each other, and the existence until now of a kind of independence in some of the smaller divisions of the same state, countenance the above supposition. At this day there is a close resemblance between the political state of Fiji and the old feudal system of the north. There are many independent Kings who have been constantly at war with each other; and intestine broils make up, for the most part, the past history of Fiji. Still,

* 4to., p. 274.

though to a much less extent, civil dissensions abound, and it is not uncommon for several garrisons on the same island to be fighting against each other. The chiefs have ever been warring among themselves, though the advantage of the victor is but precarious, often involving his own destruction.

The chiefs of Mbengga were formerly of high rank, and still style themselves *Gali-cuva-ki-lagi,* which means, "Subject only to Heaven." They do not now stand high, being subject to Rewa. On the matter of supremacy nothing is known further back than 1800, at which time, it is certain, Verata took the lead. A part of Great Fiji and several islands of importance owned its sway. At this date Na-Ulivou ruled in Mbau. He succeeded Mbanuvi, his father, and the father also of Tanoa. Na-Ulivou was an energetic Chief, and distinguished himself in a war with the sons of Savou, numbering, it is said, thirty, who contended with him the right of succession. He overcame his enemies, and was honoured with the name of Na Vu-ni-valu, that is, "The Root of War," a title which his successors have since borne. Aided by the white men named in the preceding chapter, and employing the new power supplied by fire-arms, this Chief made war on Verata, took possession of its dependencies, and left its sovereign little more to rule over than his own town. Na-Ulivou died in 1829, and was succeeded by his brother Tanoa. He died at an advanced age, a heathen and cannibal, December 8th, 1852. His reign of twenty-three years was not happy or peaceful. Rebellious subjects and rebellious sons filled it with anxiety. Once he had to fly his chief city; and for a number of years his fear of Raivalita—one of his sons—kept him a close prisoner. Several years before his death, old age disqualified Tanoa for the discharge of the active duties of his position, which were attended to by one of his sons acting in the capacity of Regent. Tanoa was a proud man: when grey and wrinkled, he tried to hide these marks of old age by a plentiful application of black powder. He was also cruel and implacable. Mothelotu, one of his cousins, was so unhappy as to offend him, and sought with tears and entreaties for forgiveness; but the purpose of the cruel Chief was fixed, that Mothelotu should die. After having kissed his relative, Tanoa cut off his arm at the elbow, and drank the blood as it flowed warm from the severed veins. The arm, still quivering with life, he threw upon a fire, and, when sufficiently cooked, ate it in presence of its proper owner, who was then dismembered, limb by limb, while the savage murderer looked with pitiless brutality on the dying agonies of his victim.

At a later period, Tanoa sentenced his youngest son to die by the club. The blow given by the brother who was appointed as his executioner, was not fatal. The father, knowing of his entreaty for mercy, shouted angrily, "Kill him! Kill him!" and the horrible act was completed. Nearly the last words spoken by this man of blood were formed into the question, "How many will follow me?" meaning, "How many women do you intend to strangle at my death?" Being assured that five of his wives would then be sacrificed, he died with satisfaction. The name of the tribe from which the Kings of Mbau are taken is Tui Kamba. The four chief personages or families in this state are the Rokotuimbau, the Tunitonga, the Vusarandavi, and the Tui Kamba.

Mbau, as has been already intimated, is the present centre of political power in Fiji. Its supremacy is acknowledged in nearly all parts of the group. The kingdoms named as subject to it are so but nominally, rendering it homage rather than servitude. The other leading powers are, Rewa, Somosomo, Verata, Lakemba, Naitasiri, Mathuata, and Mbua.

Two kinds of subjection are recognised and distinguished in Fiji, called *Qali* and *Bati*. *Qali* represents a province or town that is subject and tributary to a chief town. *Bati* denotes those which are not so directly subject: they are less oppressed, but less respected, than the *Qali*. Hence arises an awkwardly delicate point among the Fijian powers, who have often to acknowledge inferiority when they feel none. The Chiefs sometimes lay the blame of the annoyance on some one of their gods. The Somosomo Chiefs supply a ludicrous instance of this.

Of all who visit Mbau, the people of Somosomo have most to abase themselves, and all, say they, "through a foolish god." Ng-gurai—one of their gods—wished to visit Mbau; Vatu Mundre supplied him with a bamboo, as a conveyance, and, as he was ignorant of the course, engaged to direct him. Having entered into a rat, Ng-gurai took his club and started. Vatu Mundre had to direct his friend past several islands at which the latter felt disposed to call, and, although many miles from him, told him when he had reached his destination. Most pitiable was poor Ng-gurai's condition; for he had fallen off his bamboo through weakness, and was floating about at the mercy of the waves, when a woman of Mbau found him, took him into the chief's house, and placed him on the hearth with the cooks, where he sat shivering four days. In the meantime the Vuna god sailed up to Mbau in style, and was received and entertained in godlike sort by the Mbau god, who urged that his visitor should become tributary to Mbau, but without success.

The day having come for the visiting gods to return home, he in the rat went back cold and hungry to Thakaundrovi,* chagrined at the miserable figure he cut, and the corresponding reception he had met with. He of Vuna returned well fed and gaily dressed. After a short time the Mbau god, Omaisoroniaka, returned the visit from the god of Vuna, who then retaliated and demanded tribute from his guest. But first he had made the path slippery, so that when Omaisoroniaka grew animated, his heels flew up; at which moment the crafty Vuna god seized the opportunity to press his demand, to which the humbled deity yielded consent, agreeing to be called *Qali* to Vuna, but refusing to make food or do more than give up his club; whereupon the matter ended. In consequence of this, the Mbau people pay the Vuna people, who are subject to

* The island on which the Somosomo Chiefs formerly resided.

Somosomo, great respect, but exact from the latter a servile homage.

When a Somosomo canoe visits Mbau, the sail must be lowered while yet at a great distance, and the canoe sculled by the men in a sitting posture; for to stand might cost them their life. At short distances they have to shout the *tama*.* Arrived at Mbau, they are kept in the open air for four nights, before being allowed to go to their inn; all which time they have to move in a creeping posture, and at intervals to say the *tama*, with a trembling voice, in imitation of the shivering rat. After four days, they may go about and wear better dresses, but must still walk half doubled, with their hands on their breasts. When a Mbau man meets one of them, he says, "*Vekaveka, sa sa (sere) ko Qurai?*" "Ho! ho! is Ng-gurai set at liberty?" to which the other replies, "*Io, vaaca, sa sa o Qurai,*" "Yes, respectfully, Ng-gurai is allowed liberty."

Parties from other places are spared these degrading formalities, which the Somosomans are also partially evading by the aid of the Tongans and the boats of the white men.

The character of the rule exercised by the chief powers mentioned above is purely despotic. The will of the King is, in most cases, law, and hence the nature of the government varies according to his personal character. The people have no voice in the state; nevertheless, the utmost respect is paid to ancient divisions of landed property, of family rank, and official rights. "There exists," says Captain Erskine, "a carefully defined and (by the Fijians themselves) well understood system of polity, which dictates the position the different districts hold with respect to each other, as well as the degree of submission which each dependent owes to his principal."† Men of rank and official importance are generally about the person of the Sovereign, forming his council, and serving to check the exercise of his power. When these persons meet to

---

* The *tama* is described towards the close of this chapter.
† "Islands of the Western Pacific," p. 214.

consult on any grave subject, few speak; for few are qualified. In the councils, birth and rank by themselves are unable to command influence, but a man is commended according to his wisdom. A crude suggestion or unsound argument from a Chief of importance would at once be ridiculed, to his confusion. Assemblies of this kind are often marked by a respectable amount of diplomatic skill. In deliberations of great consequence, secrecy is aimed at, but not easily secured, the houses of the people being too open to insure privacy.*

No actual provision is made for the security of the life and possessions of the subject, who is regarded merely as property, and his welfare but seldom considered. Acts of oppression are common. The views of the Chiefs do not accord with those of the wise Son of Sirach; for they are not " ashamed to take away a portion or a gift; " but will seize not only the presents made to an inferior, but, in some cases, appropriate what a plebeian has received in payment for work done. So far from this being condemned as mean and shameful, it is considered chief-like !

The head of each government is the *Tui* or *Turaga levu*, a King of absolute power, who is, however, not unfrequently surrounded by those who exert an actual influence higher than his own, and whom, consequently, he is most careful not to offend. I have seen some Kings who only retained their position by laying aside the independent action of their own will.

---

* When the stone Mission-house at Viwa was finished, it became the wonder of the day, and was visited by most of the Mbau Chiefs. It comprised a ground-floor of three rooms, a first floor, and an attic. This was the first house in Fiji that had been carried so high, and elicited great admiration from the delighted Chiefs. They gazed round at the even walls, and above at the flat ceiling, and exclaimed, " Vekaveka ! Vekaveka ! " increasing the emphasis as they ascended the stairs, until they trod the attic floor, when their. delight was expressed by a long repeated " Wo, wo, wo," very strongly accented, and having a *tremolo* effect caused by striking the finger across the lips in Arab fashion. The uppermost thought in their minds was evident : this chamber was so high and so private that they all envied its possessor, " because it was such an excellent place for secret meetings, and for concocting plots."

When rule is strictly followed, the successor of a deceased King is his next brother; failing whom, his own eldest son, or the eldest son of his eldest brother, fills his place. But the rank of mothers and other circumstances often cause a deviation from the rule. I am acquainted with several cases in which the elder brother has yielded his right to the younger, with a reservation as to power and tribute becoming a man second only to the King.

In the induction to royalty there are two stages. First is the nomination, when the leading men drink *yaqona* with the King elect, presenting the first cup to him, and with it the royal title: this is generally done a few days after the death of the late King. The second stage, which is equivalent to coronation, is the anointing or bandaging, and may not take place for several months or even years. An unfolded *sala* or turban is bound, at one end, round the upper arm of the King, leaving the rest pendent. This ceremony is performed by a chief priest, while another gives various advice to the new Monarch, who is presently anointed by a coat of red paint on his shoulder. Large quantities of food are presented to the King, with some good advice from the aged men on his public entrance upon the regal office.

The person of a high-rank King (for the title is often given to the head of a village) is sacred. In some instances these Fijian Monarchs claim a divine origin, and, with a pride worthy of more classical examples, assert the rights of deity, and demand from their subjects respect for those claims. This is readily yielded; for the pride of descent which runs so high among the Chiefs is equalled by the admiration in which their lofty lineage is held by the people, who are its sincere and servile worshippers. Republicanism is held in contempt by the Fijians, and even the United States have a King when American citizens speak of their President to a native of the Islands. The King is supposed to impart a degree of sacredness to whatever he may wear or touch. Hence arise some amusing scenes. A poor man was ordered to carry a chair on which Tuithakau was accustomed to sit: he first encased the palms of his hands with green leaves, then, taking the chair by two of its legs, lifted it above his head to avoid further contact, and ran off at full speed, as though in so doing lay his only chance of completing the journey alive. One day, on leaving the house of the same Chief, I held in my hand a ripe plantain which I gave to a child outside; but an old man snatched it away with a countenance expressive of as much anxiety as if I had given the child a viper. His fear was, that the fruit had been touched by the King, and would therefore cause the child's death. This King took advantage of his hallowing prerogative in an odd way. He used to dress an English seaman in his *masi* (dress), and send the man to throw the train over any article of food, whether dead or alive, which he might happen to come near. The result was that such things were at once conveyed to the King without a word of explanation being required.

The duties of a King allow him abundant leisure, except when he is much engaged in feasting or fighting. Like potentates of ancient times, he knows how to reconcile manual labour with an elevated position and the affairs of state. With a simplicity quite patriarchal, he wields by turns the sceptre, the spear, and the spade ; and, if unusually industrious, amuses himself indoors by plaiting sinnet. Should he be one of the rare exceptions who see old age, he exists, during his last days, near a comfortable fire, lying or sitting, as his humour may prompt, in drowsy silence.

Royalty has other distinctions beside the name. In Somosomo, as in eastern countries, the King only is allowed to use the sun-shade: the two high priests, however, share the privilege by favour. In Lakemba none but the King may wear the gauze-like turban of the Fijian gentleman during the day-time. In Mbua, he only may wear his *masi* with a train. A particular kind of staff—*Matana-ki-lagi* (point-to-the-sky)—used to be a mark of royalty. Certain ornaments for the neck and breast are said to become Kings alone. Invariably His Majesty has two or three attendants about his person, who feed him, and perform more than servile offices on his behalf. A thumb-nail an inch longer than is allowed to grow on plebeian digits, is a mark of dignity. An attendant priest or two, and a number of wives, complete the accompaniments of Fijian royalty. Instances of stoutness of person in these dignitaries are very rare. The use of a throne is unknown : the King and his humblest subjects sit on the same level—on the ground. There was one exception in the case of Tuithakau, who used a chair.

The Chiefs profess to derive their arbitrary power from the gods; especially at Verata, Rewa, and Somosomo. Their influence is also greatly increased by that peculiar institution found so generally among the Polynesian tribes, —the 'tabu, which will be further noticed hereafter. The following examples, to which many more might be added, will serve to show how really despotic is Fijian government.

A Rewa Chief desired and asked for a hoe belonging to a man, and, on being refused, took the man's wife.

The King of Somosomo wished to collect the people belonging to the town in which he lived, that they might be directly under his eye. The officer to whom the order to that effect was intrusted, was commissioned to *bake* any who refused compliance.

Towards the close of 1849, I called on the young Chief of Mbau, and found him evidently out of temper. Some villagers had cut him fewer reeds than he expected, whereupon he dispatched a party to burn their village ; which was accordingly done, a child perishing in the fire.

Those who surround the person of the King are generally of various grades, some of whom, however, are merely privileged idlers, the flatterers of their Chief, and makers of mischief and cigarettes.

The *Mata-ni-vanuas* are exceedingly useful men, whose office is described by their title, which signifies either "the eyes," or "the face, of the land," and may intimate the supervision which these men maintain; or that, through them, the chiefs see the state of affairs—the face of the land. They are the legitimate medium of communication between the Chiefs and their dependencies, and form a complete and effective agency. Taking the kingdom of Lakemba as an instance, the system is worked thus. In each island and town under the rule of Lakemba there is an authorized *Mata ki Lakemba,* "Ambassador to Lakemba," through whom all the business between that place and the seat of government is transacted. Then again, at Lakemba there is a diplomatic corps, the official title of each individual of which contains the name of the place to which he is messenger, and to which all the King's commands are by him communicated. When on duty, these officials represent their Chief, after the manner of more civilized courts, and are treated with great respect. When they have to take several messages, or when one communication consists of several important parts, they help memory by mnemonic sticks or reeds, which are of various lengths. The Mata, having reached his destination, lays down one of these before him, and repeats the message of which it is the memorial. He then lays down another, proceeding in the same way, until the sticks are transferred from his hand, and lie in a row before him, each message having been accurately delivered. I have seen men of this class practise their lesson before setting out, and have heard them give the answers on their return.

In some parts there is one of the Matas who is more immediately attached to the person of the King, and is styled, *O na Mata.* It is his business to be in attendance when tribute or food is brought to the Sovereign, and to go through the customary form of acknowledgment, to receive and answer reports of all kinds, doing so in the King's presence and under his direction, and to officiate at the *yaqona* ring, with other similar duties.

Beside the Mata, there are other officials, of various duties and degrees of importance. All these, except in extreme cases, go about their duties most deliberately, as every appearance of haste in such matters is supposed to detract from true dignity.   A careful observance of established forms is deemed very essential.

In some parts of Fiji the Mata holds his post for life,
in others for only a few years.   In the latter case, when
tired of public life, he presents a large quantity of provisions to his Chief, asking for permission to retire.   On
Vanua Levu the election of a successor has the appearance
of being done by surprise.   The leading men having assembled and consulted awhile, one of their number advances
to the person chosen, and makes him their Mata by binding
a blade of the red Ti-tree leaf round his arm between the
shoulder and elbow.   It is the fashion for the man thus
bandaged to weep and protest against his election, asserting
his incompetency, and pleading low birth, poverty, indolence,
ignorance of official phraseology, etc.; all which objections
are, of course, met by the others declaring their choice to
be good.   The feast on such an occasion is prepared with
extra care.

Public business is conducted with tedious formality.
Old forms are strictly observed, and innovations opposed.
An abundance of measured clapping of hands, and subdued
exclamations, characterize these occasions.   Whales' teeth
and other property are never exchanged or presented without the following or a similar form: *"A! woi! woi!
woi!! A! woi! woi! woi!! A tabua levu! woi! woi!
A mudua, mudua, mudua!"* (Clapping.)

Whoever asks a favour of a Chief, or seeks civil intercourse with him, is expected to bring a present.

Justice is known by name to the Fijian powers, and its
form sometimes adopted; yet in very many criminal cases
the evidence is partial and imperfect, the sentence precipitate and regardless of proportion, and its execution
sudden and brutal.   The injured parties, headed by the
nearest Chief, form the "bench" to decide the case.   If
the defendant's rank is higher than their own, an appeal is
made to the King as chief magistrate, and this is final.

Offences, in Fijian estimation, are light or grave according
to the rank of the offender.   Murder by a Chief is less

heinous than a petty larceny committed by a man of low rank. Only a few crimes are regarded as serious; *e. g.*, theft, adultery, abduction, witchcraft, infringement of a *tabu*, disrespect to a Chief, incendiarism, and treason.

Punishment is inflicted variously. Theft is punished by fine, repayment in kind, loss of a finger, or clubbing. Either fine, or loss of the finger, ear, or nose, is inflicted on the disrespectful. The other crimes are punished with death, the instrument being the club, the noose, or the musket. Adultery taxes vindictive ingenuity the most. For this offence, the criminals may be shot, clubbed, or strangled; the man may lose his wife, who is seized on behalf of the aggrieved party by his friends; he may be deprived of his land, have his house burnt, his canoe taken away, or his plantations destroyed.

Young men are deputed to inflict the appointed punishment, and are often messengers of death. Their movements are sudden and destructive, like a tropical squall. The protracted solemnity of public executions in civilized countries is here unknown. A man is often judged in his absence, and executed before he is aware that sentence has been passed against him. Sometimes a little form is observed, as in the case of the Vasu to Vuna. This man conspired against the life of Tuikilakila; but the plot was discovered, and the Vasu brought to meet death at Somosomo. His friends prepared him according to the custom of Fiji, by folding a large new *masi* about his loins, and oiling and blacking his body as if for war. A necklace and a profusion of ornaments at his elbows and knees completed the attire. He was then placed standing, to be shot by a man suitably equipped. The shot failed, when the musket was exchanged for a club, which the executioner broke on the Vasu's head; but neither this blow, nor a second from a more ponderous weapon, succeeded in bringing the young man to the ground. The victim now ran towards the spot where the King sat, perhaps with the hope of reprieve; but was felled by a death-blow from the club of a powerful man standing by. The slain body was cooked and eaten. One of the baked thighs the King sent to his brother, who was principal in the plot, that he might " taste how sweet his accomplice was, and eat of the fruit of his doings." This is a fair sample of a Fijian public execution. Those who are doomed to die are never, so far as I know, bound in any way. A Fijian is implicitly submissive to the will of his Chief. The executioner states his errand; to which the victim replies, " Whatever the King says, must be done."

Injured persons often take the law into their own hands; an arrangement in which the authorized powers gladly concur. In such cases justice yields to passion, and the most unlicensed cruelty follows. For a trifling offence a man has been tied to a log, so that he could not move a limb, and then placed in the sun, with his face fully exposed to its fierce heat for several hours.

One who had removed an article which he believed to be his own, was cruelly pelted with large stones. In another case, a man threw at a duck, supposing it to be wild: it proved, however, to be tame, and the property of a petty Chief, who regarded the act as done to himself. A messenger was accordingly sent to the Chief of the offender to demand an explanation, which was forthwith given, together with the fingers of four persons, to appease the angry Chieftain. He, however, not being yet satisfied, caused the delinquent to be shut up in a house with the lame duck, informing him that his life depended upon that of the injured bird. If he restored the use of the limb, he was to live; but to die if the duck died.

Some offences are punished by stripping the house of the culprit: in slight cases, much humour is displayed by the spoilers. The *sang froid* of the sufferer is an enigma to the Englishman.

The virtue of vicarious suffering is recognised, and by its means the ends of justice are often frustrated. On the island of Nayau the following tragedy took place. A warrior left his charged musket so carelessly that it went off, killing two persons, and wounding two more; whereupon the man fled, and hid himself in the bush. His case was adjudged worthy of death by the Chiefs of his tribe; but he was absent, and, moreover, a very serviceable individual. Hence it was thought best, in point of expedition as well as economy, to exact the penalty from the offender's aged father, who was accordingly seized and strangled. Still later, a white man was killed on the island of Nukulau. The commander of the U. S. ship "Falmouth" inquired into the case, and sentence of death was passed by him on an accused native, who, when he understood his position, proposed that the Americans should hang his father in his stead.

Persons liable to punishment often escape by the aid of a *soro*, or "atonement," or something offered to obtain forgiveness. This is a provision acknowledged throughout Fiji, and in constant use. There are five kinds of *soro*. 1. The *soro* with a whale's tooth, a mat, club, musket, or other property, is in request for every kind of offence, from stealing a yam to running away with a woman, or the commission of adultery. 2. The *soro* with a reed, called *mata ni gasau*. This is not commonly resorted to in private affairs, but by civil functionaries and small Chiefs, when accused or convicted of unfaithfulness to the duties of their position. It is more humiliating than the first. 3. The *soro* with a spear, *mata ni moto*, is used to secure forgiveness in cases of civil delinquency of a graver sort. It is still more humiliating than the second kind. He who presents the spear, generally some one of importance, will stoop or nearly prostrate himself: the whole act is supposed to imply that he, and those whom he represents, have deserved to be transfixed by a spear to the earth. 4. The *soro* with a basket of earth, *a kau vanua*, is generally con‧nected with war, and is presented by the weaker party, indicating the yielding up of their land to the conquerors. Sometimes, however, the ceremony may be an expression of loyalty by parties whose fealty is suspected. 5. The *soro* with ashes, *bisi dravu*, belongs to an extreme case, involving a life or lives. A Chief or Mata-ni-vanua disfigures himself by covering his bosom and arms with ashes, and, with deep humiliation, entreats that the aggrieved person will compassionately grant the life of the offender or offenders.

On the part of the offerer, the presentation of the *soro* is a serious thing, and his faltering voice and trembling body testify the emotion within.

When a *soro* is refused, it is repeated, it may be five or even ten times; until the property given, or the importunity shown, gains the desired point.

Whatever may have been the origin of this custom, and however beneficial its right use might prove to the innocent, or the unintentional offender, its operation in Fiji seems too generally to avert deserved punishment from the criminal, and in many cases is but legalized corruption. No small proportion of the misdemeanours brought under the notice of Chiefs are deliberate acts, in which a balance has been previously struck between the fruit of the crime and the *soro* which must follow, and the commission of the act has been accordingly determined on.

In some cases those who are in danger of punishment place themselves under the protection of an influential Chief of another tribe, who receives servitude in return for the shelter thus afforded.

Fijian society is divided into six recognised classes, in the distinctions of which there is much that resembles the system of caste.

1. Kings and Queens.
2. Chiefs of large islands or districts.
3. Chiefs of towns, priests, and Mata-ni-vanuas.
4. Distinguished warriors of low birth, Chiefs of the carpenters, and Chiefs of the fishers for turtle.
5. Common people.
6. Slaves by war.

Rank is hereditary, descending through the female; an arrangement which arises from the great number of wives allowed to a leading Chief, among whom is found the widest difference of grade. The dignity of a Chief is estimated by the number of his wives, which is frequently considerable, varying from ten to fifty or a hundred. It is not to be supposed that all these are found in his domestic establishment at the same time; for rarely more than a half or fourth are there together. Some have been dismissed on account of old age, others have returned to their parents to become mothers, others again are but infants themselves.

No people can be more tenacious of distinction than are these Fijians, and few fonder of exaggerating it. When on their guard, and acting with the duplicity so strongly marked in the native character, they will depreciate themselves, as well as when surprised into a feeling of inferiority by unexpected contrast with some refined nation; but only let something occur to throw them off their guard, and they instantly become swollen with an imaginary importance which is not a little amusing. Lofty aspirings and great meanness are often found united in the same Chief, who will be haughtily demanding, one moment, why the Monarch of some great nation does not send a ship of war or large steamer to gratify *his* curiosity, and the next be begging tobacco of a shoeless seaman.

Tribes, chief families, the houses of Chiefs, and the wives of Kings, have distinctive appellations, to which great importance is attached, and by means of which the pride of the owner is gratified and the jealousy of neighbours aroused. Before the death of the King Tanoa, the whites residing in Fiji wrote to General Miller, H. B. M. Consul-General at the Sandwich Islands, complaining of their ill-treatment by Thakombau, the young Chief of Mbau and heir of Tanoa, but already exercising virtually the kingly power. General Miller sent a letter about the matter to the Chief, addressing it, " To the King of Fiji." When this letter arrived, a Tonga Chief, who had visited Sydney and could read English, was staying with Thakombau, to whom he interpreted the Consul's dispatch, translating the address, " Tui Viti." This title, till then unknown, thus became fixed, and proved of great use to the young Chief during his regency, though a cause of bitter jealousy to other Chiefs, some of whom I heard comforting themselves by saying, "It is without authority: foreigners gave it to him." At the death of the aged King, however, this proud appellation was laid aside, and Thakombau received the high hereditary title of Vu-ni-valu, though frequently addressed still as Tui Viti—a name to which his widely spread ascendancy gives him a real claim. An old Chief on Na Viti Levu, known to few, boasts that the Chiefs of Mbau and Rewa are his children; thus putting them far below himself. Common men, though esteemed for superior prowess, and rewarded with an honourable name, do not rise in rank, their original grade being always remembered. There are many inferior Chiefs, but they have little authority. Observing that the land-breeze blows most strongly in the bays, the natives have thence made a proverb, alluding to the fact just stated: *Sa dui cagi ni toba*, "Every one is a wind in his own bay."

Most prominent among the public notorieties of Fiji is the *Vasu*. The word means a nephew or niece, but becomes a title of office in the case of the male, who, in some localities, has the extraordinary privilege of appropriating whatever he chooses belonging to his uncle, or those under his uncle's power. Vasus are of three kinds: the *Vasu taukei*, the *Vasu levu*, and the *Vasu*: the last is a common name, belonging to any nephew whatever. *Vasu taukei* is a term applied to any Vasu whose mother is a lady of the land in which he is born. The fact of Mbau being at the head of Fijian rank gives the Queen of Mbau a pre-eminence over all Fijian ladies, and her son a place nominally above all Vasus. No material difference exists between the power of a *Vasu taukei* and that of a *Vasu levu*, which latter title is given to every Vasu born of a woman of rank, and having a first-class Chief for his father. A *Vasu taukei* can claim anything belonging to a native of his mother's land, excepting the wives, home, and land of a Chief. Vasus cannot be considered apart from the civil polity of the group, forming as they do one of its integral parts, and supplying the high-pressure power of Fijian despotism.

In grasping at dominant influence the Chiefs have created a power which, ever and anon, turns round and gripes them with no gentle hand. However high a Chief may rank, however powerful a King may be, if he has a nephew, he has a master, one who will not be content with the name, but who will exercise his prerogative to the full, seizing whatever may take his fancy, regardless of its value or the owner's inconvenience in its loss. Resistance is not thought of, and objection only offered in extreme cases. A striking instance of the power of the Vasu occurred in the case of Thokonauto, a Rewa Chief, who, during a quarrel with an uncle, used the right of Vasu, and actually supplied himself with ammunition from his enemy's stores. But it is not in his private capacity, but as acting under the direction of the King, that the Vasu's agency tends greatly to modify the political machinery of Fiji, inasmuch as the Sovereign employs the Vasu's influence, and shares much of the property thereby acquired. Great Vasus are also Vasus to great places, and, when they visit these at their superior's command, have a numerous retinue and increased authority. A public reception and great feasts are given them by the inhabitants of the place which they visit; and they return home laden with property, most of which, as tribute, is handed over to the King. When thus " on commission," a Vasu is amenable for his conduct, and, should his personal exactions affect the revenue, incurs the displeasure of his King, which can only be removed by a *soro* of the most costly kind, such as a first-class canoe; and this he may have to load with riches before it is deemed a sufficient atonement.

The reception of one of these important personages, as witnessed by myself at Somosomo, may be worth detailing. The Vasu, who was from Mbau, had arrived with a suite of ten canoes, six days before. On the seventh day, several hundreds of people were assembled in the open air to give the important visitor a greeting worthy of his dignity. After waiting a short time, the Vasu and his suite approached them, and performed a dance, which they finished by presenting their clubs and upper dresses to the

Somosomo King; after which they retired, seating themselves at a distance, opposite to him. Two Matas were
then sent by the King, holding by either end a coarse mat,
and passing over the ground with a motion compounded of
squatting and crawling, until they reached the Vasu and
spread the mat before him, upon which he and another
Chief forthwith seated themselves. An Ambassador, near
the King, now shouted, in a high key, the proper greeting,
" *Sa tio!* (He sits.) *Sa tio! Sa tio! Sa tio!* " repeating the cry with increasing rapidity and in descending tones
for about a dozen times. Having rested long enough to
recover breath, the man shouted again, " *Sa tawa!* "
(" Inhabited :" a compliment to the Vasu, intimating that
before his arrival it was empty.) " *Sa-ta-wa! Sa-ta-wa!* He
comes, nobly descended from his ancestors! *Sa tawa!* "
(Repeated many times quickly.) After a short pause, an
aged Mata left the King, advancing towards the Vasu in a
sitting posture : when he had gone about two yards from the
King, a second Mata followed in the same style, and so on,
until there were six of them in a line, at equal distances
from each other. They now faced to the S.W., but,
turning as they sat, simultaneously swung themselves
half round, thus facing the N.E., having managed at the
same time, by help of their hands, to advance a yard ;
repeating the painful evolution, until the front man was
within six feet of the Vasu. Whereupon the sitting Matas
bowed themselves sideways, so as to make their beards
touch the earth : again they rose, and gently inclined their
heads from the Vasu, clasping their beards with both
hands, and crying out several times, " Furled are your
sails ! (*Sa uru.*) Furled are your sails ! " (" *A! woi! woi!
woi !* ") This done, they returned to their places. The Vasu
then walked up to the King, having two whales' teeth in his
hand, which—after a short speech, referring to his coming
and its object—he presented, receiving in return an
expression of the King's wishes for prosperity and peace.
All the people then clapped their hands several times, and
the ceremony was concluded. Such then is the· *Vasu*

levu; such is the power he exercises, and such the honours paid him. Where else shall we find his parallel?

Descending in the social scale, the Vasu is a hindrance to industry, few being willing to labour unrewarded for another's benefit. One illustration will suffice. An industrious uncle builds a canoe, in which he has not made half-a-dozen trips, when an idle nephew mounts the deck, sounds his trumpet-shell, and the blast announces to all within hearing that the canoe has, that instant, changed masters.

There are Vasus to the gods; or rather to the basket in which the god's share of food is kept. But these have no power.

Persons of rank generally manifest a strong feeling of jealousy towards each other, and studiously avoid meeting unnecessarily. On more than one occasion I have had a Chief of rank in my house, when another has been seen approaching the door; whereupon the first would at once retire into a private room. After the last arrival had sat a few minutes, I intimated to him the position of affairs, at which he smiled and made his visit very short. Their conduct is often a strange mixture of vanity, cupidity, and liberality. When, however, they do meet, and are not too reserved, they display a courteous demeanour, which betokens a recognition of rank in others, as well as a consciousness of it in themselves.

The Chiefs demand a large amount of homage from the people, expressed both by language and action. As in the Malayan, so in the Fijian, there exists an aristocratic dialect, which is particularly observable in the windward districts, where not a member of a Chief's body, or the commonest acts of his life, are mentioned in ordinary phraseology, but are all hyperbolized. Respect is further indicated by the *tama*, which is a shout of reverence uttered by inferiors when approaching a Chief or chief town. The *tama* varies in different places, and the women have a formula distinct from that of the men. Sometimes, in uttering this shout, the people place their hands behind them, and stoop forward. Chiefs look for the *tama* from

those they meet, whether on land or sea, and expect it
when inferiors pass their houses. At the close of the day,
or when a Chief is superintending the making or repairing
of a sail, and in some other cases, the *tama* is improper,
and would be answered by a laugh, or regarded as an insult.
In some districts the *tama* is "long drawn out," and in others
half sung, so as to produce a somewhat pleasing effect,
when raised by fifty or a hundred voices at once. Generally the Chiefs acknowledge courteously the salutation of
one of the lower orders of the people.*

Equally expressive of respect are many of the actions
prescribed by Fijian etiquette. An armed man lowers his
arms, takes the outside of the path, and crouches down
until the Chief has passed by. When a person has given
anything, say a cigar, to a Chief, he claps his hands respectfully. The same form is observed after touching a Chief's
head, or when taking anything from a place over his head;
on receiving any trifle from him; always at the close of his
meals, and sometimes to applaud what he has said. In
some parts the men do not crouch, but rub the upper part
of the left arm with the right hand. Some take hold of their
beards and look to the earth: this is very common when
conversing with a Chief, or begging; hence great beggars
are called "beard-scratchers." The speaker also inter-
sperses his address with respectful expletives, of which they
have many. If any one would cross the path of a Chief,
or the place where he is sitting or standing, he must pass
before, and never behind, his superior. Standing in the
presence of a Chief is not allowed: all who move about the
house in which he is creep, or, if on their feet, advance
bent, as in an act of obeisance. As in some other countries
where the government is despotic, no one is permitted to
address the Chief otherwise than in a sitting posture.

* The following are specimens of the *tama*:—

PLACE.	MEN.	WOMEN.
Mbau.	Muduo! wo!	M-a-i-n-a-v-a-k-a-d-u-a!
Lakemba.	O-o! Oa!	N-i-q-o!
Somosomo.	Duo! wo!	M-a-i-n-a-v-a-a-d-u-a!
Vanua Levu.	Dua! dua! dua!	M-a-i-n-a-v-a-a-d-u-a!

Seamen are cautious not to sail by a Chief's canoe on the outrigger side, which would be considered worse than a person on land passing behind the back of his Sovereign.

Most singular among these customs is the *bale muri,* "follow in falling," the attendant falling because his master has fallen. This is to prevent shame from resting on the Chief, who, as he ought, has to pay for the respect. One day, I came to a long bridge formed of a single cocoa-nut tree, which was thrown across a rapid stream, the opposite bank of which was two or three feet lower, so that the declivity was too steep to be comfortable. The pole was also wet and slippery, and thus my crossing safely was very doubtful. Just as I commenced the experiment, a heathen said, with much animation, "To-day I shall have a musket!" I had, however, just then to heed my steps more than his words, and so succeeded in reaching the other side safely. When I asked him why he spoke of a musket, the man replied, "I felt certain you would fall in attempting to go over, and I should have fallen after you;" (that is, appeared to be equally clumsy;) "and, as the bridge is high, the water rapid, and you a gentleman, you would not have thought of giving me less than a musket."

The best produce of the gardens, the seines, and the sties in Fiji, goes to the Chiefs, together with compliments the most extravagant and oriental in their form. Warrior Chiefs often owe their escape in battle to their inferiors— even when enemies—dreading to strike them. This fear partly arises from Chiefs being confounded with deities, and partly from the certainty of their death being avenged on the man who slew them. Women of rank often escape strangling, at the death of their lord, because there are not at hand men of equal rank to act as executioners. Such an excess of homage must of course be maintained by a most vigorous infliction of punishment for any breach of its observance; and a vast number of fingers, missing from the hands of men and women, have gone as the fine for disrespectful or awkward conduct.

In Fiji, subjects do not pay rent for their land, but a

kind of tax on all their produce, beside giving their labour occasionally in peace, and their service, when needed, in war, for the benefit of the King or their own Chief. Tax-paying in Fiji, unlike that in Britain, is associated with all that the people love. The time of its taking place is a high day; a day for the best attire, the pleasantest looks, and the kindest words; a day for display: whales' teeth and cowrie necklaces, orange-cowrie and pearl-shell breast ornaments, the scarlet frontlet, the newest style of neck-band, white armlets, bossed knee and ancle bands, tortoise-shell hair pins, (eighteen inches long,) cocks' tail feathers, the whitest *masi*, the most graceful turban, powder of jet black, and rouge of the deepest red, are all in requisition on that festive day. The coiffure that has been in process for months is now shown in perfection; the beard, long nursed, receives extra attention and the finishing touch; the body is anointed with the most fragrant oil, and decorated with the gayest flowers and most elegant vines. The weapons also—clubs, spears, and muskets—are all highly polished and unusually gay. The Fijian carries his tribute with every demonstration of joyful excitement, of which all the tribe concerned fully partake. Crowds of spectators are assembled, and the King and his suite are there to receive the impost, which is paid in with a song and a dance, and received with smiles and applause. From this scene the tax-payers retire to partake of a feast provided by their King. Surely the policy that can thus make the paying of taxes "a thing of joy" is not contemptible.

Whales' teeth always form a part of the property paid in. Those smooth and red with age and turmeric are most valued; and the greater the quantity of these, the more respectable is the *solevu* (tribute). Canoes, bales of plain and printed cloth, (*tapa*,) each bale fifteen or twenty feet long, with as many men to carry it, musquito curtains, balls and rolls of sinnet,* floor-mats, sail-mats, fishing

---

* Braid or flat string made with the cocoa-nut fibre, and in general use for every kind of fastening. An average roll of sinnet, wound with beautiful neatness, is three feet six inches high, and five feet in circumference.

nets, baskets, spears, clubs, guns, scarfs or turbans, *likus*,* pearl-shell breast-plates, turtles, and women, may be classed under the head of tribute. In some of the smaller states, pigs, yams, taro, arrow-root, turmeric, yaqona, sandal-wood, salt, tobacco, and black powder, are principal articles.

The presentation of a canoe, if new and large, is a distinct affair. Tui Nayau, King of Lakemba, gave one to Thakombau in the following manner. Preliminaries being finished, Tui Nayau approached the Mbau Chief, and knelt before him. From the folds of his huge dress he took a whale's tooth, and then began his speech. The introduction was an expression of the pleasure which Thakombau's visit gave to Tui Nayau and his people. As he warmed, the speaker proceeded: "Before we were subject to Mbau, our land was empty, and no cocoa-nuts grew on its shore; but since you have been our Chiefs, the land is full of people, and nuts and food abound. Our fathers were subject to Mbau, and desired so to be; and my desire, and that of my friends and my subjects, is towards Mbau, and it is very intense." The sentences here strung together were picked out from among a great number of petitions, praying that "Tui Nayau and his people might live." Neither was this omitted in the peroration: "Therefore let us live, that we may chop out canoes for you; and that we may live, I present this earnest" (the whale's tooth) "of the *Ta ivei*" (the name of the canoe) "as our *soro*, and the *soro* of our friends." On receiving the tooth Thakombau expressed a wish, almost like an imperial permission, that all might live; whereupon all present clapped their hands. Custom required of the receiver a form like this: "Woi! Woi! Woi! The sacred canoe! Yi! Yi! Yi!" and a long shrill shout in conclusion.

All love to make as much display as possible on these occasions; food is provided in abundance, and on all hands is seen a liberality approaching to a community of goods: but where there exists anything like equality between those who give and those who receive, the return

* Women's dresses or girdles.

of similar gifts and entertainment is anxiously expected, and calculated carefully beforehand.

Sometimes the property or tribute is taken to the King; sometimes he chooses to fetch it. In the latter case, he makes those he visits a small present, the time of so doing being made the opportunity for his public reception, after which he and his attendants dance. Such visits are very burdensome to the people thus honoured; for the King's fleet may comprise twenty or thirty canoes, the crews of which, as well as the King's attendants, have to be fed by the visited, however long they remain.

When the tribute is carried to the King, those who take it—varying in number from fifty to three hundred—are detained several weeks, well fed the first few days, and, in some parts, left to live as they can the remainder. By means of them and their canoes the King verifies the native proverb, "Work is easily done when strangers help." The strangers voyage and garden for the Chiefs of the place, receive a present, and are then sent home.

Chiefs of power exact largely and give liberally, only a small portion of what they receive remaining in their own hands; which fact will help to explain the following speech of a Mata on the occasion of one of these presentations of property: "We have a wish for eternal friendship: see this in our labours to procure cloth for you: we are wearied: we have left ourselves without clothing, that you may have it all. We have a Chief who loves peace: we also love it. War is an evil: let us not fight, but labour. Do not let difficulties or jealousies arise out of sharing this property. Our minds regard you equally. You are all our friends. Any difference in the quantity shared to each tribe is to be referred to the proportion of service rendered by the tribe. There has been no partiality."

CHAPTER III.

WAR.

ANOTHER and most strongly marked feature in the political aspect of Fiji has yet to be noticed: it is war. Much has been set forth on this subject, with which my own long and close observation forbids me to agree.

It is said of the Fijians, as of most savage nations, that they are warlike; and they have been pictured as fierce, ferocious, and eager for bloodshed and battle. But this is a caricature, resulting from too hasty and superficial an estimate of the native character. When on his feet, the Fijian is always armed; when working in his garden, or lying on his mat, his arms are always at hand. This, however, is not to be attributed to his bold or choleric temper, but to suspicion and dread. Fear arms the Fijian. His own heart tells him that no one could trust him and be safe, whence he infers that his own security consists in universal mistrust of others. The club or spear is the companion of all his walks; but it is only for defence. This is proved by every man you meet: in the distance you see him with his weapon shouldered; getting nearer, he lowers it to his knee, gives you the path, and passes on. This is invariable, except when the people meet purposely to fight, or when two enemies come unexpectedly together. Such conduct surely is the opposite to offensive, being rather a show of inferiority, a mere point of etiquette.

Nevertheless Fiji is rarely free from war and its attendant evils. Several causes exist for this, such as the pride and jealousy of the Chiefs, and the fact of there being so many independent governments, each of which seeks aggrandizement at the expense of the rest. Any misgiving

as to the probability of success proves the most powerful
motive for peace; and superstition asserts the cackling of
hens at night to be a sure prognostic of fighting. The
appearance of restless haste for war is often assumed, when
no corresponding anxiety is felt. When war is decided upon
between two powers, a formal message to that effect is inter-
changed, and informal messages in abundance, warning each
other to strengthen their fences and carry them up to the
sky. Councils are held, in which future action is planned.
Before going to war with men, they study to be right with
the gods. Ruined temples are rebuilt, some half-buried in
weeds are brought to light, and new ones erected. Costly
offerings are brought to the gods, and prayers presented
for the utter destruction of the enemy, and every bowl of
yaqona is quaffed with an expression of the same wish.
Kanakanai yarua, to eat with both contending parties, is very
tabu, and punished, when discovered, with death. On one
occasion I saw offered to the god of war, forty whales'
teeth, (fifty pounds of ivory,) ten thousand yams, thirty
turtles, forty roots of yaqona, some very large, many
hundreds of native puddings, (two tons,) one hundred and
fifty giant oysters, (*chama gigas*,) fifteen water melons,
cocoa-nuts, a large number of violet land-crabs, taro, and
ripe bananas. Much confidence is placed in the gods'
help thus purchased. On remarking to a small party on
their way to war, "You are few;" they promptly replied,
"Our allies are the gods."

Frequently the men separate themselves from their wives
at such times, but sometimes the wives accompany them to
the war. Orders are sent by the Chief to all under his
rule to be in readiness, and application is made to friendly
powers for help. A flat refusal to comply with the
summons of the Chief, by any place on which he had a
claim, would, sooner or later, be visited by the destruction
of the offenders. Efforts are made to neutralize each
other's influence. *A* sends a whale's tooth to *B*, entreating
his aid against *C*, who, hearing of this, sends a larger
tooth to *B*, to *bika*—" press down "—the present from *A*;

and thus *B* joins neither party. Sometimes two hostile Chiefs will each make a superior Chief the stay of their hopes: he, for his own interest, trims between the two, and often aids the weaker party, that he may damage the stronger, yet professing, all the time, a deep interest in his welfare.

When many warriors are expected to help in an expedition, slight houses are built for their accommodation. Tongans who may be visiting the Chief at the time are expected to assist him; to which they rarely object, their services being repaid in canoes, arms, mats, &c. In some rare cases Tongan Chiefs have had small islands ceded to them.

When an appeal for help to a superior Chief is favourably received, a club or spear is sent to the applicant with words such as these: "I have sent my club: by and bye I will follow." This form of earnest, I understand, is modern: the old fashion was to return a spear with a floating streamer, which the successful petitioner planted conspicuously, to indicate his fair prospects.

The military in Fiji do not form a distinct class, but are selected from every rank, irrespective of age or size; any who can raise a club or hurl a spear are eligible. At the close of the war, all who survive return to their ordinary pursuits. During active service, a faithful follower owns no tie but that which binds him to his tribe, and the command of the Vu-ni-valu—General—is his only law.

Instances of persons devoting themselves specially to deeds of arms are not uncommon. The manner in which they do this is singular, and wears the appearance of a marriage contract; and the two men entering into it are spoken of as man and wife, to indicate the closeness of their military union. By this mutual bond the two men pledge themselves to oneness of purpose and effort, to stand by each other in every danger, defending each other to the death, and, if needful, to die together. In the case of one of the parties wishing to become married, in the ordinary style, to one of the other sex, the former contract is duly declared void. Between Mbetelambandai and Mbombo. of Vatukarakara such a union existed. The former was slain in war. Mbombo, on hearing that his friend was in danger, ran to the rescue; but, arriving too late, died avenging his comrade's death.

Forces are gathered by the *taqa*, a kind of review. Of these there is a series,—one at every place where the army stops on its way to the scene of action. If any part of Fijian warfare has interest, it is this; and to the parties engaged, it is doubtless glorious. They defy an enemy that is far away, and boast of what they will do on a day which has not yet come; and all this in the midst of their friends. The boasting is distinct from, though associated with, the *taqa*, which means, "ready, or on the move," namely, for challenging. The challenging is called *bolebole*; and the ceremony, when complete, is as follows. If the head of the party of allies just arrived is a great Chief, his approach is hailed with a general shout. Taking the lead, he conducts his followers to a large open space, where the Chief, to whose help he comes, waits with his men. Forthwith shouts of respect are exchanged by the two companies. Presently a man, who is supposed to represent the enemy, stands forth and cries out, " Cut up! cut up! The temple receives; " * intimating, probably, that the enemy will certainly be cut up, cooked, and offered to the gods. Then follow those who *bole*, or challenge. First comes the leader, and then others, singly at the beginning, but afterwards in companies of six, or ten, or twenty. It is impossible to tell all that is said when many are speaking at once; but there is no lack of bragging, if single challengers may be taken as specimens. One man runs up to the Chief, brandishes his club, and exclaims, "Sir, do you know me? Your enemies soon will!" Another, darting forward, says, "See this hatchet, how clean!

* " *Sai tava! Sai tava! Ka yau mai ka yavia a bure.*" Several Chiefs of whom I asked the precise meaning of this sentence, acknowledged that they could not tell, saying, " It has come down to us from past ages." Nor is this the only instance I have noticed of language having outlived thought,—the form being preserved when the primitive idea is lost.

To-morrow it will be bathed in blood!" One cries out, "This is my club, the club that never yet was false!" The next, "This army moves to-morrow; then you shall eat dead men till you are surfeited!" A man, striking the ground violently with his club, boasts, "I cause the earth to tremble: it is I who meet the enemy to-morrow!" "See," exclaims another, "I hold a musket and a battle-axe! If the musket miss fire, the hatchet will not!" A fine young man stepped quietly towards a King, holding a pole used as an anchor for a canoe, and said, "See, Sire, the anchor of Natewa!* I will do thus with it!" And he broke the pole across his knee. A man, swinging a ponderous club, said, "This club is a defence, a shade from the heat of the sun, and the cold of the rain." Glancing at the Chief, he added, "You may come under it." A fiery youth ran up, as though breathless, crying out, "I long to be gone! I am impatient!" One of the same kind said, "Ah, ah! these boasters are deceivers! I only am a true man: in the battle you shall find me so." These "great swelling words" are listened to with mingled laughter and applause. Although the speeches of the warriors are marked with great earnestness, there is nothing of the horrifying grimace in which the New Zealander indulges on similar occasions. The fighting men have their bodies covered with black powder; some, however, confine this to the upper part only. An athletic warrior thus powdered, so as to make his skin wear a velvet-like blackness, has a truly formidable appearance, his eyes and teeth gleaming with very effective whiteness.

Fijians make a show of war at the *taqa*, but do no mischief, and incur no danger: and this is just what they like. The challenging is their delight; beyond it their ambition does not reach, and glory is without charms.

Notwithstanding the boasts of the braves, the Chief will sometimes playfully taunt them; intimating that, from their appearance, he should judge them to be better

* The place against which they were going to fight.

acquainted with spades than clubs, and fitter to use the digging-stick than the musket.

Incentives to bravery are not withheld. Young women, and women of rank, are promised to such as shall, by their prowess, render themselves deserving. A woman given as a reward for valour is called, "The cable of the land;" and the Chief who gives her is esteemed a benefactor, his people testifying their gratitude by giving him a feast and presents. Promises of such rewards are made in a short speech, the substance of which is the same in all cases: "Be faithful to my cause; do not listen to those who call you to desert me. Your reward will be princely."

The forces collected for war rarely exceed in number a thousand men. An army of four or five thousand is only assembled by an immense effort. Sometimes flags are used, but they are only paltry affairs.

When all is ready, the army is led probably against some mountain fastness, or a town fortified with an earth rampart, about six feet thick, faced with large stones, surmounted by a reed-fence or cocoa-nut trunks, and surrounded by a muddy moat. Some of their fastnesses well deserve the name. One was visited by myself, where ten men might defy a host. After wearily climbing up a rugged path, hidden and encumbered with rank vegetation, I reached the verge of a precipice. This was the end of the path, and beyond it, at the distance of several yards, in the face of the cliff, was the entrance to the fortress. To get to this opening it was necessary to insert my toes in the natural crevices of the perpendicular rock, laying hold with my hands on any irregularity within reach, and thus move sideways until a small landing at the doorway was reached. Some of these strongholds have, in addition to their natural difficulty of access, strong palisades and stone breastworks pierced with loopholes. Sometimes a fortress has only one gateway, with a traverse leading to it; but from four to eight entrances are generally found. At the top of the gateway, on the inside, there is sometimes a raised and covered platform for a look-out. The gates are

formed by strong sliding bars inside : without, on either
side, are substantial bastions. Visitors capable of judging
give the Fijians credit for skill in arranging these several
parts, so as to afford an excellent defence even against
musketry. The garrisons are often well provisioned, but
ill watered.

Since the introduction of orange and lemon trees, some
fortifications have a row of these in lieu of the wicker-like
fence, and the naked natives fear these prickly living walls
greatly. It is in garrisons that drums are used, and, by
various beats, warning is given to friends outside of the
approach of danger or an attack. By the same means they
defy the foe, as also by banners, and gaudy kite-like things
which, when the wind favours, are flown in the direction of
the enemy.

If a place, when attacked, is likely to hold out, an
encampment is formed and a vigilant guard kept by the
besiegers, and by each party the steps of the other seem to
be counted. Such a position is not liked; but great
advantages and easy conquest best suit the aggressors.
An attack being decided upon, a command to that effect is
issued by the Vu-ni-valu, who names the order in which
the several companies are to advance, and specifies which is
to have the honour of the first assault. The assailants
then join in a sort of slogan and set off. If the country
be favourable, they prefer a stealthy approach, and, when a
little beyond gun-shot from the fort, each man acts as
though his chief duty were to take care of himself. Not a
stone, bush, or tree, but has a man behind it, glad of anything to come between him and the fort; whence a strict
watch is kept, until some straggler—perhaps a child—is
exposed, and falls a victim. If the defenders of the place
remain obstinate, the besiegers repeat the war-cry, to
encourage each other and alarm the enemy. Numerous
shots are now exchanged; and if those within are many and
valorous, they make a sally, each man singling out his
antagonist, and so the battle resolves itself into a number
of single combats. Should the first detachment shoot and

E

shout themselves tired, without drawing the enemy out,
they are relieved by a second, who, if they succeed no
better, are followed by a third, and so on. A rush from
within generally makes the assaulting party run. ·This
conduct is excused by a native proverb, which, in some
shape or other, is to be found in almost every language,
and which in Fiji, in the form of a couplet, waits ready on
every warrior's lip.*

> " 'T is certain death to brave it out ;
> And but a jest to join the rout."

Nevertheless, obstinate resistance is sometimes made.
Death or victory was declared in a striking way by the
Chief of Mbua, Ngoneseuseu, at the beginning of the present century. He and his second in command—Ndunga-
wangka—ordered the heads of two stately nut-trees to be
cut off, and sent a messenger to the enemy, the Chief of
Raviravi, to tell what was done, and defy him to do his worst.
Both sides exerted themselves to the utmost, and a bloody
battle ensued. The symbolic act of the Mbua Chiefs pr
ominous of their own fate ; for their own heads oand
hundreds more of their followers (an eye-witness says, a
thousand) were cut off and placed in a row, and desolation
was spread by the victors over all the western coast of
Vanua Levu.

Sharp and irritating remarks are exchanged by hostile
parties previous to an engagement. Thus a commander
will cry out loudly, so that both sides may hear, " The
men of that fort have been dead a long while ; those who
occupy it now are a set of old women." Another, addressing his followers, says derisively, "Are they gods who
hold yonder guns? Are they not mere men? They are
only men. We have nothing then to fear ; for *we are truly*
men." Such speeches elicit others of like kind from the
enemy. " You are men ! But are you so strong that,
if speared to-day, you will not fall until to-morrow?"
"Are you stones, that a bullet will not enter you?

* " *A vosota, na mate :*
A dro na ka ni veiwale."

Are your skulls iron, that a hatchet will not cleave them?"

Under the excitement of the time, indiscreet men have been known to utter special threats against the leader of the enemy. Shouting his name, they declare their intention to cut out his tongue, eat his brains, and make a cup of his skull. Such boasters become at once marked men: orders are given to take them alive, and woful is their lot, if captured. On Vanua Levu, the punishment awaiting such is called *drewai sasa*, after the manner in which women carry fuel. A large bundle of dry cocoa-nut leaves is bound across the shoulders of the offender, so as to pinion him effectually. The ends of the bundle, which project several feet on either side, are then ignited, and the bearer of the burning mass is turned loose to run wherever his torment may drive him. The exultation of the spectators rises in proportion as the agony of the sufferer becomes more intense.

Wars in Fiji are sometimes bloodless, and result only in the destruction of property; but in cases where the contest is of a purely civil kind, fruit-trees are often spared until the obstinacy of the enemy exhausts the patience of the rest, and a general destruction takes place. An opinion has frequently been expressed that the natives are sharp enough to dodge the bullets; which means that they watch the flash of the gun, and instantly fall flat on the ground. Of their ability to dodge stones, thrown thickly and with good aim, I am a witness.

Open attack is less esteemed in Fiji than stratagem or surprise, and to these their best men trust for success and fame. Their plots are often most treacherous, and exhibit heartless cruelty, without ingenuity.

A Rakiraki Chief named Wangkawai agreed to help the Chief of Na Korovatu, who was engaged in war. Of course Wangkawai and his party must *bole;* and the ceremony was finished joyously. As the earnest for payment was being presented by the Na Korovatu Chief, Wangkawai struck him dead with his club; at which preconcerted signal his armed attendants attacked and murdered the friends of the fallen Chief,—a catastrophe which the treacherous ally had been meditating for years.

Mbau wished to take the town on Naingani, but could not. The Viwa Chief, Namosemalua, being applied to, readily undertook the task. He went to the people of Naingani as their friend, offering to place them out of the reach of Mbau, by removing them to a place under his own power. They assented, and followed him to the seaside, where he helped the Mbau people to murder them. Other similar instances might be related. Relatives within a garrison are often bribed to befriend the besiegers by burning the town or opening the gates. By the use of such means, far more than open fighting, wars are sometimes very destructive. Old natives speak of as many as a thousand being killed in some of the battles when they were young men; but I doubt whether the slain ever amounted to more than half that number. From twenty to a hundred more commonly cover the list of killed. The largest number, within my own knowledge of Fiji, was at Rewa, in 1846, when about four hundred—chiefly women and children—were slain. Horrifying beyond description is the scene when a town is taken, and instances are narrated of the inhabitants seeking deliverance from such horrors by self-destruction. A remarkable shelf of rocks is pointed out on the island of Wakaya, whence a Chief, unable to resist his enemies, precipitated himself. Many of his people followed his example. The shelf is called, "The Chieftain's Leap." In sacking a place, every man regards what he can pick up as his own. The spoil is generally small; for nearly every town and village has a natural magazine, where they store everything valuable on the slightest alarm. I have several times been myself the cause of towns being thus emptied. The sight of my canoe in the distance suggested the thought of oppressive Chiefs or cruel foes, and the wisdom of secreting property. On one occasion, I met a string of laden women thus employed, whose undisguised terror was soon followed by every mark of joy, when assured that we were only friends. Once I saw a Chief with seven balls of sinnet, several dogs, and five female slaves, as his share of spoil; but I believe that part of this was pay, and part plunder.

In a pitched battle comparatively little mischief is done. Flesh wounds are inflicted by spears or bullets, until one of the combatants falls, when his friends run away with him, the enemy following for a short distance; when, if the wounded or dead man is not cast away, they return to exaggerate their own prowess, and the numbers of killed and wounded on the other side. Yet, altogether the total loss of life in consequence of war, amounting probably to 1,500 or 2,000 *per annum*, has hitherto told heavily on the population of Fiji; and perhaps the number here stated does not include the widows who are strangled on the death of their lords. The introduction of fire-arms has tended to diminish war. The fact that bullets are so promiscuous in their work, striking a Chief as well as commoner men, makes the people less disposed than ever to come to fighting, while their faith in the diviner qualities of their commanders is much shaken.

Captives are sometimes taken, and are treated with incredible barbarity. Some have been given up to boys of rank, to practise their ingenuity in torture. Some, when stunned, were cast into hot ovens; and when the fierce heat brought them back to consciousness and urged them to fearful struggles to escape, the loud laughter of the spectators bore witness to their joy at the scene. Children have been hung by their feet from the mast-head of a canoe, to be dashed to death, as the rollings of the vessel swung them heavily against the mast.

The return of a victorious party is celebrated with the wildest joy; and if they bring the bodies of the slain foes, the excitement of the women, who go out to welcome the returning warriors, is intense. This custom of the women greeting the conquerors at once suggests a comparison with eastern, and especially Hebrew, usage. But among the Fijians, all that could be admired in the other case is brutalized and abominable. The words of the women's song may not be translated; nor are the obscene gestures of their dance, in which the young virgins are compelled to take part, or the foul insults offered to the corpses of the slain, fit to be described. And who that has witnessed the scene on the canoes at such a time, can forget it, or help shrinking with horror from the thought of its repetition? Dead men or women are tied on the fore-part of the canoe, while on the main deck their murderers, like triumphant fiends, dance madly among the flourishing of clubs and sun shades, and confused din. At intervals they bound upon the deck with a shrill and terrible yell, expressive of unchecked rage and deadly hatred. The corpses, when loosed, are dragged with frantic running and shouts to the temple, where they are offered to the god, before being cooked. On these occasions, the ordinary social restrictions are destroyed, and the unbridled and indiscriminate indulgence of every evil lust and passion completes the scene of abomination.

Modes of treating for peace vary. In some instances a woman of rank is dressed in highest Fijian style, and presented, with whales' teeth in her hand, to the hostile Chief, to procure peace. More generally an ordinary Ambassador is deputed, who offers a whale's tooth, or some other *soro*, in the name of the people. The terms dictated to the conquered are severe, including, generally, the destruction of their town and its defences, and the abject servitude of its inhabitants. In the Mbua district, hostilities are closed very appropriately. On a set day, the two parties meet, and throw down their arms at each other's feet. At the time, dread of treachery often makes them fear, as they give up their weapons; but afterwards a security is felt which nothing else could produce.

Fijian warfare is very expensive, especially when foreign aid is called in; for the allies have not only to be fed, but enjoy full licence to overrun the territory of their friends, and appropriate whatever they choose, beside committing everywhere acts of the most wanton mischief and destruction.

"O!" said an old man to me after the departure of a host of such subsidiaries, "our young men have been to the gardens, but the sight dispirited them, and they have returned home to weep."

It is customary throughout Fiji to give honorary names to such as have clubbed a human being, of any age or either sex, during a war. The new epithet is given with the complimentary prefix, *Koroi.* I once asked a man why he was called Koroi. "Because," he replied, "I, with several other men, found some women and children in a cave, drew them out and clubbed them, and then was *consecrated.*" If the man killed has been of distinguished rank, the slayer is allowed to take his name; or he is honoured by being styled the *comb,* the *dog,* the *canoe,* or the *fort* of some great living Chief. Warriors of rank receive proud titles; such as, "the divider of" a district, "the waster of" a coast, "the depopulator of" an island; the name of the place in question being affixed. A practice analogous to this is recorded frequently in both sacred and classical history. I had an opportunity of witnessing the ceremony of consecration, as carried out in the case of a young man of the highest rank in Somosomo. The King and leading men having taken their seats in the public square, fourteen mats were brought and spread out, and upon these were placed a bale of cloth and two whales' teeth. Near by was laid a sail mat, and on it several men's dresses. The young Chief now made his appearance, bearing in one hand a large pine-apple club, and in the other a common reed, while his long train of *masi* dragged on the ground behind him. On his reaching the mats, an old man took the reed out of the hero's hand, and dispatched a youth to deposit it carefully in the temple of the war-god. The King then ordered the young Chief to stand upon the bale of cloth; and while he obeyed, a number of women came into the square, bringing small dishes of turmeric mixed with oil, which they placed before the youth, and retired with a song. The *masi* was now removed by the Chief himself, an attendant substituting one much larger in its stead. The King's Mata next selected several dishes of the coloured oil, and anointed the warrior from the roots of the hair to his heels. At this stage of the proceedings one of the spectators stepped forward and exchanged clubs with the anointed, and soon another did the same; then one left him a gun in place of the club; and many similar changes were effected, under a belief that the weapons thus passing through his hands derived some virtue. The mats were now removed, and a portion of them sent to the temple, some of the turmeric being sent after them. The King and old men, followed by the young men, and two men sounding conchs, now proceeded to the sea-side, where the anointed one passed through the ancients to the water's edge, and, having wet the soles of his feet, returned, while the King and those with him counted one, two, three, four, five, and then each threw a stone into the sea. The whole company now went back to the town with blasts of the trumpet-shells, and a peculiar hooting of the men. Custom requires that a hut should be built, in which the anointed man and his companions may pass the next three nights, during which time the new-named hero must not lie down, but sleep as he sits : he must not change his *masi*, or remove the turmeric, or enter a house in which there is a woman, until that period has elapsed. In the case now described, the hut had not been built, and the young Chief was permitted to use the temple of the god of war instead. During the three days, he was on an incessant march, followed by half a score lads reddened like himself. After three weeks he paid me a visit, on the first day of his being permitted to enter a house in which there was a female. He informed me that his new name was *Kuila,* " Flag."

In some parts of Fiji, after each conflict, the parties tell each other of their losses ; but more generally they conceal them. If a valiant man has fallen, his friends place his *masi* on a pole in sight of the enemy, thereby declaring their intention to be revenged. If an enemy come by sea, he is defied by men running into the water and striking it with their clubs.

The arms chiefly used by the Fijians are the club, the spear, the battle-axe, the bow, the sling, and the musket. The club is the favourite weapon, and has many varieties, some of which, however, answer more to the mace, and others, of very hard, heavy wood, wrought with a broad blade-like end and sharp edge, are more fitly classed with the battle-axe. A variety of the *dromo* resembles the spiked mace of the Scythians; the *dui* approaches the double axe of the Phrygians, and the *totokea* is like a spiked hammer, while very many are like the club described by Spenser, as

"All armed with ragged snubbes and knottie graine."

Of Fijian spears or javelins there is a great variety, having from one to four points, and showing a round, square, or semicircular section. Some are armed with the thorns of the sting-ray, some are barbed, and some formed of a wood which bursts when moist, so that it can scarcely be extracted from a wound. They are deadly weapons, generally of heavy wood, and from ten to fifteen feet long. One variety is significantly called, *"The priest is too late."* In hard sieges the bow is sometimes used with effect by women. Fiery arrows are occasionally employed to burn a place into submission. The sling is wielded by powerful hands. I saw a musket which had been struck by a slung stone. The barrel was considerably indented andýbent nearly half an inch in its length. Another weapon much used is the missile club, which is worn stuck in the girdle, sometimes in pairs, like pistols. It resembles the *induku* of the Kaffirs, a short stick with a large knob at one end, either plain or ornamented. This is hurled with great precision, and used formerly to be the favourite implement of assassination.

Clubs—the most primitive weapon—are, as already stated, greatly prized by the Fijian. Those which belong to distinguished warriors have emphatic names, e. g.: *A sautu, lamolamora,* "For war, though all be at peace." *Na tagi, ka kere bole,* "The weeping" (i. e., for the dead I slew) "urges me again to action." *Veitalakote,* "The disperser." *Kadiga ni damuni,* "Damaging beyond hope."

Defensive armour is not used. Security is sought by many in disguise. This is especially the case with men of rank. Bamboo spikes are set in the approaches to a fort, and burnt cross-wise so as to break off into the foot. Sometimes these are planted in a shallow trench, and lightly covered over with earth.

Regarding it from any point of view whatever, there is scarcely anything to excite admiration in Fijian warfare; and the deeds of which they boast most proudly, are such as the truly brave would scorn. Nevertheless I own to having felt keenly when taking leave of Chiefs who were going direct to war. Although nearly naked, their step was proud, and their carriage truly martial. More than one I have known, who paced haughtily forth like a war-horse to the battle, to be soon after dragged ignobly to the oven. Here and there·an instance occurs of manly daring, intelligent activity, and bold enterprise; but such are very few. Of these memorable few was a Chief of Wainunu. A short time before I settled in Vanua Levu, this man drove from him all his influential friends, by a resolution to destroy a place which they desired to save. An enemy of Tui Wainunu, hearing that he was deserted, deemed this a good opportunity to make a descent upon him, and prepared accordingly. His purpose, however, reached the watchful Chief, who determined at once to meet the emergency by acting himself on the offensive. Depending on his own prowess and that of a youthful nephew, he gathered a few old men, whom age, rather than inclination, had kept near him, and proceeded by night to storm his enemy's position. He and his young comrade entered the village about day-break, and, while the old men shouted amain outside, plied their clubs on the panic-struck inhabitants within. Twenty-seven dead bodies were quickly scattered over the place. The club of Tui Wainunu was raised to slay another, when the nephew recognised, in the intended victim, a playfellow, and saved his life. This deed was soon blazed abroad, and the Chief's friends hastened back to him through very fear.

In the greater proportion, however, of the most distinguished cases, perseverance in effecting his purpose, by *some* means, is all to which the Fijian attains. If it be pleaded on his behalf that his valour has no artificial supports,—no helmet or steel breast-plate to shield him from danger, and no fleet horse to carry him from it,—that he opposes a naked body to the dangers of the battle, all this is admitted; yet, after all, the low estimate at which he rates life negatives his valour, and robs the mass of the people of all claim to be regarded as acting under the impulse of nobler emotions. In addition to mutual suspicion and distrust, that pride which rules in every savage nature, keeps the Fijian at war. He likes to take another's property without asking for it, and to trample the owner under foot with impunity; and hence goes to war. Few of this kind care for glory, and fewer still are susceptible of a noble or really patriotic impulse. They make pretensions to bravery, and speak of strife and battle with the tongues of heroes; yet, with rare exceptions, meet the hardships and dangers of war with effeminate timidity.

CHAPTER IV.

INDUSTRIAL PRODUCE, ETC.

PRIESTS' BOWLS.

It is pleasing to turn from the horrible scenes of barbarous war, to the gentler and more profitable occupations of peace, of which the tillage of the soil seems always the attractive type.

At this point there is observable one of the strange and almost anomalous blendings of opposite traits in the Fijian character. Side by side with the wildest savageism, we find among the natives of this group an attention to agriculture, and a variety of cultivated produce, not to be found among any other of the numerous islands of the western Pacific. It is observed that the increase of cultivated plants is regular on receding from the Hawaiian group up to Fiji, where roots and fruits are found that are unknown on the more eastern islands.* The natives raise large quantities of taro, yams, kawai, banana, kumera, and sugar-cane. Rows of maize and ti-tree, and patches of tobacco, are often seen, and the papua-apple is cultivated. Some of these things are too familiar to need any minute description.

Of yams there are in Fiji the usual varieties, and, in some parts of the group, two crops are raised in the year. Ordinary tubers of this valuable plant weigh from six to twelve pounds; extraordinary, from thirty to one hundred pounds. I have raised yams in my own garden nearly six feet in length, and weighing eighty pounds. A teacher on the island of Ono gave a yam nearly nine feet long to a Missionary's child, as a birth-day present. The soil is well cleared for the reception of the plants, which are placed in mounds, and the vines prevented from touching the ground, or playing too freely with the wind, by reeds planted cross-wise beneath, or piled like sticks for peas. Some of the yams grown in Fiji are for barter, and keep well for several months.

The tubers of the *kumera*, or sweet potato, vary in weight from half a pound to five pounds. The *kawai*, or sweet yam, resembles a kidney potato about eight or ten inches long. The vine is more woody than either of the two preceding, and armed with spines. It is prolific, and yields tubers of an average weight of one pound and a half.

Dalo (*Arum esculentum*) is the *taro* of sea-faring men, and the Fijian's "staff of life," surpassing all his other esculents in nutritious value. One kind is grown on dry soil. Irrigated taro beds are generally oblong, and prepared with much labour. The most approved soil is a stiff, rich clay, which is worked into the consistency of mortar, and watered carefully, and often with skill. Valleys are preferred for these beds; but sometimes they have to be cut on the mountain slopes, which, when thus terraced with mature taro patches, present as beautiful a spectacle as any kind of agriculture can furnish. The deep, rich green of

---

* Pickering's " Races of Man," p. 153.

the broad leaves, which rise three feet or more from their
watery beds in rank and file, contrasts beautifully with the
profuse but irregular vegetation of the uncultivated ground.
The root is oval in outline, and of a dark or light slate-
colour, showing in section an appearance like finely veined
marble.   It is propagated by setting the tops of the ripe
roots in deep holes prepared in the clay, and bringing to
mind the celery-beds at home in England.   In ten or
twelve months the taro is fit to be drawn up, and yields
well.   From one to four pounds is a common weight; not
unusually eight, ten, or twelve pounds.   I weighed one
head without the skin, and it reached twenty-one pounds
and a half.   The acrid taste of the raw root is removed by
cooking, which renders the taro a useful and delicious food,
the substitute for bread to the natives, and greatly esteemed
by foreigners.   As a vegetable, it is served up entire, and,
made into paste, forms the chief ingredient in many native
puddings.   The leaves, when boiled, eat like those of the
mercury, and the petiole is little inferior to asparagus.

Qai or masawe (Dracæna terminalis)—the ti-tree—
costs little care.   Its slight stem, crowned with a tuft of
lanceolate leaves, is sometimes seen in rows on the edge
of a yam bed.   The root weighs from ten to forty pounds,
and is used, after being baked, as liquorice, or for sweeten-
ing made dishes.

The banana and plantain are well known, and have been
frequently described.   The beautiful leaf of the former,
when young, becomes the "mackintosh" of Fiji, by being
warmed over the fire, and made into water-proof covers for
the head.   It is also used as a sort of cloth in which to tie
up certain kinds of food, in the preparation of which oil
has been used.   On a remarkably fine specimen of this tree,
I counted as many as one hundred and eighty in one bunch of
the fruit.   The natives cultivate at least thirty varieties, the
fruits of which vary in form and size.   It is propagated by
suckers, four or six of which rise from the roots of the old
tree.   Beside its use as a simple vegetable and a fruit, it
forms a stew with the expressed juice of the cocoa-nut, and

stuffed with the grated nut makes a pudding. The white residents use it in pies, and procure from it by fermentation a superior vinegar. Dried in balls, it is little inferior to cured figs. This, with the bread-fruit tree, is among the most useful productions of the islands. The fibrous stem has never been used by the natives for cordage.

Sugar-cane is grown in large quantities, and thrives well, ripening in twelve or fourteen months. The canes girt from three to seven inches, and their juice appeases both hunger and thirst; it is also used in cookery. The leaves are largely employed for thatch.

Considerable care is bestowed in some parts of the islands on the cultivation of the *yaqona*, (*Piper methisticum*,) the *cava* of voyagers. The root, prized for its narcotic properties, and yielding the native grog, is the part most valued, and that which consequently receives the most care. So successfully is this root cultivated, as to be brought sometimes to a great weight. I had one at Somosomo weighing one hundred and forty pounds.

Another and very important object of agricultural attention in Fiji is the paper mulberry, (*Broussonetia*,) known to the natives as *masi* or *malo*. A *malo* plantation is like a nursery of young trees, having an average height of ten feet, and a girth of three and a half inches. It supplies the people with their principal clothing.

Other vegetables, of immense value to the native, but yielding their benefit spontaneously, and without adding to his toil, will be noticed in connexion with the parts where they severally most abound.

The agricultural implements of the Fijians are few and simple; yet a notice of them may please the curious.

A tool, lancet-shaped, and about a yard long, made of hard wood, is used in breaking down and clearing away the brushwood and coarse grass, which, when dry, is burnt. The ground thus cleared is ready for the digging-stick—the plough of Fiji. This tool is generally made of a young mangrove tree, not larger or longer than the handle of an ordinary hay-fork. The bark is kept on, except at the end which is used for digging, and which is tapered off on one side after the shape of a quill tooth-pick. In digging, this flattened side is kept downwards. When preparing a piece of ground for yams, a number of men are employed, divided into groups of three or four. Each man being furnished with a digging-stick, they drive them into the ground so as to enclose a circle of about two feet in diameter. When, by repeated strokes, the sticks reach the depth of eighteen inches, they are used as levers, and the mass of soil between them is thus loosened and raised.

Two or three lads follow with short sticks, and break the clods, which are afterwards pulverized by hand, and formed into mounds, in the summits of which the yam-set is placed. Thus the best use is made of the light soil, and the training of the vines facilitated, which run from mound to mound, until nothing is seen but an expanse of matted verdure. Before this is the case, the land has to be weeded several times; an operation which is accomplished by means of a tool used like a Dutch hoe, the workman squatting so as to bring the handle nearly level with the ground. The blade used formerly to be made of a bone from the back of a turtle, or a plate of tortoise-shell, or the valve of a large oyster, or large kind of pinna. An oval iron blade or toy spades are fast superseding these.

Among the taro beds of the windward group I saw a large dibble in use, eight feet long, and the lower part eighteen inches in circumference at about two feet from the point, to which it tapered.

A pruning knife was made of a plate of tortoise-shell lashed to the end of a rod ten feet long. This implement was also a mark of rank. But Sheffield blades have long since taken its place, and hatchets, plane-irons, spades, and butchers' knives have produced a great change, and given the present generation a vast superiority over those preceding it, in the facilities thus gained for producing food.

An annual or triennial change of their planting grounds, with occasional drainage or irrigation, constitute the entire system of tilth throughout the islands.

While the men are busy gardening, the women have important work to perform in-doors, a great part of the manufactured produce of Fiji coming from their hands, though receiving some addition from the mechanical skill of the men. In respect of its manufactures, also, Fiji has always had a pre-eminence over other groups; a fact which did not escape the observant eye of Captain Cook, who thus writes about some Fijians whom he saw at Tonga: "It appeared to me that the Feejee men whom we now saw were much respected here: they seem to excel the inhabitants of Tongataboo in ingenuity, if we might judge from several specimens of their skill in workmanship which we saw; such as clubs and spears, which were carved in a masterly manner, cloth beautifully chequered, variegated mats, earthen pots, and some other articles; all of which had a cast of superiority in their execution." The Captain certainly formed a correct idea of the points wherein the Fijian is superior to his neighbours. In printing cloth he particularly excels; but very large quantities of this article are used in its white state. The process of manufacturing the native cloth, or *masi*, has peculiar interest, inasmuch as in some parts—New Zealand, for instance—where it was once made, the art is now lost; and among the Fijians, also, the manufacture must inevitably cease, as the demand for the *masi* declines before the more durable textures of English looms.

The bark of the malo tree is taken off in strips as long as possible, and then steeped in water, to facilitate the separation of the epidermis, which is effected by a large volute shell. In this state the *masi* is kept for some time, although fit for immediate use. A log flattened on the top side is so fixed as to spring a little; and on this the strips of *masi* are beaten with an *iki*, or mallet, about two inches square, and grooved longitudinally on three of its sides. Two lengths of the wet *masi* are generally beaten together, in order to secure greater strength; the gluten which they contain being sufficient to keep their fibres united. A two-inch strip can thus be beaten out to the width of a foot and a half; but the length is at the same time reduced. The pieces are neatly lapped together with the starch of the taro, or arrow-root boiled whole, and thus reach a length of many yards. I measured a dress intended for a King on a festive day, and found its length to be one hundred and eighty yards. The "widths" are also joined by the same means laterally, so as to form pieces of fifteen or thirty feet square; and upon these the ladies exhaust their ornamenting skill. The middle of the square is printed with a red brown, by the following process. Upon a convex board, several feet long, are arranged parallel, at about a finger-width apart, thin straight strips of bamboo, a quarter of an inch wide : by the side of these, curved pieces, formed of the mid-rib of cocoa-nut leaflets, are arranged. Over the board thus prepared the cloth is laid, and rubbed over with a dye obtained from the *lauci* (*Aleurites triloba*). The cloth, of course, takes the dye upon those parts which receive pressure, being supported by the slips beneath, and thus shows the same pattern in the colour employed. A stronger preparation of the same dye, laid on with a sort of brush, is used to divide the square into oblong compartments, with large round or radiated dots in the centre. The *kesa*, or dye, when good, dries bright. Blank borders, two or three feet wide, are still left on two sides of the square ; and to elaborate the ornamentation of these, so as to excite applause, is the pride of every Fijian lady. There is now an entire change of apparatus. The operator works on a plain board ; the red dye gives place to a jet black ; her pattern is now formed by a strip of banana leaf placed on the upper surface of the cloth. Out of the leaf is cut the pattern— not more than an inch long—which she wishes to print upon the border, and holds by her first and middle finger, pressing it down with the thumb. Then taking a soft pad of cloth steeped in the dye in her right hand, she rubs it firmly over the stencil, and a fair, sharp figure is made. The practised fingers of the women move quickly, but it is, after all, a tedious process. When finished, these large squares are used as mosquito-curtains, a comfort which the Fijian enjoys, but of which his neighbours are ignorant. In the work above described the Lakemba women excel. On the island of Matuku very pretty curtains are made; but the pattern is large, and covers the entire square, while the spaces between the black lines are filled in with red and yellow.

On Kandavu a strong kind of *masi* is made, called *liti*, which is the work of men, who leave the women to do the garden labour.

The becoming turban worn by Fijian men is a finely prepared *masi* of only one thickness, and of a gauze-like appearance.

Women's dresses—*liku*—are braided by the women. The bark of the *vau*, (a kind of *hibiscus*,) the fibre of a wild root, and some kinds of grass, are used in making the *liku*, which, while in progress, the women hold by the great toe of the right foot. This dress is a cincture, or broad band of beautiful variegated braid-work, with a fringe from three to ten inches deep.

A variety of this dress is made from the stem of a parasite, called *waloa*, which, when in use, is a bright jet black, and very pliable.

Second in importance to the beating of cloth, is the making of mats. Of these there are many varieties, and the number used is considerable. An intelligent native, on seeing a mat, can generally tell whence it was brought, each island showing a peculiarity, either in the material used, or the manner in which it is plaited. Beside the rough mat made of the cocoa-nut leaf, the women make floor, sail, sleeping, and nursing mats. Large floor mats are twenty-six by sixteen feet, the square of the plait varying from one to two inches. Ornamental borders are from one braid to six inches wide, and display considerable taste. Shreds of coloured English print or worsted, and white feathers, are often worked in the edges. Sail-mats vary in width from eighteen inches to four feet, and in length from nine to three hundred feet: the usual length is fifteen or twenty feet. The worst plait comes from Rewa, the best from Moala. Bed-mats may be divided into mats for lying on, and soft ones for lying in : these are often eight feet long, by five wide. The mats thus far named are sometimes chequered with black. A valuable kind is made at Ono, with a plait from one-eighth to a quarter of an inch in width. The native name of this kind intimates that its use is prohibited to common people. Sometimes a neat angular ornament is wrought into the matting, and one rare kind has a ridge running down the middle of each braid.

The materials used in the construction of these useful articles, are the leaf of the dwarf *pandanus*, of the *pandanus odoratissima,* and a rush gathered from swamps.

Closely connected with the above is the art of basket-making. The baskets made of the same materials as the matting, are flat and oblong, presenting an unending variety of pattern. Sometimes double baskets are seen, some covered, and some neatly edged with sinnet. "The wicker-work baskets of Fiji," writes the Rev. W. Lawry,

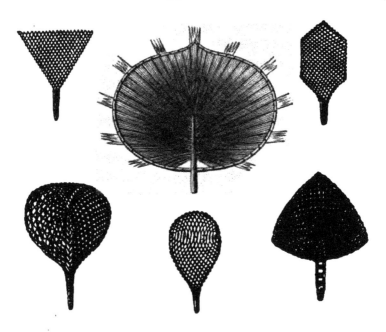

FANS AND SUN-SCREENS.

"are strong, handsome, and useful, beyond any I have seen at home or abroad." Baskets of this kind are made small, and also exceedingly large. Another branch of the art of braid-work is fan-making. These things, in Fiji, are marked by variety, neatness, and utility.

The making of nets next demands notice. The women make theirs of the vine of a creeper known as the *yaka*, which, after sundry steepings and scrapings, is twisted into a strong twine, and then netted. Nets are from three feet to more than three fathoms long, and from eighteen inches to six feet deep. The turtle-fishers make their nets of sinnet; or, when this is not to be had, of the bark of the *hibiscus*. All have the same plan of netting in every respect as that used in England : the needle is the same, and the mesh flat. Shrimping-nets, seines, and turtle-nets, are used all over the group, and are weighted, when necessary, with shells closely strung along the bottom.

Sinnet is a very valuable production, and many tons of it are made annually. It is composed of the fibre of the cocoa-nut husk, dried by baking, combed out and braided, and has hitherto furnished the Fijian with a universally applied means of fastening, lashing, and wrapping : large quantities of it are used about canoes, the houses of Chiefs, and the temples. The kind used for turtle-nets is peculiarly strong. In winding this article, the native love for variety shows itself. There is the plain hank, the variegated roll, the double cone, the oval and round balls, and the honey-comb ball. The usual size of sinnet-balls has been stated ; but this is, at times, exceeded. I measured a roll which was nine feet high and thirteen feet in circumference. One double cone of fine sinnet was twelve feet from point to point, and twenty feet in circumference. Sinnet is used in making the best ropes : inferior ones are made of the *vau*. In size, the cordage ranges from one strand to a cable, and its strength surprises persons familiar with such articles.

The Fijian is also distinguished from all the South S islanders eastward in his potteries, where are produce various utensils of red and brown ware. The drinking vessels are often prettily designed, some being globular, some urn-shaped, others like three or four oranges joined together, the handle springing from each and meeting at the top; others, again, are made in the form of canoes. Earthen arrow-root pans, dye-bowls, and fish-pots, are in great demand. A very neat bowl is made in imitation of the section of a ribbed flower. The greatest call, however, is for cooking-pots. Several of these are found in every house; and as they are not very durable, the demand is brisk. I saw one large pot capable of holding a hogshead,

FIJIAN POTTERY.

and having four apertures, to facilitate its being filled or emptied. Ordinary cooking-vessels contain from five to ten gallons, and their shape seems to have been suggested by the nest of a sort of black bee common in the islands. In the manufacture of their pottery, the Fijians employ red and blue clays tempered with sand : their apparatus consists merely of a ring-like cushion, four flat mallets, (*tata*,) and a round flat stone; and yet the pots are often made with as true an outline as if they had been turned with a wheel. Lines and figures are traced on the vessels while yet moist; and after drying a few days, a number of them are placed together, and covered over with very light fuel, such as reeds, nut leaves, grass, etc.: this is set on fire, and by the time it is burnt out, the pots are baked. While yet hot, such as are to be glazed are rubbed over with the resin of a species of pine. They are now fit for the market. Women have the making of pottery entirely in their own hands, and the art, moreover, seems to be confined to the women of sailors and fishermen.

On Vanua Levu, good salt, but of a sandy colour, is procured by evaporation, and preserved near the fire in baskets made for the purpose. In the same locality small quantities of sugar are boiled.

Fish is cured by smoking, after which, in some parts, it becomes an article of exchange.

Many natives find employment in canoe-building. It seems that formerly none but persons of a certain tribe were permitted to do this work; but now many others are attempting it successfully, and the importance of these artificers in such an archipelago as Fiji may be readily conceived. The carpenters of the present day, however, are somewhat inferior to those who preceded them : neither is it difficult to account for this fact; for they are ill paid, and a vigorous competitor has entered the field, with whom the present race are too dispirited to cope. The Tongans crowd the path of the carpenter, and, as the Chiefs of Fiji like to employ them, seem likely to thrust the native mechanic out of place and work.

Carpenters (*matai*, literally, "mechanics") constitute a caste, which bears in Fiji the sounding name of "King's carpenters," having Chiefs of their own, for whom and their work they show respect. A poor man whom I once saw on the beach, weeping bitterly as he caressed the prow of a large canoe, proved to be one of this class. The canoe was the master-piece of his Chief, who, soon after its completion, was lost at sea. The sight of the vessel awoke recollections of his master's skill and untimely end, and he thus publicly honoured the one and lamented the other.

Near by was another man, who for the same cause silently wept.

Four classes of canoes are found in Fiji : the *velovelo,* the *camakau,* the *tabilai,* and the *drua.* All these have various modifications of the outrigger, (*cama,*) and are distinguished by peculiarities in the hulk. The *velovelo,* or, more properly, the *takia,* is open throughout its length like a boat, and the spars to which the *cama* is secured rest on the gunwale. The *camakau,* as its name imports, has a solid spar for its *cama :* the hulk has a deck over the middle third of its length, twice its own width, and raised on a deep plank built edgeways on each gunwale. Between the edge of this deck and the outrigger all is open. The projecting ends of the canoe, which are lower than the main-deck or platform, as much as the depth of the plank on which it is raised, are each covered with one solid triangular piece of wood, hollowed underneath, and thickest at the broad end next the centre deck, to which it thus forms a gradual ascent. The two ridges, formed by the hollowing underneath on the sides of the triangle, are

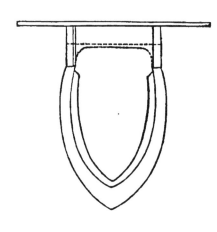

TRANSVERSE SECTION OF
CAMAKAU.

united to the edge of the hulk, so as completely to box it up. The rig of the *camakau* is the same as that of the double canoe described presently; and from the small resistance this build offers to the water, it is the " clipper" of Fiji, and the vessel described under the name of *pirogue* in the Imperial Dictionary.

The *tabilai* is a link between the *camakau* and *drua,* and is made with the outrigger of either. It is often of great length, several feet at each end being solid wood, cut away something like the hull of a ship sternward, the stern-post of the ship representing the cut-water of the canoe, which, instead of being sharp, presents a square perpendicular edge to the water. This is the same at both ends, and is the distinctive of the class.

The *drua*, or double canoe, differs from the rest in having another smaller canoe for its outrigger, and the deck is laid across both.

When not more than thirty or forty feet long, canoes are often cut out of a single tree, and require comparatively little skill in their construction. When, however, a first-class canoe is to be built, the case is far otherwise, and its creditable completion is a cause of great triumph.

A keel is laid in two or three pieces carefully scarfed together. From this the sides are built up, without ribs, in a number of pieces varying in length from three to twenty feet. The edge of each piece has on the inside a flange; as the large pieces are worked in, openings of very irregular form are left to be filled in, as suitable pieces may be found. When it is recollected that the edges of the planks are by no means straight, it will be seen that considerable skill is required in securing neat joints; yet the native carpenters effect this with surprising success. After the edges are fitted together, holes of about three-eighths of an inch in diameter are bored a hand-breadth apart in them, having an oblique direction inwards, so as to have their outlet in the flange: the holes in the edge of the opposite board are made to answer these exactly. A white pitch from the bread-fruit tree, prepared with an extract from the cocoa-nut kernel, is spread uniformly on both edges, and over this a strip of fine *masi* is laid, which is burnt through with a small fire-stick where it covers the holes. The piece or *vono* is now ready for fixing, which is done by what is commonly but wrongly called "sewing:" the native word better describes the process, and means, "*to bind*." The *vono* being lifted to its place, well plaited but not large sinnet is passed through the hole in the top flange, so as to come out through the lower one: the end is then inserted in the sinnet further on, and the sinnet run rapidly through the hole, until eight or twelve loose turns are taken: the inserted end is then sought and laid on the round projection formed by the united flanges, and fastened there by drawing one turn of the sinnet tightly over it; the other turns are then tightened, the last but one being made a tie to the last. The spare sinnet is now cut off close, and the operation repeated at the next hole. The bindings, already very strong, have their power increased by fine wedges of hard wood, to the number of six or seven, being driven in opposite directions under the sinnet, whereby the greatest possible pressure is obtained. The ribs seen in canoes are not used to bring the planks into shape, but are the last things inserted, and are for securing the deep side-boards described below, and uniting the deck more firmly with the body of the canoe. The outside of the *vono* is now carefully adzed into form, and the carpenter has often to look closely to find the joint. When the body of the canoe is cleaned off and rubbed down with pumice-stone, the surface is beautifully smooth. Of course no signs of the fastenings are seen outside. This process is not used in fixing the deep planks which support the main deck, or the triangular coverings of the two ends already described. These, as shown in the section, being on the top of the gunwale, and above the water-mark, the sinnet is seen, at regular intervals passing, like a band, over a flat bead which runs the whole length of the canoe, covering the joint and making a neat finish. Into the upper edge of planks, two or three feet deep, fixed along the top of the sides perpendicularly, the cross beams which join on the outrigger are let and lashed down, and over these a deck of light wood is laid. The scuttle holes for baling are left at each corner. The deck also has six holes forward, and six aft, through which to work the sculling-oars, used in light winds to help the sail, or when dead calm or foul wind makes the sail useless. A small house or cuddy is built amid-ships, in which boxes or bales are stowed, and on a platform over it persons can lie or sit; a rack behind it receives guns and spears, and clubs or baskets are hung upon it. The projecting ends of the canoe are beautifully finished at the expense of immense labour, and are sometimes thickly covered with white shells (*Ovula oviformis*). Any aperture inside not filled with the sinnet is tightly caulked with cocoa-nut husk, and such as are next the water are flushed up with the white pitch or resin.

The lines of the two canoes forming the *drua* differ considerably. A long bow, slackly strung, would represent the longitudinal section of the outrigger, both ends of which finish in a circle less than the palm of the hand. The keel of the main canoe has not so much curve, and the ends differ. The small end is heart-shaped or circular, and several inches over; the large end is like a great wedge, presenting its sharp perpendicular edge to cut the water.

Such canoes seldom exceed one hundred feet in length. The following are the dimensions of the largest canoe I know. Its name was *Rusa i vanua*, "Perished inland," signifying that it would be impossible to launch it.

	FEET.
Extreme length	118
Length of deck	50
Width of deck	24
Length of mast	68
Length of yards	90

The measurement of another *drua*, the *Lobi ki Tonga*, is as follows :—

	FEET.	INCHES.
Length	99	3
Length of deck	46	4
Width of deck	20	3
Height from keel to housetop	14	0
Draught of water	2	6
Length of mast	62	3
Length of yards	83	0

A good canoe in good condition makes very little water, and such as have been just described would safely convey a hundred persons, and several tons of goods, over a thousand miles of ocean.

. A queer thing, called *ulatoka*—a raised platform on two logs—and a catamaran made of bamboos, are used in the bays and rivers.

The well built and excellently designed canoes of the Fijians were for a long time superior to those of any other islanders in the Pacific. Their neighbours, the Friendly Islanders, are more finished carpenters and bolder sailors, and used to build large canoes, but not equal to those of Fiji. Though considering the Fijians as their inferiors, yet the Tongans have adopted their canoes, and imitate them even in the make of their sails. This change was in process when Captain Cook first visited Tonga in 1772. The Fijians whom he saw there were probably the companions of Tui Hala Fatai, who had returned, a short time before, from Fiji in a canoe built by the people there, leaving in its place his own clumsy and hardly manageable *togiaki*. A glance at the new canoe convinced the shrewd Chiefs of Tonga that their own naval architecture was sadly at fault. Their *togiaki*, with its square, upright mast, the spars for stays, projecting like monster horns, the bevelled deck, the loose house, and its broad, flat ends, contrasted with the smart Fijian craft much as a coal barge with a clipper yacht. The *togiaki* was forthwith doomed to disuse, and is now seen no more among the fair isles of Tonga. Not the slightest change has been made in the model thus adopted, and which has now been used for more than a century by the best seamen in these regions; but the Tongans have the praise of executing the several parts with superior care and finish.

Another branch of Fijian manufacture is seen in their various weapons, to which reference has already been made. Most of the clubs are made in the house, but not all. The *kau loa* is preserved just as it comes from the woods, and one side of the *waka* is formed while the tree is growing, and requires attention for several months. The *mada* and the *dromu* are young trees, torn up by the roots, which are cut off nearly close, so as to form a knotty mace. Others are the result of days and weeks of patient toil. The handles of some, and the entire surface of others, are covered with fine and elaborate carving; a few are inlaid with ivory and shell. A very fine and beautifully plaited braid of white and black is made for wrapping some of the clubs, scarlet feathers being worked in with it. Some few of the handles are cased with a kind of wicker-work. The knob of the small *ula* is often cut with exact symmetry, and the projections sometimes inlaid with ivory or human teeth. Some clubs are made merely for scenes of amusement, and not for war.

The variety of spears is very great, and shows the best specimens of native carving, many of the fine open patterns being beautifully executed.

The bows, which are about seven feet long, are made from the pendent shoots of the mangrove. When the arrows are for killing fish, they have several points, with the barbs cut inwards. A spear is also made on the same principle for the same purpose.

With the artisans employed in the above manufactures may be classed those who make pillows—fillets of iron-wood supported on two claw-feet—the makers of breast-plates, rings, combs, necklaces, and other ornaments.

Fancy oil dishes and yaqona bowls, chiefly for the priests, are cut, as well as the cannibal forks, out of very hard wood, and the former in a great variety of forms. I have seen one carved like a duck, another like a turtle,

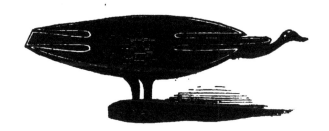

PRIEST'S BOWL.

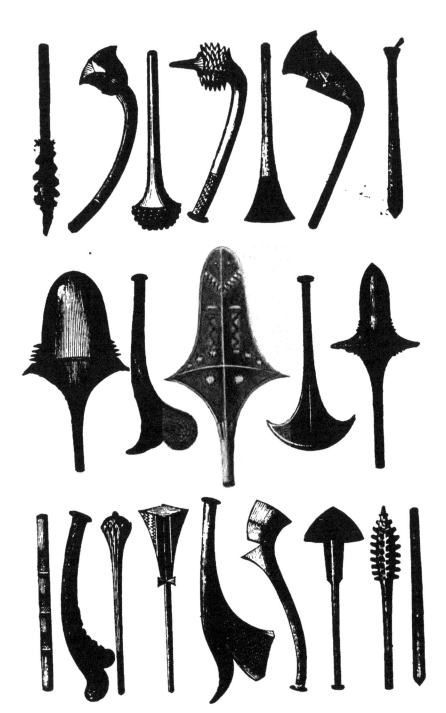

CLUBS.

the Fijian had with which to hew out his posts and planks, to cut down trees, or make the nicest joints, or, together with shells, to execute most marvellous carving. Fire-sticks and the long spines of echini supplied his boring apparatus. With rats' teeth set in hard wood, he executed his more minute carving or engraving; and for a rasp or file he still uses the mushroom coral, or the shagreen-like skin of the ray-fish, and pumice-stone for general finishing pur-poses. With no other aids than these, the workman of Fiji was able to accomplish feats of joinery and carving— the boast of mechanics provided with all the steel tools and other appliances which art can furnish. Now, however, as it has already been intimated, the good blades and chisels of Sheffield, and axes from America, and plane-irons, which the natives still prefer to any other tool, since they can fix and use them after the fashion of the old stone-adze, are, with similar articles, fast superseding the primitive imple-ments of Fiji.

The form of the houses in Fiji is so varied, that a description of a building in one of the windward islands would give a very imperfect idea of those to leeward, those of the former being much the better. In one district, a village looks like an assemblage of square wicker baskets; in another, like so many rustic arbours; a third seems a collection of oblong hayricks with holes in the sides, while in a fourth these ricks are conical. By one tribe, just enough frame-work is built to receive the covering for the walls and roofs, the inside of the house being an open space. Another tribe introduces long centre posts, posts half as long to receive the wall-plates, and others still shorter, as quarterings to strengthen the walls : to these are added tie-beams, to resist the outward pressure of the high-pitched rafters, and along the side is a substantial gallery, on which property is stored. The walls or fences of a house are from four to ten feet high; and, in some cases, are hidden on the outside by the thatch being extended to the ground, so as to make the transverse sec-tion of the building an equilateral triangle. [3.] The walls

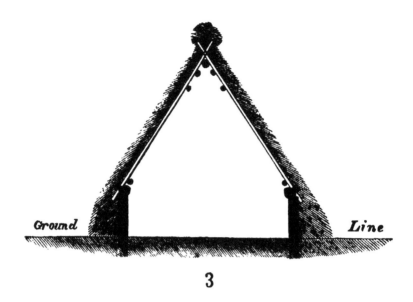

Ground   Line

3

range in thickness from a single reed to three feet. Those
at Lau (windward) have the advantage in appearance ;
those at Ra (leeward) are the warmest. At Lau the walls
of Chiefs' houses are three reeds thick, the outer and inner
rows of reeds being arranged perpendicularly, and the
middle horizontally, so as to regulate the neat sinnet-work

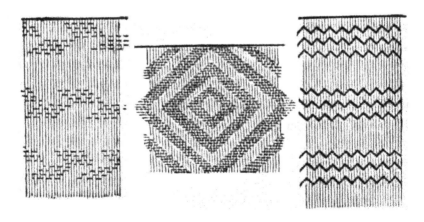

SINNET WORK OF FENCES.

with which they are ornamented. At Ra, a covering of grass or leaves is used, and the fastenings are vines cut from the woods; but at Lau sinnet is used for this purpose, and patterns wrought with it upon the reeds in several different colours. A man, master of difficult patterns, is highly valued, and his work certainly produces a beautiful and often artistic effect. Sometimes the reeds within the grass walls are reticulated skilfully with black lines. The door-posts are so finished as to become literally reeded pillars; but some use the naturally carved stem of the palm-fern instead. Fire-places are sunk a foot below the floor, nearly in the centre of the building, and are surrounded by a curb of hard wood. In a large house, the hearth is twelve feet square, and over it is a frame supporting one or two floors, whereon pots and fuel are placed. [1.] Sometimes an elevation at one end of the dwelling serves as a divan and sleeping place.

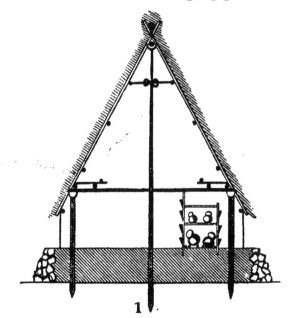

Slight houses are run up in a short time. When at Lakemba, I passed a number of men who had just planted the posts of a house twenty feet long. I was away, engaged with a Tongan Chief, for about an hour and a half, and on my return was amazed to see the house finished, except the completing of the ridge.   An ordinary house can be built in a fortnight; the largest require two or three months. A visitor, speaking of Tanoa's house, says, " It surpasses in magnitude and grandeur anything I have seen in these seas. It is 130 feet long, 42 feet wide, with massive columns in the centre, and strong, curious workmanship in every part." Excellent timber being easily procured, houses from 60 to 90 feet long, by 30 feet wide, are built, with a framework which, unless burnt, will last for twenty years.   The wood of the bread-fruit tree is seldom used; *vesi*, the green-heart of India, *buabua*, very like box-wood, and *cevua,* bastard sandal-wood, being more durable.

A peculiarity of the Fijian pillar spoils its appearance. Where the capital is looked for, there is a long neck just wide enough to receive the beam it supports. A pillar two feet in diameter is thus cut away at the top to about six inches.

Ordinary grass houses have no eaves; [2] but there is over the doorway a thick semicircular projection of fern and grass, forming a pent. [*a.*] Some houses have openings for

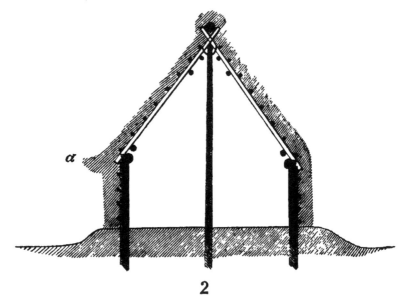

2

windows. The doorways are generally so low as to compel those who enter to stoop. The answer to my inquiry why they were so, often reminded me of Proverbs xvii. 19. Although the Fijian has no mounted Arab to fear, he has often foes equally subtle, to whom a high doorway would give facility for many a murderous visit.

Temples, dwelling-houses, sleeping-houses, kitchens, (Lau,) inns, or receiving houses for strangers, (*bure ni vulagi,*) and yam stores, are the buildings of Fiji.

SLEEPING BURES.

For thatching, long grass, or leaves of the sugar-cane and stone-palm, are used. The latter are folded in rows over a reed, and sewn together, so as to be used in lengths of four or six feet, and make a very durable covering. The leaves of the sugar-cane are also folded over a reed; but this is done on the roof, and cannot be removed, as the other may, without injury. The grass or reed thatch is laid on in rather thin tiers, and fastened down by long rods, found ready for use in the mangrove forests, and from ten to twenty feet long, and secured to the rafters by split rattans. Some very good houses are covered first with the cane leaves, and then with the grass, forming a double thatch. Sometimes the eaves are made two feet thick with ferns, and have a good effect; but, when thicker, they look heavy, and, by retaining the wet, soon rot.

The ridge of superior buildings receives much attention. The ends of the ridge-pole project for a yard or more beyond the thatch, having the extremities blackened, and increasing with a funnel-shape, and decorated with large white shells (*Cyprea ovula*). The rest of the ridge is finished as a large roll bound with vines, and on this is fixed a thick, well-twisted grass cable: another similar cable is passed along the under side of the roll, having hung from it a row of large tassels. All foreigners are struck with the tasteful character of this work, and lament that its materials are not more durable. I have seen several houses in which the upper edge of the eaves was finished with a neat braid. The thatchers, contrary to the statement in the "U. S. Exploring Narrative," always begin at the eaves and work upwards.

A more animated scene than the thatching of a house in Fiji cannot be conceived. When a sufficient quantity of material has been collected round the house, the roof of which has been previously covered with a net-work of reeds, from forty to three hundred men and boys assemble, each being satisfied that he is expected to do some work, and each determined to be very noisy in doing it. The workers within pair with those outside, each tying what another lays on. When all have taken their places, and are getting warm, the calls for grass, rods, and lashings, and the answers, all coming from two or three hundred excited voices of all keys, intermixed with stamping down the thatch, and shrill cries of exultation from every quarter, make a miniature Babel, in which the Fijian—a notorious proficient in nearly every variety of halloo, whoop, and yell —fairly outdoes himself. All that is excellent in material or workmanship in the Chiefs' houses, is seen to perfection and in unsparing profusion in the *bure*, or temple.

An intelligent voyager observes, "In architecture the Fijians have made no mean progress; and they are the only people I have seen, among those classed by Europeans as 'savages,' who manifested a taste for the fine arts; while, as with the ancient Greeks, this taste was universal."*

Sailors—an important part of the Fijian community—are found throughout the group; and not among the men only, for many women are able to discharge the duties of "ordinary seamen." The Levuka and Mbutoni tribes are especially nautical, and, their roving habits inducing irregular practices, their character is not very fair : they are insolent or officious, as self-interest may dictate. As much may be said of the fishermen's caste, to which the others are closely allied. Fijians do not make bold sailors, and none have yet taken their canoes beyond the boundaries of their own group. One old man I knew, who freighted his canoe with pots and *masi*, sought the help of his god, and sailed away for a land which his fancy, or some equally foolish informant, told him lay to the west of the Exploring Isles, and with which he rejoiced to think he should open a trade. But after an absence of two or three days, Toa-levu (the Great Fowl) returned crest-fallen and disappointed, and his failure was pointed out as a warning to all ambitious navigators. I never heard of but one Fijian Chief who had attempted to steer his canoe to Tonga, though the people of that grou , having the wind in their favour, pay yearly visits to Fiji.p

Though deficient in boldness, the native sailors display great skill in managing their vessels. When ready for sea, the mast, which is "stepped on deck in a chock," stands erect, except that it is hauled to bend towards the outrigger. It is secured by fore and back stays, the latter taking the place of shrouds : when the sail is hoisted, the halyards also become back-stays : these ropes, as long as the canoe is under sail, may be called her standing rigging, not being loosed in tacking. The halyards are bent on the yard at less than a third of its length from the upper end, and passed over the top of the mast, which has generally a crescent form. The great sail is allowed to swing a few feet from the deck, or to lie upon it, until orders are given to get

* Pickering's " Races of Man," p. 153.

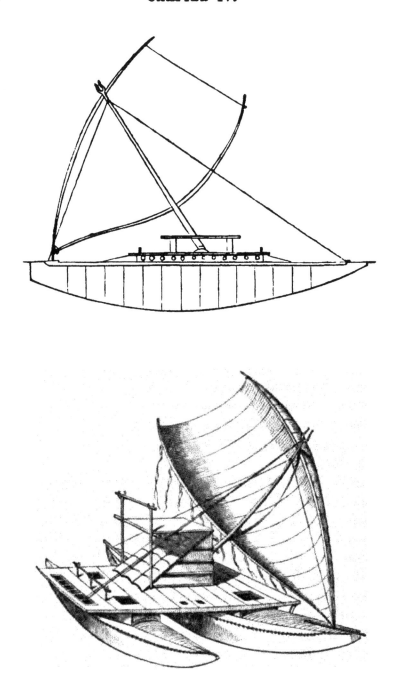

under way. The yard is now hoisted hard up to the mast-
head; but, as the length of the yard from the halyards to

the tack is longer than the mast, the latter is slacked off so as to incline to that end of the canoe to which the tack is fixed, thus forming with the lower length of the yard a triangle, of which the line of deck is the base. The ends of the deck-beams on the *cama* side serve for belaying pins on which a turn of the halyards is taken, the loose ends being passed round the "dog," or belaying pole. The steersman, holding a long oar, stands nearly on a line with the tack on the far edge of the main-deck, while in the opposite corner is the man who tends the sheet. The sheet is bent on the boom about two-thirds up, and, by giving it a couple of turns on a beam, one man can hold it even in a breeze. Like the felucca of the Mediterranean, the helm is used at either end, and, on tacking, is put up instead of down, that the outrigger may be kept to windward : the wind being brought aft, the tack is carried to the other end, which is thus changed from stern to bow, the mast being slacked back again to suit the change; the helmsman and sheet-holder change places, and the canoe starts on her new tack. Unless the outrigger be kept to the weather side, the canoe must be swamped ; for, so soon as it gets to leeward, the wind drives the sail against the mast, and the *cama* is forced under water. If the man at the sheet does not slack away promptly, when a gust of wind strikes the sail, the *cama* is raised into the air, and the canoe capsizes. These craft are easily overturned by carelessness ; but, when properly managed, will carry sail in a brisk breeze. The weight of the sail with the force of the wind being imposed on one end, strains the canoe.

A steer-oar for a large canoe is twenty feet long, with an eight-feet blade sixteen inches wide. Being made of heavy wood, the great difficulty of handling it is eased by a rope which is passed through the top of the blade, and the other end of which is made fast to the middle beam of the deck. "Rudder-bands," too, are attached to the handle of the oar, and carried towards the *cama*; yet two, and sometimes three, men are needed to keep the canoe on her course. Violent blows on the side are often received

from the helm, and I have known them cause a man's
death.

In a calm, the canoe is propelled by vertical sculling.
Four, six, or eight sculls, according to the size of the canoe,
are used.   The men who work them throw their weight on
the upright oar from side to side, moving together, and
raising their feet alternately, so as to give, at a distance,
the appearance of walking over the water.

In smooth weather, canoe-sailing is pleasant enough;
but in a sea and heavy wind, the deck inclines at a most
uncomfortable angle to the water.   When running with
the small end foremost, a beautiful jet of water, ever
changing its form, is thrown up in front to the height of a
yard; or, sometimes, the body of the canoe is driven along
beneath the surface, and only seen occasionally,—a dark
outline in a bed of foam.   When this is the case, a
landsman is safest sitting still, but the native sailors move
about with surprising security.

Canoe-sailing is not silent work.   The sail is hoisted and
the canoe put about with merry shouts; a brisk inter-
change of jest and raillery is kept up while poling over
shoal reefs, and the heavier task of sculling is lightened by
mutual encouragement to exertion, and loud thanks to the
scullers, as each set is relieved at intervals of five or ten
minutes.   A dead calm is enlivened by playful invitations
addressed to the wind most wanted, the slightest breath
being greeted with cries of, "Welcome! welcome on
board!" and when, with full sail, the canoe bounds
along,—

> "The merry seamen laugh to see
> Their fragile bark so lustily
> Furrow the green sea-foam."

If there should be drums on board, their clatter is added to
the general noise.   The announcement to the helmsman of
each approaching wave, with the order to *lavi*,—keep her
away,—and the accompanying "one, two, and another to
come," by which the measured advance of the waves is
counted, with passing comments on their good or ill

demeanour, keep all alive and all in good humour. If the canoe is sound, nothing but bad weather can spoil the enjoyment of such voyaging. The duties of the *ship* are not attended to in the perfunctory style of a hired crew, but in just the same spirit as actuates friends on a pleasure-trip, where each feels his own happiness involved in the happiness of all.

Generally my crews were careful to avoid the dangers of the deep : but sailors are allowed occasional freaks, and mine had theirs. On more trips than one they broke off their course, and, forgetful of the primary object of the voyage, engaged in an absorbing chase after a shark, or sting-ray, or turtle, apparently willing to wreck the canoe, rather than lose the fish.

The heathen sailors are very superstitious. Certain parts of the ocean, through fear of the spirits of the deep, they pass over in silence, with uncovered heads, and careful that no fragment of food or part of their dress shall fall into the water. The common tropic-bird is the shrine of one of their gods, and the shark of another ; and should the one fly over their heads, or the other swim past, those who wore turbans would doff them, and all utter the word of respect. A shark lying athwart their course is an omen which fills them with fear. A basket of bitter oranges put on a *vesi* canoe is believed to diminish its speed. On one of their canoes it is *tabu* to eat food in the hold ; on another, in the house-on-deck ; on another, on the platform over the house. Canoes have been lost because the crew, instead of exerting themselves in a storm, have quitted their posts to *soro* to their god, and throw yaqona and whales' teeth at the waves to propitiate them.

The fishermen, though associated with the sailors, move about still nearer home. They take great quantities of fish ; and the chief work of some is the catching of turtle. The principal fishing-tribes are those of Lasakau and Malaki ; but nearly every influential Chief has a company of fishermen at command. Various means are employed for taking fish, including nets and a sort of weir formed like the creels and crab-pots used along the British coasts, and baited and secured in the same way. Another kind has two apertures; a third contrivance is an intricate fence, either fixed or portable. Stone pens, hooks, and fish-spears, are in use throughout Fiji. Some drowsy fish of the shark family are taken by passing a noose over their heads, and a vegetable poison from a climbing glycine is employed to stupify smaller kinds. In some parts the *rau* is used, which is a fringe formed by winding split cocoa-nut leaves round a number of vines, to the length of hundreds or even thousands of feet. This being stretched in a straight line, the canoes to which the ends are attached approach until they meet, thus making a vast enclosure within which the fish are then speared or netted. One kind of net is used in the same way. The native seines are like our own, and are well made.

Turtle-fishers generally act under orders from the Chief of whose establishment they form a part, and often receive presents of food and property on their return from a successful trip. At times they engage themselves to other people, when it is understood that they are to fish ten times. When they take nothing, they receive no payment; but each time they bring in one or more turtles, food and property are given them, and the employer must make them a handsome present on the completion of the engagement. For this work nets are used, made of sinnet, and very inferior ones of *vau*. They should not be less than sixty yards long; the best are two hundred. Sixteen meshes, each seven or eight inches square, give a depth of about ten feet. The floats are of light wood, about two feet long, and five feet apart: pebbles or large trochus shells are used to weight the lower edge. This net is carried out on a canoe into deep water, and let down just outside the reef: both ends are next brought close to the reef, or, should there be water enough, a little way upon it: thus there is formed a semi-circular fence, which intercepts the turtle on its way back from feeding. If the

animal turns from the net, it is frightened back by the
fishermen, who shout, strike the water with poles, and
stamp furiously on the deck of the canoe, until their prey
becomes entangled by its attempts to pass through the net.
A plan, not generally known, is practised at night by some
of the Malakis. The net is then said to be *nursed*: that
is, several persons, stationed at intervals along the net,
which is fully stretched out, hold it gathered up in their
arms. The approach of the turtle is then listened for, and
the man towards whom it comes drops the net, and the
animal is secured. But the most difficult part of the business—that of getting actual possession—yet remains.
The men have to dive and seize their captive in an element
where he is more at home than they. The struggle is
sometimes violent, and the turtle, if large, requires the
exertions of four or five men. The first diver aims to
secure the extremity of the fore-fin, it being thought that
by depressing the fore-part of its body the turtle is made
more eager to ascend: to lay hold of the body-joint of the
fin would endanger a man's hand. If their captive is very
troublesome, the men try to insert a finger and thumb in
the sockets of the eyes, so as to insure a firmer hold.
Finding resistance vain, the creature moves upward, and
his enemies rise too, glad enough to leave the unnatural
element which has been the scene of conflict. On their
appearance above water, the men on the canoe help to drag
the prize on board, where it is turned on its back, its flat
buckler preventing its regaining its natural position.
Loud blasts on the conch-shell announce the triumph of
the fishermen.

The heathen fishers of Mbua take with them a consecrated club, which, when a turtle is caught, is dipped
by a priest into the sea, and so held by him that the
water may drip off it into the animal's mouth: during
this ceremony he offers prayers, beseeching the god to
be mindful of his votaries, and give them a successful
season.

Turtle-fishing is not without danger, and lives are sometimes lost in it by deep openings in the reef, or the savage attacks of the shark. Sometimes the sail of the canoe is made to cast its shadow behind the swimming turtle, which is thus frightened and pursued until exhausted, when it is easily captured. The people on land sometimes take the female when she comes ashore to deposit her eggs. But man is not the turtle's only enemy. Sharks, as well as Aldermen, have a *penchant* for green fat, and, selecting the finest specimen, surround the harmless creature and tear it in pieces. I have often seen turtles which have been mangled in these attacks. I once weighed a pound and a half of turtle-shell, which was found in a shark's stomach, in fragments so large as to enable me to decide to what part of the buckler they belonged, and to justify the con-clusion that the whole "head" must have weighed between three and four pounds. The entire weight of the turtle could not have been less than two hundred-weight. The head, fins, and most of the body were found in an undi-gested state in this one shark, which paid for its gluttony dearly; for it was found dead. An old fisherman of my acquaintance, whose word I have no reason to doubt, assured me that only four moons previously he took a turtle whole, and weighing about one hundred-weight, from the stomach of a shark, in which receptacle he also found a common parrot. Yet sharks, in these waters, are rarely more than twelve feet in length, and very seldom as large.

The fishermen of Fiji might supply the naturalist with many interesting facts, did not their superstition urge them to avoid, as quickly as possible, the presence of anything extraordinary, believing it to be supernatural, and · fearing lest they should be guilty of unpardonable temerity in remaining in its presence.

After successful fishing, the canoes return in nearly the same order, and with as much noise, as when they come home from war laden with their slain foes. The women meet them with dancing and songs, which, I remember, in one instance they finished by a smart volley of bitter oranges, which the men returned by driving the women from the beach.

The turtle caught are kept in stone or paled pens. Three or four may be taken in a day; but many days are quite without success. Fifty or a hundred turtle caught in a season, constitute very good fishing. According to Fijian fishermen, the female only yields the tortoise-shell of commerce. Traders name the thirteen plates which cover the back, " a head." A head of shell weighs from one to four pounds; the latter is not common. One or two heads have been taken weighing five pounds; and one, seven pounds. Fishermen make offerings to their gods, and obtain promise of success before leaving home. Tuikila-kila once thought fit to accompany his men. The priestess promised five turtles, and the party set out in high spirits. Some days after, we saw them returning, but in profound silence: an unwelcome omen for the poor priestess, who forthwith fled and hid herself in the forest, and thus prevented the enraged King from cooking her instead of a turtle.

The commercial transactions of the Fijians, though dating far back, have been on a small scale, consisting of a barter trade, which is chiefly in the hands of the Levuka, Mbutoni, and Malaki people, who regard the sea as their home, and are known as " the inhabitants of the water." Although wanderers, they have settlements on Lakemba, Somosomo, Great Fiji, and other places. They exchange pottery for *masi*, mats, and yams. On one island, the men fish, and the women make pots, for barter with the people on the main. Their mode of exchange is very irregular. The islanders send to inform those on the mainland that they will meet them, on such a day, at the trading-place,— a square near the coast paved for the purpose. The people of the continent bring yams, taro, bread, &c., to exchange for fish. The trade is often left to the women, among whom a few transactions take place quietly, when some misunderstanding arises, causing excited language, and ending in a scuffle. This is the signal for a general scramble, when all parties seize on all they can, and run off with their booty amidst the shouts and execrations of the less successful.

The inland tribes of the Great Fiji take *yaqona* to the coast, receiving in exchange mats, *masi*, and fine salt.

For nearly one hundred years past the Friendly Islanders have traded with Fiji. The scarlet feathers of a beautiful paroquet were a leading attraction. These birds abounded in one part of Taviuni, where they were caught by nets, and purchased by the Tongans, who traded with them in exchange for the fine mats of the Samoans. They paid the Fijians for the paroquets with small articles of European manufacture, bowls, and the loan of their women. Iron goods were thus introduced among the Somosomans. The first article of steel owned by them seems to have been the half of a ship-carpenter's draw-knife, ground to an edge at the broken end. This was fixed as an adze, and greatly prized, receiving the name of *Fulifuli*, after the Chief who brought it to Fiji. One of their first hatchets came through the Tongans, and was named *Sitia*. This intercourse between the Friendly Islanders and Mbua came to an end in consequence of the quarrels and bloodshed to which it gave rise. A Tongan canoe—the *Ndulu-ko-Fiji*—was appropriated by the natives of Mbua, who had murdered the crew.

The inhabitants of the Friendly Islands still depend on Fiji for their canoes, spars, sail-mats, pottery, and mosquito curtains. They also consume large quantities of Fijian sinnet and food, bringing in exchange whales' teeth, the same made into necklaces, inlaid clubs, small white cowries, Tonga cloth, axes, and muskets, together with the loan of their canoes and crews, and, too often, their services in war. This kind of intercourse has greatly increased of late years, and its injurious effects on the morals of the Tongans, and the advance of Christianity in Fiji, are incalculable. A plan for so regulating this commerce, as to secure to the Tongans its advantages, and to the Fijians a protection from its evils, is yet needed.

Commercial intercourse between Europeans and the people of Fiji was commenced about the year 1806, probably by vessels of the East India Company visiting the northeast part of Vanua Levu to procure sandal-wood for the Chinese market. The payments in exchange were made with iron hoop, spikes, beads, red paint, and similar trifles. On the failure of sandal-wood, biche-de-mar—the *trepang* of old books—began to be collected, and the natives were encouraged to preserve the turtle-shell. Traffic in these articles has been, and is still, chiefly in the hands of Americans from the port of Salem. Biche-de-mar, to the value of about 30,000 dollars, is picked annually from the reefs, principally on the north coast of Vanua Levu, and the north-west of Viti Levu.

Quite recently small lots of arrow-root, cocoa-nut oil, and sawn timber have been taken from the islands. The supply of oil is not likely to be so far in advance of the home demand as to yield any great quantity for exportation, although proper attention and an improved process of manufacture may effect a considerable alteration in this particular. At present the biche-de-mar is the great inducement to speculation. It is yet found in great quantities on the reefs just named, especially on such as have a mixture of sand and coral. There are several kinds, all of the holothuria family. The native name is *dri*, all kinds of which are occasionally eaten in Fiji. There are six valuable species, of which the black sort is the most esteemed. These molluscs, especially one prickly kind, are unsightly objects, being great slugs from nine inches to a foot in length. They are somewhat hard to the touch, and in drying are reduced two-thirds in size. When cured, they are like pieces of half-baked clay, from two inches to a foot long, of a dull black or dirty grey colour, occasionally mixed with sandy red. The section of the solid part looks like light india-rubber. After long soaking in water, the Chinese cooks cut them up, and use them in making rich soups.

Those who visit these parts for a cargo of biche-de-mar,

complain of the tricks played upon them by the natives, forgetting that they themselves have set the example, and that the hard dealings of the islanders may be regarded as retributive.

Driving a hard bargain is one of the first arts of civilized life which the savage acquires, and the records of voyagers show it to be the first taught. Many have noticed that these people, and others in like position, have shown an utter ignorance of the relative value of articles; and the most amusing instances have come under my own notice of their offering goods in exchange for some desired object, with an utter disregard of any proportion whatever.

There are some other resources of the inhabitants of Fiji which yet demand notice. In addition to the black and brown dyes already mentioned, the natives are acquainted with others of various colours, chiefly of vegetable origin, and the knowledge of which is almost confined to the women. To them, also, is intrusted the management of the pits in which the native bread—*madrai*—is fermented. These pits are round holes three feet deep, thickly lined at the bottom and sides with layers of banana leaves; and into them are put about two bushels of either taro, kawai, arrow-root, bread-fruit, or bananas stripped of their skins. Inferior kinds of bread are made from the fruit of the mangrove, a large arum, and the stones of the *dawa* and *kaveka*. The two last, with *boro* or *pulaka* bread, are used only in certain districts. The root of the carrion-flower and some wild nuts are employed to bring the mass into a proper state of fermentation. Banana bread is the best, and, when fit for use, is very like hard milk curds; but the sour, fetid smell of the pits is most offensive to a European. After the fruit is put in, the pit is covered by turning down over each other the projecting leaves used for lining the sides, and thus keeping out the rain. Large stones are then placed on the top to press all down. When ready for use, a quantity is taken out, mashed, and mixed with either scraped cocoa-nut, papuan apple, or ripe banana, and then folded in leaves in small balls or rolls, when it is either boiled or baked. The unpleasant odour is greatly dissipated by cooking; but the taste remains slightly, though not unpleasantly, sour. Opinions differ as to the amount of nutriment contained in this food. It is certainly very useful to the natives, though many of them suffer from its too constant use. The inhabitants of rocky and unproductive islands receive effectual aid, in the form of baskets of native bread, from such as have an over abundant vegetable supply. Destructive gales sometimes sweep over the cultivated grounds, cutting off the ripening fruits, which, however, in their green state are fit for bread-making; and thus in another way the *madrai*, which disgusts strangers, serves to keep off famine, otherwise inevitable.

Beside the supplies which are reared under the care of the native agriculture, the Fijian has an exhaustless store of food in the uncultivated districts of the larger islands, where, among the wildest and most prolific luxuriance, he may gather refreshing fruits, or dig valuable esculents. Here he finds a large spontaneous supply of arrow-root, which, with cultivation and improvement in its manufacture, he will soon be able to send in large quantities to the home market, so as to compete successfully with the best West Indian samples. The *bulou* is a wild root, very like an old potato, and weighing from one to eight pounds. The *yaka* is a creeper, with a root very like liquorice, and used in the same way. The ti-root and turmeric grow wild, together with two sorts of yams, in abundance. The fruit and bulbous roots of the *kaili*—a sort of climber—are used in times of scarcity. Two kinds of tomato (*solanum*) are found, and eaten by the natives, boiled with yams, etc. The leaves of the *bele* are used as greens. The nutmeg grows here unnoticed and unprized. Among other resources open to the Fijian, without any trouble but that of gathering, may be mentioned the *lagolago* and the *vutu*, —two kinds of nuts. Concerning the latter, which tastes like our English earth-nut, the natives believe that if the young leaves are split, the husk of the nut will be tender.

H

There are also gathered in plenty the *wi*, or Brazilian plum, (*Spondias dulcis*,) the wild fig, the *kavika*, or Malay apple, (*Eugenia Malaccensis*,) and the shaddock. The *tomitomi*, *tarawau*, and *dawa* are different kinds of wild plums. The fruit of the *pandanus* is also used by the natives. This remarkable tree, with its curious self-grown props or shores, is too familiar to need description. I have met with several instances in which the original root had no longer any connexion with the ground, while the tree was supported on a cluster of its supplementary props.

PANDANUS.

The trunk is sometimes used in small buildings, but is chiefly valued for handles of garden-tools. The leaf makes good thatch and rough mats; the flower gives scent to oil; and the fruit is sucked, or strung into orange-coloured necklaces.

The importance and value of the cocoa-nut is well known, and the uses to which it is put in Fiji are too numerous to detail. A remarkable fact, however, concerning this tree, may here be recorded. I am acquainted with two well authenticated cases of the nut-tree sending out branches. One at Mothe, after reaching a good height, branched off in two directions, and was consequently regarded with great veneration. The second and more remarkable case was found on the island of Ngau. Having grown about twenty-four feet high, a cocoa-nut tree struck out into five branches. A man told me that when he saw it, one of the branches had been blown off in a gale, and lay on the ground. He climbed up the trunk to the point of separation, but feared to ascend the branches lest they should break beneath his weight. He guessed them to be eighteen feet long, and some struck off obliquely for a few feet, and then resumed a perpendicular direction. The nuts were never gathered.

A few words are due to the native forest-trees, which yield valuable timber, both hard and soft, in considerable plenty. Among the hard timbers, the *vesi*—supposed to be the *green-heart* of India—is important, as giving to the canoes of Fiji their superiority over those of other groups. The wood is very compact and resinous, often resembling good mahogany in colour and curl. My own experience proves it to be little less durable than English oak. The tree is often four feet in diameter, with a white bark, and small scaly leaves.

The *bau* is about the same size as the former, but more valuable for cabinet-work. It is of deep red colour, close and straight grain, sometimes as compact as ebony, and susceptible of a high polish. The *dilo* (*Calophyllum*)—the *tamanu* of Tahiti—abounds in Fiji, and often reaches a great size, being a durable wood of pretty grain. The *damanu* is a fine tree, and its timber fit for every department of carpentry. The natives prize it, on account of its toughness, for masts. The *nokonoko*, or iron wood, (*Casuarina*,) is used chiefly for clubs. The *caukuru* is equally hard, but has a grain more like wainscot. It is used for the upper parts of houses, but soon perishes in the ground. The *gayali*, I think, is lance-wood. *Cevua*, or bastard sandal-wood, is hard, yellow, of rich silky grain like satinwood, and full of aromatic oil. The most durable wood I have met with in the islands, is the *buabua,* which is very heavy, and resembles boxwood. When being wrought, it gives out a peach-like smell, and works quite fresh after having been cut for years. *Yasidravu* and *mali* are two useful woods, the former like cedar in colour, and the latter a little browner. *Dakua* and *dakua salusalu* are varieties of the *Damaria Australis,* or *Pinus kauri :* a very useful pine, when kept from the wet. The *vaivai* is something like the tamarind : its wood is yellowish, and works very smooth; it is as light as pine, but much more lasting, and is the best of all woods for decks, since it will bear exposure to the sun better than any. The white residents greatly value it. There is also the *viriviri,* which is very light ; and the *rara,* little heavier than cork. All the timbers here mentioned I have either used myself, or had them worked under my direction. Twice the number of useful woods growing in Fiji might be added to this short list.

It will thus be seen that the natives of this group are furnished with a most abundant and diversified supply of all their wants, a supply which, with the addition of proper care, would yield a considerable and remunerative overplus for commerce. Many valuable products of other countries, greatly in demand at home, are already found wild and uncared for in Fiji, or might be introduced with certain success. Arrow-root has already been mentioned. Cotton, of superior quality, grows without attention, and might be cultivated to a very large extent. Many parts of the group are peculiarly adapted for coffee ; and, throughout, tobacco of the finest kind could be produced. Sugar-canes, with but imperfect attention, already flourish ; and rice might, perhaps, be grown in the broad swampy flats of the larger islands. There is good reason to hope that the enlightened enterprise of a better class of white settlers will, ere long, serve to develope the indigenous resources of Fiji, as well as to introduce, on an important scale, other valuable produce. The perils which have hitherto attended a residence among this people, have, in many of the islands, already gone; and, in the rest, are giving way to the better influences of Christianity.

This chapter may be fitly closed by an attempt to give a compendious view of the Fijian year, which has no distinctly marked seasons analogous to those of more temperate climes.

> "For here great spring greens all the year,
> And fruits and blossoms blush in social sweetness
> On the self-same bough."

JANUARY.—A few early yams dug. Bananas planted. Old bananas plentiful. Ivi-nuts and a few wis come in.

FEBRUARY.—Wis and ivis plentiful. Dawa ripe. "First-fruit" of yams offered. Men fishing for turtle. Women making ivi-bread. Sugar-cane planted.

MARCH.—Yams ripe, and yam-stores built. Oranges ripe. New leaf of the ivi puts out. Turtle-fishing. Torrents of rain, with thunder and lightning. Native name, *vulai botabota, i. e.,* "the month when leaves are dry."

APRIL.—Turtle-fishing. Yams dug. Oranges, shaddocks, and kavikas ripe. House-building. March and April are the native *vulai kelikeli,* "digging moons," and, with February, *vulai uca,* "rainy moons."

MAY.—Building. Men out with *vau* seine for fish. Arrow-root dug and prepared. Tarawaus ripe. Yam-digging ends. New plots cleared, and a few early yams set.

JUNE.—Oranges, kavikas, wis, and dawas ripe. The kawai and bolous dug. *Vau* seine in use.

JULY.—Patches of ground broken up for yam-beds. June and July are *vulai liliwa,* "cold moons."

AUGUST.—All hands busily employed planting yams. Now, and in the following month, flowers most plentiful.

SEPTEMBER.—Planting yams, kawais, and kumeras. From May till now are *vulai teitei,* "planting moons."

OCTOBER.—Kawai planting continued. Bulous set; wild ones dug. Kavikas and bread-fruit plentiful. Ivi in bloom, filling the air with scent of violets.

NOVEMBER.—Large kavikas. Bread-fruit. Wild yams dug.

DECEMBER.—Bananas planted. Some bread-fruit.

CHAPTER V.

THE PEOPLE.

VEINDOVI.

THE population of the Fiji Islands has been stated by some authorities at 300,000; and by Commodore Wilkes, of the United States Exploring Expedition, at 133,500, which is nearer the truth, though somewhat too low; 150,000, I am convinced, being a truer estimate. My opinion of Wilkes's computation is based upon the following considerations. Several islands, which he states to be uninhabited, have a small population; and he is wrong in giving sixty-five as the number of inhabited islands, eighty being the real number. Speaking of the larger islands, he correctly remarks that the climate of the mountains is unsuited to the taste and habits of the natives; but he is not so correct in confining the production of their food to the low ground. The cocoa-nut only is restricted to the coast; yams, taro, and other esculents, flourish several hundred feet above sea-level, and the dwellers on the heights purchase fish of those on the coast, or supply its lack with fowls and pork. His deduction therefore does not hold good, that the interior of the large islands is thinly populated; that there are not, for instance, more than 5,000 inhabitants in the inland districts of Great Fiji. Adding therefore to the above considerations my own personal observation and inquiry, I must regard Wilkes's number as too low, and am persuaded that, whatever necessity had to do originally with the selection of the inland districts, the tribes dwelling there remain now from choice.

Native tales about the great size and ferocity of the mountaineers, and of their going naked, deserve no credit; the chief difference between them and the rest of the people being that they bestow less care on their persons, and are more rustic in their manners. On visiting these highlanders, I always found them friendly, nor do I remember that they ever used me unkindly, though their opportunities of doing so were many.

Both on the coast and inland, the population has diminished, within the last fifty years, probably one third, and in some districts as much as one half. The Chiefs do not migrate, as it is said was formerly the custom with the Hawaiians; so that every town ruined in war is a proof of a minished population. Another strong evidence is the large quantity of waste ground which was once under cultivation, —more than can be accounted for on the principle of native agriculture. Except where the smaller islands have been entirely depopulated, the larger ones show the clearest signs of decrease in the number of inhabitants—a decrease which has been very great within the memory of men now living, and the causes of which, beyond doubt, have been war and the murderous customs of heathenism. Those who have thus passed away, if we may judge from their posterity, were, physically, a fine race of men. Some familiarity is needed to picture a Fijian justly; for strangers cannot look on him without prejudice. They know that the history of

his race is a scandal to humanity, and their first contact
with him is certainly startling. Fresh from highly civilized
society, and accustomed to the well-clad companions of his
voyage, the visitor experiences a strange and not easily
described feeling, when first he sees a dark, stout, athletic,
and almost naked cannibal, the weird influence of whose
penetrating glance many have acknowledged. To sensitive
minds the Fijian is an object of disgust; but as this feeling
arises from his abominable practices only, personal intercourse with him seldom fails to produce at last a more
favourable impression.

The natives of the group are generally above the middle
height, well made, and of great variety of figure. They
exceed the white race in average stature, but are below the
Tongans. Men above six feet are often seen, but rarely so
tall as six feet six inches. I know only one reliable case of
a Fijian giant. Corpulent persons are not common, but
large, powerful, muscular men abound. Their mould is
decidedly European, and their lower extremities of the
proportion generally found among white people, though
sometimes narrower across the loins. Most have broad
chests and strong, sinewy arms, and the prevailing stoutness of limb and shortness of neck is at once conspicuous.
The head is often covered by a mass of black hair, long,
frizzled, and bushy, sometimes encroaching on the forehead,
and joined by whiskers to a thick, round or pointed beard,
to which moustaches are often added. The outline of the
face is a good oval; the mouth large, with white and
regular teeth; the nose well-shaped, with full nostrils, yet
distinct from the Negro type; the eyes are black, quick,
and restlessly observant. Dr. Pickering, of the United
States Exploring Expedition, observes concerning the Fijian
countenance, that it was "often grave and peculiarly im-
pressive." * He further remarks, "The profile in general
appeared to be as vertical, if not more so, than in the white
race; but this, I find, is not confirmed by the facial angle
of the skull, and it may possibly be accounted for by some

* " Races of Man," p. 147.

difference in the carriage of the head. The Fijian skulls brought home by the Expedition, will not readily be mistaken for Malayan; they bear rather the Negro outline; but they are much compressed, and differ materially from all other skulls that I have seen."* The peculiar harshness of skin, said to be characteristic of the Papuan race, is more observable among the wilder inland tribes of Fiji, where less attention is paid to the constant bathing and oiling of the body. The complexion of the people varies, but the pure Fijian seems to stand between the black and the copper-coloured races. Dr. Pickering thought that he noticed "a purplish tinge in the Fijian complexion, particularly when contrasted in the sunlight with green foliage;" and adds, "The epithet of 'purple men' might be given to this race, if that of 'red men' be retained for the Malayan." † The nearest approach to the Negro is found on the island of Kandavu. An intermixture of the Tongan and Fijian blood has produced a variety called "Tonga-Fiji," some members of which are good-looking; but the class has not always been distinguished by its admirers from the true Friendly Islanders.

Thakombau, the Chief known as "King of Fiji," is thus described by an American gentleman : "He is extremely good-looking, being tall, well made, and athletic. He exhibits much intelligence both in his expression of countenance and manners. His features and figure resemble those of a European, and he is graceful and easy in his carriage." This opinion agrees with Captain Erskine's description of the same Chief. He says, "It was impossible not to admire the appearance of the Chief : of large, almost gigantic, size, his limbs were beautifully formed and proportioned ; his countenance, with far less of the Negro cast than among the lower orders, agreeable and intelligent ; while his immense head of hair, covered and concealed with

* " Races of Man," p. 147.
† Ibid., p. 149. Captain Erskine, of H.M.S. " Havannah," attributes what he calls " a bluish black tinge," in the colour of the Fijians, to " the quantity of hair on their bodies."

gauze, smoke-dried and slightly tinged with brown, gave him altogether the appearance of an eastern Sultan. No garments confined his magnificent chest and neck, or concealed the natural colour of the skin, a clear but decided black; and in spite of this paucity of attire—the evident wealth which surrounded him showing that it was a matter of choice and not of necessity—he looked 'every inch a King.'" These descriptions will apply to many of the Fijian dignitaries; and the difference between Chiefs and people is not so marked as in some groups: the lower ranks have neither the sleek skin nor portly mien of their superiors, yet supply a fair ratio of fine men, supple in joint, strong in limb, and full of activity.

There is a prevailing opinion, that Albinoes occur more frequently among the Papuan race than elsewhere. My own observation tends somewhat to confirm this, as, during my residence in Fiji, I met with five specimens of this exceptional variety. In three of these, who were adults, the skin had an unnatural appearance; it was whiter than that of an Englishman who had been exposed to the sun, and smooth and horny to the touch. Through the heat of the sun it was deeply cracked and spotted with large brown freckle-like marks, left by old sun-sores. All these persons suffered much from exposure to the sun, and never, as far as I could learn, became accustomed to the heat. The skin had a slight tinge of red, and hair, together with that of the head, of a flaxen colour. In two cases the iris was blue, and in the third there was a sandy tinge. The eyes were kept half closed, as though unable to bear much light. One man of this class I knew well. He lived for four years near me, and was industrious and good-tempered, and eventually became a Christian. Natives are sometimes seen with white hands or feet, the effect of disease; but this blanched appearance never spreads over the body, neither are the parts affected painfully sensitive to the sun's heat. The last Albino that I saw, was a child of two or three weeks old, born of Christian parents who were young and healthy. It was a remarkable object, the skin being much whiter than the generality of English infants, and very clear. A twin case occurred in the village of Na Vavi—a boy and girl, both of whom reached maturity.

The aspect of the Fijian, considered with reference to his mental character, so far from supporting the decision which would thrust him almost outside of mankind, presents many points of great interest, showing that, if an ordinary amount of attention were bestowed on him, he would take no mean rank in the great human family, to which, hitherto, he has been a disgrace. Dull, barren stupidity forms no part of his character. His feelings are acute, but not lasting; his emotions easily roused, but transient; he can love truly, and hate deeply; he can sympathize with thorough sincerity, and feign with consummate skill; his fidelity and loyalty are strong and enduring, while his revenge never dies, but waits to avail itself of circumstances, or of the blackest treachery, to accomplish its purpose. His senses are keen, and so well employed, that he often excels the white man in ordinary things. Tact has been called " ready cash," and of this the native of Fiji has a full share, enabling him to surmount at once many difficulties, and accomplish many tasks, that would have "fixed" an Englishman. Tools, cord, or packing materials, he finds directly, where the white man would be at a loss for either; and nature seems to him but a general store for his use, where the article he wants is always within reach.

In social diplomacy the Fijian is very cautious and clever. That he ever paid a visit merely *en passant*, is hard to be believed. If no request leaves his lips, he has brought the desire, and only waits for a good chance to present it now, or prepare the way for its favourable reception at some other time. His face and voice are all pleasantness, and he has the rare skill of finding out just the subject on which you most like to talk, or sees at once whether you desire silence. Rarely will he fail to read your countenance; and the case must be urgent indeed, which obliges him to ask a favour when he sees a frown. The more important he feels his business, the more earnestly he protests that he has none at all; and the subject uppermost in his thoughts comes last to his lips, or is not even named; for he will make a second or even a third visit, rather than risk a failure through precipitancy. He seems to read other men by intuition, especially where selfishness or lust are prominent traits. If it serves his purpose, he will study difficult and peculiar characters, reserving the results for future use : if, afterwards, he wish to please them, he will know how; and if to annoy them, it will be done most exactly.

His sense of hearing is acute, and by a stroke of his nail he judges of the ripeness of fruits, or soundness of various substances.

Great command of temper, and power to conceal his emotions, are often displayed by the Fijian. Let some one, for instance, bring a valuable present to a Chief from whom he seeks a favour, it will be regarded with chilling indifference, although it is, of all things, what the delighted superior most wished to possess. I well recollect how an old Chief on Lakemba received from my lips an important piece of information, just arrived from Mbau. I communicated it, under the impression that no one else in his village knew of it. His manner strengthened this belief; for, by simply naming the source of my report, I secured his ear, and, as I proceeded, his jaw fell, his eyes dilated, the muscles of his face worked strongly, and long before I finished, the old man was a very impersonation of admiring attention. The effect was complete, and I paused at the end of my story, expecting the usual outburst of exclamation; but, to my mortification, the old Chief's features relapsed into their wonted placidity, as he coolly replied, "The messenger of the King had just finished telling us this news as you approached the house."

The conduct of Absalom towards his brother Amnon is exactly descriptive of what often happens in Fiji : " And Absalom spake unto his brother Amnon neither good nor bad ; for Absalom hated Amnon." I have often witnessed such outward calmness and apparent indifference, when within—

" Slumber'd a whirlwind of the heart's emotions."

I was personally acquainted with the chief parties in the following tragedy, which serves to illustrate the characteristic
just noted. Tui Wainunu, the principal actor, was himself
my informant. In the year 1851, his cousin Mbatinamu
of Mbua was slain. Shortly after Mbatinamu's death, part
of a tribe from the district where he fell visited Tui
Wainunu with a present of pottery, and were entertained by
him for several days. One day, when the party from Na
Mbuna were conversing with Tui Wainunu, their Chief,
ignorant of their entertainer's connexion with Mbua,
mentioned Mbatinamu, saying that he was a fine young
Chief. Tui Wainunu's suspicions were at once excited, and
he, pretending entire ignorance of the deceased Chief, made
several inquiries about him. This had the desired effect.
The Mbuna Chief gave Mbatinamu's history, concluding
thus: "I struck him to the earth, and was deaf to his
entreaties for life." After describing how the corpse lay,
he added, "I turned it upon its back, cut out the tongue
by the roots, and ate it myself! And see this cord, by
which my chest key is suspended from my neck; it was
braided of the ornamental tufts of hair cut from his head."
"And did you eat his tongue?" calmly asked the listener.
"Yes," was the reply, "I killed him, and ate his tongue."
The guest was already a dead man in Tui Wainunu's estimation; but the execution of his vengeance was deferred until
the eve of the visitor's departure. Then, after midnight,
Tui Wainunu called round him a few trusty men, and
walked with them to the house where the victims slept. A
blow on the wall from the Chief's heavy club woke the
inmates, who, before they could recover from their surprise,
were ordered out to die, while the wrathful avenger cried,
"And can you fly, that you will escape from me?" The
first who came out was placed in the custody of an attendant.
The next fell with his skull smashed, and the next, and the
next, until eleven dead or dying men lay at the feet of the
executioners. Two women of the party were kept as slaves,
and the man who came out first managed to escape in the
confusion. All the rest, without the slightest warning,

were suddenly butchered, and their bodies shared and devoured by the friends of Tui Wainunu, who "spake" to his ill-fated guests "neither good nor bad."

It is a trite observation, that the character of a people is shown in their proverbs. The proverbs of Fiji are plentiful, and in agreement with this rule. Of those which grow out of local or other peculiarities there are many, and some have been already quoted. A great number might be added, did they not entirely lose their force by translation, while some cannot be rendered into another tongue at all. The following proverbial saying is often heard, when the setting sun casts long shadows :—

> "*Sa coka na dabea;*"

literally, "The dabea darts forth." The dabea is a large sea-eel which thrusts out its head from beneath the beds of coral, as the afternoon advances.

Greediness is reproved in this couplet :—

> "*Votavota ko lewa, matn ca :*
> *Digitaka ka levu, ka visa ;*"

which may be thus paraphrased :—

> "Your evil eye esteems your share too small,
> And prompts you greedily to aim at all."

The spirit of another, used to shame a cruel husband, may be represented thus :—

> "O what a valiant man you are,
> Who beat your wife, but dare not go to war!"

An ill-regulated tribe, or family badly provided for, is sneered at as, "*A mataqali yauta,*" "A family on whom the dew falls;" *i. e.*, unprotected. The result of wealth in adding care is thus set forth :—

> "*E dua nomu waqa levu,*
> *E dua nomu vusi levu:*"

> "If you have a great canoe,
> Great will be your labour too."

The arithmetical skill of goddesses is an article of Fijian faith, and very high numbers are thus spoken of:—

"Sa wili seva na alewa-kalou:"

"Goddesses, in counting them, would err." Gay attire, and trifling employment, are reproved as follows:—

"Sa sega na lovo e buta kina:"

"No food is cooked thereby." I once heard a man say jeeringly to another of small means, who was looking wishfully at a costly box,—

"Sa sarasara na ika maravu:"

"Becalmed, and looking at fishes." The proverb supposes a person becalmed, and longing for the fish which sport securely round his canoe.

"Sa taumada na vana kai Nakodo:"

"The Nakondo people cut the mast first." Improvidence and want of forethought are thus censured, which would prepare the mast before securing the canoe.

"A medra wai na vosa a tamata cidroi:"

"The saucy take reproof like water," i. e., swallow it without thought.

"Sa tuba leca na siga o qo:"

"An unimproved day is not to be counted:" and,—

"A kena laya sa vakaoqo, sa drau na kena votu:"

"This is like its bud;" (or calyx;) "its results will appear a hundred-fold." These need no comment, and show that the Fijian can be serious, though he is very rarely so, except about trifles.

The people have more than average conversational powers, and chattering groups while away the early night by retailing local news or olden legends. In sarcasm, mimicry, jest, and "chaff," they greatly excel, and will keep each other on the broad grin for hours together. A Mr. Hadley, of Wenham, cited by Dr. Pickering, says, "In the course of much experience, the Fijians were the only 'savage people' he had ever met with who could give reasons, and with whom it was possible to hold a connected conversation."*

* "Races of Man," p. 173.

That considerable mechanical skill exists among the Fijians will have been already evident, and their cleverness in design is manifest in the carved and stained patterns which they produce.   Imitative art is rarely found, except in rude attempts to represent, on clubs or cloth, men, turtles, fishes, guns, etc.   Almost all their lines are straight or zigzag; the curve being scarcely ever found in ornamental work, except in outlines.

Of admiring emotion, produced by the contemplation of beauty, these people seem incapable; while they remain unmoved by the wondrous loveliness with which they are everywhere surrounded.

But the savageism of the Fijian has a more terrible badge, and one whereby he is principally distinguished by all the world,—his cruelty is relentless and bloody.   That innate depravity which he shares in common with other men, has, in his case, been fostered into peculiar brutality by the character of his religion, and all his early training and associations.   Shedding of blood to him is no crime, but a glory.   Whoever may be the victim,—whether noble or vulgar, old or young, man, woman, or child,—whether slain in war, or butchered by treachery,—to be somehow an acknowledged murderer is the object of the Fijian's restless ambition.   This, however, has more to do with the moral character of the people.

It will already be manifest, that the Chiefs who have to rule subjects like these, must be shrewd and sagacious men; and it will be seen more clearly presently, that only such men can insure respect and obedience.

As the character of a people's mind will, of course, reveal itself in their language, a few words are due to that subject here, although its fuller consideration is reserved to a future chapter.   All, therefore, that need be mentioned now concerning the Fijian language is, that it is full, vigorous, of considerable internal resources, flexible, and bold.

Poetry, too, for the reason just named, deserves notice; but of Fijian poetry, strictly so called, there is but little to be said. What has been remarked about the insensibility of the natives to all that is beautiful, will show that a true poet among them is indeed a *rara avis*. Living amidst an "unimaginable luxuriance of herbage, in a greenhouse-like atmosphere," surrounded with "the fresh flush of vegetable fragrance, calculated to regale the senses, exhilarate the spirits, and diffuse through the whole soul a strange delirium of buoyant hope and joy," the mind of the Fijian has hitherto seemed utterly unconscious of any inspiration of beauty, and his imagination has grovelled in the most vulgar earthliness.

The islands named as the most favoured abodes of the muses are Nairai and Thikombia-i-ra: on the former a man, and on the latter a woman, is blessed with the spirit of poesy—a poesy most difficult to define or describe, and which refuses to come within even the widest signification to which that much abused term is often stretched. The account which the poets give of themselves and their productions is amusing. They say that, while asleep, they visit the world of spirits, where a poetic divinity teaches them a poem, while, at the same time, they learn a dance corresponding to the song. The heaven-taught minstrels then return to their mundane home, and communicate the new acquisition to their friends, by whom, on their trading or festive visits, it is spread far and wide through every town and island. No alteration is ever made in the *meke* —a word applied indifferently to both song and dance— however the language may differ from the dialect of the people among whom it is introduced: hence the natives are often ignorant of the meaning of many of their most popular songs, and express surprise if any one should expect them to understand them. The privilege of visiting the spirit-world is said by some to be hereditary. But there are many composers in Fiji who lay no claim to this distinction, but whose productions are nevertheless quite equal to those of the more honoured bards. These are generally a detailing of common events, varied with an occasional episode of fiction. Metre and rhyme are both

aimed at, but neither secured with invariable success. As
far as I have been able to ascertain, the natives judge of
the merit of a composition by the uniformity of metre
throughout, and the regularity with which each line in a
stanza ends with the two same vowels. The great difficulty
of such style is partly removed by the plentiful use of
expletives, abbreviated or prolonged words, the omission of
articles, or other most free poetic licence; but a stanza of
any length is rarely completed without some change of
rhyme. Frequently the first of the two vowels is dropped,
and the rhyme sustained with the last only. The best
specimen I have seen, was the production of a youth under
my own care at Tiliva: it contained eighteen lines, each of
which, without the use of expletives, ended in the diphthong
au. One example from the Fijian Hades is rhymed by a
consonant followed with the vowel *a;* this fails in four
lines. Some *mekes* are in triplets. Fijian poems may be
divided into dirges, serenades, wake-songs, war-songs, and
hymns for the dance. The last class is most numerous,
and includes many that might be termed historic. In
legendary songs, the native love for exaggeration is freely
indulged. One, for instance, tells of a crab so large that
it grasped in its claw a man, who, though between
the forceps, received no injury. A bold fellow who
climbed the monster's shell was not so fortunate, being
dashed to pieces by a back-stroke from one of its
limbs.

The following story, which is the basis of a very popular
meke, will give some idea of the general character of such
compositions, and also illustrate Fijian customs. Nai
Thombothombo, it is said, is a land of gods, among whom
a few human beings are allowed, by privilege, to reside.
One of the gods, Rokoua, gave his sister in marriage to
another divinity, named Okova. The match was one of
unusual happiness; but, in confirmation of the adage, "The
course of true love never did run smooth," Okova had
shortly to mourn the loss of his wife, and that under circumstances of peculiar distress. The lady had accompanied

her lord to the reef on a fishing excursion, when she was
seized by a vast bird, surpassing the Rok of the Arabian
tale, and carried away under its wing. The bird which
thus took Tutuwathiwathi, is known to some as Nga-ni-
vatu, "Duck of the rock," and to others as Ngutulei.
Okova hastened, in an agony of distress, to his brother-
in-law Rokoua, and, presenting a root of yaqona,
besought his assistance. They set off in a large canoe in
pursuit of the lady, and, on their way, came to an island
inhabited by goddesses, where, says the song, "there
existed no man, but they while away their time in sports."
Rokoua thought to make this their journey's end, saying
to Okova, "Let us not sail further in search of Tutuwathiwathi: here is a land of superior ladies, and abounding in
precious cowries." But these had no charms for the faithful and disconsolate husband, who replied, "Nay, Rokoua,
not so; let us seek Tutuwathiwathi only." Arriving at
the Yasawas, the brothers inquired where the Duck-of-the-
rock could be found, and were directed to Sawailau, but
did not find the bird in its cave. On looking round, they
perceived one of Tutuwathiwathi's little fingers, which
Okova took as a precious relic, rightly concluding that his
wife had been devoured. Having rested awhile, the two
gods saw the devourer approaching; "for his fog-like shade
shut out the face of the sun." In his beak he carried five
large turtles, and in his talons ten porpoises, which, on
reaching the cave, he began to eat, without regarding the
intruders. Rokoua proposed to spear the monster, but
Okova entreated him to pause while he prayed to three
other gods to aid them by causing the wind to blow. The
prayer was heard, and a wind blowing into the cave spread
out the bird's tail: Rokoua seized the opportunity, and
struck his spear through its vitals. The spear, though
very long, was entirely hidden in the body of the bird. It
was now proposed to make a new sail of one of the wing-
feathers; but as its weight would endanger the canoe, a
smaller feather was selected, by means of which they sailed
safely home. Before starting, however, they cast the dead

bird into the sea, thereby causing such a surge as to
"flood the foundation of the sky."

This is given as a fair specimen of a Fijian *meke* of the
common kind. Many more might be cited, were it
necessary; but only such will be brought forward as are
strikingly illustrative of style, or of the rise of a better
state of things among the people.

A sort of dialogue or antiphony is common in the
mekes; but one in regular triplets is not usual. The
following is a good example :—

> MATA.—"*Ai tukutuku ka muri wailala,*
> *Muria mai na tubu levu lala,*
> *Vakavuravura, e mata ni darava.*"

> DOMO MAI LOMA.—"*Vura ca oqori, se vura vinaka ?*
> *Lalaqila sa yadra cala*
> *Cabo dali, Keitou vakatama.*"

> MATA.—"*Na Viti-levu, ka sa samu lala,*
> *Sa dravutaki na kena tamata,*
> *Me tou se ki tubu levu lala.*"
>   *Dulena.*
> "*Ka vuki na bosulu, ka yau*
> *Na Dilolevu ka vakatautau,*
> *Me qorica toka ko Tuicakau,*
> *Ka bara curu loloma koi au :*
> *Mo curu mai ko Adi kea Bau,*
> *Na rerega ko solia vei au,*
> *Qoqoli sili a lewa ni Lasakau,*
> *Bogi mai ko ligoligoci au.*"

In the above, a *Mata* or herald is supposed to proclaim an
official message, when "a voice from within" inquires as
to its purport, to which he replies by announcing some
disastrous occurrences on Viti Levu. The *dulena*, which
is found in many *mekes*, is a sort of epode, rarely having
any reference whatever to the preceding subject, but
being generally, as in the present instance, the vehicle of
indelicate allusions, in which the point and beauty of the
song are thought to consist. Hence when a native yields
to the purer influence of Christianity, he bids farewell to
the nocturnal dance; and a knowledge of the above fact
will enable those to form a better judgment, who have

condemned the practice of the Missionaries in discountenancing the native dances.

Some few of the *mekes* rhyme fairly throughout, and preserve a uniform measure. This, however, is rare. The lines are sometimes, though not often, iambic; in other instances, trochaic, frequently with a remaining syllable. The anapæst and dactyl are sometimes introduced.

The subjoined is a literal translation of a native poem on the Sepulture and Resurrection of our Lord, and will serve as an example of a more elevated style of Fijian poetry :—

> " The Saviour of mankind has expired ;
> And the gloom of an eclipse covers the world.
> The Sun is ashamed, and ashamed is the Moon !
> Joseph carried away the body,
> And buried it in a new tomb.
> The world's atonement buried lies :
> Three nights it lay in the grave,
> And the inhabitants of Judæa rejoiced !
> Then of the angels there came two :
> The faces of these two flamed like fire,
> And the children of war fell down as dead.
> They two opened the sepulchre of stone,
> And the Redeemer rose again from the dead.
> The linen lay folded in its place.
> I stamp underfoot the tooth of the grave !
> And where now, O Death, is thy might ?
> Take to thyself thy envenomed sting :
> I pledge a wide-spread exemption.
> Shout triumphantly, sons of the earth ;
> For feeble now is the tooth of the law !"

CHORUS.—" *Suvaia suva.*"

In chanting, the chorus is repeated at the end of each line. The love of the natives for their poetry amounts to a passion. They assemble nightly for recitation exercises, and enliven their daily tasks by frequent snatches of songs, sung to a sort of plaintive chant, limited to a few notes, and always in a major key. Some have thought it to resemble the singing in a Jewish synagogue.

In detached fragments, frequentl and often appropriately introduced, the poetry of Fiji is certainly shown to the greatest advantage. Indeed, there is no lack of poetic phraseology in the language, and all but the professed poets make use of it. Death is often spoken of as a sleep, and the same figure is used with reference to fluids in a congealed state. Dying is described by the same terms as the sunset. A swearer is said to be "armed with teeth," and ignorance is "the night of the mind." The native describes the furling of a sail in the same language as the bird folding its wings for rest; and the word which expresses "modesty" (*lumaluma*) suggests the softened, retiring light of evening.

Epigrammatic couplets are abundant in Fiji, and some have already been given. One or two more may be added. The first is made for confederates in sin :—

> " *O iko ko tagi ;*   " You must cry ;
> *Oi au kau caki.*"   And I 'll deny."

The next speaks for itself :—

> " *Turaga o qo e dauvuvu,*
> *Mai baria na vatu ka tu.*"

"This Chief is jealous : let him nibble a stone." Another sets forth the fame of the Viwa people for propagating a report :—

> " *Tukutuku e rogo malua ;*
> *Rogo ki Viwa eacavakabuka.*"

"Reports go slowly ; but, on reaching Viwa, spread like fire." A man's claim on his friend is thus put :—

> " *Noqui tau,*   " My friend,
> *Solia noqu yau.*"   Give me some property."

With reference to children, the jingling question is asked and answered,—

> " *Uci cei ?*   " Like whom ?
> *Uci lei.*"   Like his father."

The people often force their words into a sort of rhyming correspondence. For example :—

> " *Manini sautanini.*"   " A miser will tremble."
> " *Malua marusa.*"   " Delay is ruin."

The material for a higher class of poetry evidently exists both in the Fijian mind and language ; and there can be no doubt that as the former becomes refined, so will the latter be exalted by means of Christianity. As the spirit of the Fijian escapes from the fetters of a most tyrannous superstition, and his imagination is no longer defiled by unchecked appetite, or dwarfed by selfishness, or darkened by cruelty; as his heart yields to the softening and hallowing power of the Gospel, a purer passion and loftier sentiment will find utterance in higher and holier strains; God's works of beauty shall no longer appeal in vain for a tribute of loving wonder; a great and widening feeling of brotherhood shall kindle a strange glow in the heart, which, like some harp that has long been cast aside, shall, strung with new and grander chords, give forth music most excellent. The Christian *meke* already quoted may be referred to as, at least, a promise and earnest of that better poetry which the Fijian will have to number among the abundant blessings brought to him by the religion of Jesus.

The transition is easy from this point to the moral aspect of the people of Fiji. In these islands, the theory of those who teach the innate perfectibility of man—an improvement ever developing itself with all the certainty of a fixed law—has had a thorough test, resulting in most signal failure. The morality of the heathen has been a pet subject with a certain class; but experience teaches that the morality of which he often makes an imposing show, is negatived by the principle of evil within him. Every law of the Second Table is, more or less, acknowledged; and every one is habitually and flagrantly broken. The movement apparent in the moral history of Fiji has been steadily and uniformly from bad to worse. Old men speak of the atrocities of recent times as altogether new, and far surpassing the deeds of cruelty which they witnessed fifty years ago.

Pride and covetousness exercise a joint tyranny over the native mind. The Fijian is proud of his person. If he can add a clean *masi* to a well-oiled body and a bushy head of hair, his eye, his step, his every attitude is proud. Conversing one day with an old Somosomo priest, I mentioned the destitute condition of some of the natives of the

New Hebrides, adding that they thought themselves very wise, and had many gods. The priest could not conceal his displeasure at the latter part of my remark. "Not possessed of *masi*, and pretend to have gods!" he muttered repeatedly with great contempt, evidently thinking that the few yards of *masi* round his own loins gave him an immense superiority over those poor creatures, whose presumption seemed so great in pretending to have any gods!

An amusing case occurred near my house. A heathen woman complained of being subject to the solicitations of some god, who was always standing near to entice her to him. Her husband appealed to me, either to drive away the god or his wife's delusion. The Rev. John Hunt was staying with me at the time, and we went together to the dwelling of the woman, he armed with a large dose of Epsom salts, and I with a bottle of spirits of hartshorn. On our arrival, we found the house filled with people, and the woman on her back in the midst, shouting lustily, "Let me alone, that I may return!" The excitement was very great; but the shouting was considerably checked by the sudden application of the hartshorn to her nose. When a light was brought, we discovered that our patient was by no means a Venus, which led Mr. Hunt to observe, with dry gravity, "Truly she is a beauty: what a fancy the god must have who can desire her!" A burst of laughter from the spectators, in which the husband out-laughed the whole, followed this remark. The treatment was most successful. The woman's pride was so stung, that she at once sat up, assuring us that the god had gone away, and that she needed no more medicine.

The Fijian is very proud of his country. Geographical truths are unwelcome alike to his ears and his eyes. He looks with pleasure on a globe, as a representation of the world, until directed to contrast Fiji with Asia or America, when his joy ceases, and he acknowledges, with a forced smile, "Our land is not larger than the dung of a fly;" but, on rejoining his comrades, he pronounces the globe a "lying ball." The process by which a savage has his lofty views of his own country humbled gives him pain, which a feeling mind cannot witness without sharing. There is a danger, too, of the assurance and energy springing from his falsely conceived dignity giving way to listlessness and discouragement, as the pleasing error departs. Many, however, struggle against this feeling. They listen to the reports of foreigners about their own countries, and, knowing that on such a subject *they* could not speak the truth, comfort themselves by believing that the white man is, of course, telling lies. They repeat a common saying,—"The lie of a far away path,"—and hope the best for Fiji.

It will not, therefore, excite surprise that a travelled Fijian commands little respect from his countrymen. His superior knowledge makes him offensive to his Chiefs, and irksome to his equals. A Rewa man who had been to the United States, was ordered by his Chiefs to say whether the country of the white man was better than Fiji, and in what respects. He begged them to excuse him from speaking on that subject, but without avail. He had not gone far in telling the truth, when one cried out, " He is a prating fellow;" another, " He is impudent;" some said, " Kill him! It is natural that a foreigner should thus speak, but unpardonable in a Fijian." The luckless traveller, finding his opinions so little relished, made a hasty retreat, leaving his enraged betters to cool down at leisure, —a process considerably hastened by his absence.

Anything like a slight deeply offends a native, and is not soon forgotten. Crying is a favourite method of giving utterance to wounded pride. If the suffering individual is a woman, she will sit down,—the more public the place the better,—she will sigh, sob, whine, until she gets a good start, when she will trust to the strength of her lungs to let every one within hearing know that one of their species is injured. A reflection on a woman's character, her rank, her child, her domestic qualifications, or any one of a hundred other things, gives sufficient occasion for a wearisome cry. Nor is this demonstration restricted to

the sex: men adopt it also.   I once saw four villages
roused, and many of the inhabitants under arms, in consequence of a man crying in this style: "War! war!
Will no one kill me, that I may join the shade of my
father?   War! war!"   This was the cry which, one clear
day, sounded with singular distinctness through the air,
and drew many beside myself to the top of a hill, where we
found a little Mata goaded to desperation, because his
friend, without consulting him, had cut several yards
from some native cloth which was their joint property.
To be treated so rudely made the little man loathe life;
and hence the alarm.   A native of Mbua put together the
frame of a house, and then applied to his friends, in due
form, for help to thatch it.   They readily assented; but
in the course of the conversation which ensued, a remark
was made that touched the pride of the applicant, who
angrily resolved to make the unfinished house a monument
of his high stomach, by leaving it to rot; as it actually
did, in front of my own dwelling.

Few things go more against a native's nature than to be
betrayed into a manifestation of anger.   On the restraint
and concealment of passion he greatly prides himself, and
forms his judgment of strangers by their self-control in this
particular.   When the hidden flame bursts forth, the transition is sudden from mirth to demon-like anger.   Sometimes they are surprised into wrath, or vexed beyond
endurance; when they throw off all restraint, and give
themselves up to passion.   The rage of a civilized man,
in comparison with what then follows, is like the tossings
of a restless babe.   A savage fully developed—physically
and morally—is exhibited.   The forehead is suddenly
filled with wrinkles; the large nostrils distend and smoke;
the staring eye-balls grow red, and gleam with terrible
flashings; the mouth is stretched into a murderous and
disdainful grin; the whole body quivers with excitement;
every muscle is strained, and the clenched fist seems eager
to bathe itself in the blood of him who has roused this
demon of fury.   When anger is kept continually under

curb, it frequently results in sullenness. Pride and anger combined often lead to self-destruction. A Chief on Thithia was addressed disrespectfully by a younger brother: rather than live to have the insult made the topic of common talk, he loaded his musket, placed the muzzle at his breast, and, pushing the trigger with his toe, shot himself through the heart. I knew a very similar case on Vanua Levu. But the most common method of suicide in Fiji is by jumping over a precipice. This is, among the women, the fashionable way of destroying themselves; but they sometimes resort to the rope. Of deadly poisons they are ignorant, and drowning would be a difficult thing; for, from infancy, they learn to be almost as much at home in the water as on dry land.

Boasting generally attends upon pride, and in Fiji reaches to a very high growth. As among more civilized people, pride of pedigree is largely indulged; and should a native imagine that you are ignorant of his real origin, he will take care to fix it high enough, and support his pretensions by affecting to treat you as his inferior. Toki, a Chief of Raviravi, used to speak of himself as the offspring of a turtle, regarding all other Chiefs as the progeny of inferior fishes. The ruler of a few little islands finds no difficulty in exalting himself above European Monarchs, and designates any of their subjects who may live within his domain, as "his animals." It is a very rare and difficult thing for a Fijian to give an impartial account of any transaction in which he took part, the most trifling incident being always greatly magnified. Had not this been natural, yet would the natives have learned to brag from the example of their gods, who take advantage of their visits to earth to boast of their mighty deeds. The Fijian language supplies a smart jest against these self-trumpeters, in the onomato-poetic name of their parrot,— *kaka*; hence they accost the boasting egotist: "Ah! you are like the kaka; you only speak to shout your own name."

Where there is habitual boasting, there must be occasional lying. Among the Fijians the propensity to lie is so strong, that they seem to have no wish to deny its existence, or very little shame when convicted of a falsehood. Ordinary lies are told undisguised, but, should it be necessary, a lie is presented with every appearance of truth. Adroitness in lying is attained by the constant use made of it to conceal the schemes and plots of the Chiefs, to whom a ready and clever liar is a valuable acquisition. The universal existence of this habit is so thoroughly taken for granted, that it is common to hear, after the most ordinary statement, the rejoinder, " That's a lie," or something to the same effect, at which the accused person does not think of taking offence. Anything marvellous, on the other hand, meets with ready credence. Walking with a shrewd old native for my guide, on Vanua Levu, he directed my attention to some stones at the side of the path : " These," said he, " mark the place where a giant was slain while I was a little boy. This stone marks where his head lay, that where his knees, and these where his feet reached." Measuring the distance with my walking-staff, I found it twenty-five feet six inches ! " Well done, Fiji !" I shouted. The old man was startled at my incredulity; for he evidently believed the tale. Natives have often told me lies, evidently without any ill-will, and when it would have been far more to their advantage to have spoken the truth. The Fijians hail as agreeable companions those who are skilful in making tales, but, under some circumstances, strongly condemn the practice of falsehood. As "shocking-accident-makers," these people would greatly excel; they could supply every variety without limitation, and the most tragic and mournful without compunction. "A Fijian truth" has been regarded as a synonym for a lie, and foreigners, wishing to be rightly informed, caution the native not to speak " after the fashion of Fiji," a reflection which he turns to his own advantage when brought before the stranger for some misdemeanour, by assuring him that his accusers speak " after the fashion of Fijians." On matters most lied about by civilized people, the native is the readiest to speak the truth. Thus, when convicted of some offence, he rarely attempts to deny it, but will generally confess all to any one he esteems. Upon the whole, I am disposed to attribute the remarkable prevalence of falsehood to frivolous indifference, and the universal tendency of the people to pry into each other's affairs. This habitual concealment or disguise of the truth presents a great difficulty to the reforming labours of the Missionary, causing him some-times the bitterest disappointment. After the actual un-truth of the lips is laid aside, the principle of misrepre-sentation survives in the heart, and often leads to prevari-cation, or such a modifying of the truth as to make it seem other than it is. The following incident shows that lying, *per se*, is condemned and considered disreputable. A white man, notorious for falsehood, had displeased a powerful Chief, and wrote asking me to intercede for him. I did so; when the Chief dismissed the case briefly, saying, " Tell —— that no one hates a foreigner; but tell him that every one hates a liar ! "

The Fijian is a great adept in acting as well as telling an untruth. The expectation of an order to set about some difficult job, often makes a man wear his arm in a sling : another, while seeming to work with fearful exertion, is all the time careful not to strain a single muscle; and the appearance of seeking their neighbour's benefit, while intent only on their own, is shown continually. It has already been seen that the Fijian can be cruelly deceitful. Here is an instance in which foreigners were concerned. Four seamen left Fotuna for Fiji in a canoe less than thirty feet in length. They sighted land after being one night at sea, and, in a few hours, were in communication with the natives of Thikombia-i-ra. One of the sailors, having formerly lived in the group, knew a little of the language, and went ashore to ask where they were. A native, who had adjusted his *masi* in the style of a *lotu* dress, said, "This is Somo-somo; we are Christians, and I am Teacher in this place." This was pleasant news to the inquirer; but, on looking round, he saw the wreck of a boat on the beach, and on one of the natives a pea-jacket which had belonged to a white man who had miserably perished by the hands of the savages. Though his suspicions were thus aroused, the sailor preserved his self-command, and very composedly replied, " This is good ; this is the land I seek : I will return and bring my companions on shore." Directly on reaching the canoe, he announced their danger to his comrades, and the sail was immediately hoisted. A native who had laid hold on the end of the canoe was frightened off, by having a rusty musket presented at him. Those on shore, seeing their prey likely to escape, gave a loud shout, when many more rushed out from their ambush, and a shower of bullets followed the canoe. Several passed through the sail ; but as the savages fired high, the little party escaped uninjured, and one of them afterwards related the circumstances to me.

Here is another true tale of Fijian vengeance and deceit. Nalila, a late Chief of Lasakau, evaded the sentence of death for three years by keeping himself a close prisoner on the island of Viwa. At the close of this term, a reconciliation having been effected, and his enemies professing a sincere affection for him, the exile ventured to return to Mbau, where his restored friends lived, and passed a comfortable day with them. Ngavindi, his chief foe, was said to be sick, yet spent a little time in Nalila's company. On the second night, as they and several of their friends sat socially round the yaqona bowl, the report of a musket was heard, and Nalila fell. Ngavindi sprang on his feet to finish the deed with his club, when Nalila's father, hoary with age, begged him to show mercy, but only drew to himself the fury of the Chief, who, with one fierce blow of his club, struck the old man to the earth a corpse. The heart, liver, and tongue of Nalila were quickly cut away and devoured, and the mutilated body given up to the tears of the widow.

Covetousness, begetting envy, theft, and ingratitude, and leading to the blackest crimes, is strong in the Fijian. Prompted thereby, the natives have murdered white traders, to gain property of small value. The known prevalence of the same vice has caused the enactment of stringent regulations among the people themselves, such, for instance, as the *tabu kalawatha*. This means, to stride over, and, by accommodation, to pass by, as a canoe in sailing by a town. If the town is one to which those on the canoe are subject, it is expected that they will stop and report their errand : should they neglect this, they are regarded as smugglers, trading for their own independent advantage; an offence sometimes punished with death.

Covetousness will not even let the dead rest. On my last visit to Nai Vuki, I found the *lotu* people in trouble about a disturbed grave, wherein they had buried a Christian female, wrapping the body in a few yards of calico. The shroud of the dead woman excited the cupidity of the heathen, who resolved to strip the corpse, in which attempt they were surprised and defeated.

Theft is regarded in Fiji as a very small offence, and even as none at all when practised on a foreigner. When I was preparing once to visit the Yaro district on Vanuambalavu, a Chief who had some influence there kindly gave me a letter of introduction to the Yaro Chiefs, in which he requested them to "treat me kindly, to prevent their people being impudent, and stealing the poles, sculls, and ropes belonging to my canoe."

Meaner men steal under the direct sanction of the Chiefs, who are quite ready to punish them if detected, as, by so doing, they effect a threefold object: they appear to discountenance the practice, satisfy the plaintiff, and chastise the thief for his unskilfulness. Success, without discovery, is deemed quite enough to make thieving virtuous, and a participation in the ill-gotten gain honourable.

The Rewa Chief who told a gentleman of the United States Navy that he wished to send his daughters to the Mission school, but could not, because the attendants there were such thieves, used to supply the Missionaries with servants, who had special charge from him to rob those with whom they lived. Boats are often robbed by parties visiting them for that express purpose, but ostensibly for barter. Although these cannot be out of sight, and are closely watched, yet, under such circumstances, they are adroit enough to steal a musket or a pig of lead, and drop it overboard. When the boat is gone, a diver brings up the booty.

A master of a vessel lately complained of some natives stowing away an iron pot in their sleeping mats; and the truth of this unlikely trick is countenanced by one played upon us at Lakemba, where a native managed to secrete a dinner-plate under his narrow *masi*. A list of things stolen from the Missionaries would not be a short one; and the surprise of Europeans at some of the articles named, would not exceed the perplexity of the pilferers in endeavouring to discover their use.

Early visitors to savage lands tell of the willingness with which the people gave up their goods for the gratifi-cation of the strangers; but they expected a similar gene-rosity in return, and simply supposed that they would be allowed to claim whatever they might fancy. On finding, however, that this was not the case, they helped them-selves. Whatever excuse is in this, ought to be granted to the islanders, whose practical lessons from the whites on the distinction of *meum* and *tuum* have been cruelly and bloodily enforced.

As to the power of envy in the Fijian nature—an emotion so fruitful of trouble to its subject, and injustice and ill-will towards his neighbours—I would merely give an illustrative and striking confession of Ratu Lewe-ni-lovo, with whom I was conversing on this topic near the sea-shore. I inquired, "When will you Chiefs cease from your envious plottings?" "I cannot tell," he replied; "envy will not let us heathen rest. We see our likeness in the ocean before us; it ebbs and then it flows again, and rests not: we are like to it; we know no peace."

Ingratitude deeply and disgracefully stains the character of the Fijian heathen. A book might be filled with instances. Four years' experience.among the natives of Somosomo taught me that, if one of them, when sick, obtained medicine from me, he thought me bound to give him food; the reception of food he considered as giving him a claim on me for covering; and, thàt being secured, he deemed himself at liberty to beg anything he wanted, and abuse me if I refused his unreasonable request. I treated the old King of Somosomo, Tuithakau II. for a severe attack of sickness, which his native doctors failed to relieve. During the two or three days on which he was under my care, he had at his own request tea and arrow-root from our house; and, when recovered, his daughter waited on me to say that he could now eat well, and had sent her to beg an iron pot in which to cook his food! One more example. The master of a biche-de-mar vessel took a native under his care, whose hand was shattered by the bursting of a musket. The armourer amputated the injured part, and the man was provided for on board the vessel for nearly two months. On his recovery, he told the master that he was going on shore, but that a musket must be given him, in consideration of his having been on board so long. Such a request was, of course, refused; and, after having been reminded of the kindness shown him, to which he probably owed his life, the unreasonable fellow was sent ashore, where he showed his sense of obligation by burning down one of the Captain's drying-houses, containing fish to the value of three hundred dollars.

Intense and vengeful malignity strongly marks the Fijian character. When a person is offended, he seldom says anything, but places a stick or stone in such a position as to remind him continually of his grudge, until he has had revenge. Sometimes a man has hanging over his bed the dress of a murdered friend; or another will deprive himself of some favourite or even necessary food; while another will forego the pleasures of the dance; all being common ways of indicating sworn revenge. Sometimes a man is seen with the exact half of his head closely cropped, to which disfigurement another will add a long twist of hair hanging down the back; and thus they will appear until they have wreaked vengeance on those who slew their wives while fishing on the reef. From the ridge-pole of some Chief's house, or a temple, a roll of tobacco is suspended; and there it must hang, until taken down to be smoked over the dead body of some one of a hated tribe., A powerful savage, of sober aspect, is seen keeping profound silence in the village council. To ordinary inquiries he replies with a whistle. His son, the hero of the village, fell by a treacherous hand, and the father has vowed to abstain from the pleasures of conversation, until he opens his lips to revile the corpse of his son's murderer, or to bless the man who deprived it of life. Irritating songs are employed to excite the hatred of those who are likely to let their vengeance sleep. The youths of the place assemble before the house, and *leletaka,* or lament, that none revenge the death of their friend. The effect of such a song, framed so as to appeal to the most sensitive points of the Fijian's nature, is to awaken the malice and fury of those to whom it is addressed with all their original force, and vows of bloody retribution are made afresh.

Impatient to accomplish their purpose of revenge, the natives sometimes have recourse to witchcraft. Reeds or sticks, imbued with evil power by the necromancer's art, are placed in the path of the victim, that he may be wounded thereby, and stricken with disease or death, according to the potency of the charm. Instead of the reeds, leaves are sometimes used. Chiefs countenance a kind of Thuggism, availing themselves of the assassin's help to get rid of a rival, or punish an enemy. The Fijian Thug is named *Bati-Kadi* ("Tooth of the black ant"). One of this class was employed by Thokonauto, the Rewa Chief, to kill his rival Nanggaraninggio. In the stillness of the night, the assassin stole into a lone house belonging to his intended victim; but which happened to be occupied only by a powerful Tahitian, named Aboro, a faithful friend of Nanggaraninggio, who was sleeping nearer to the town. Groping round in the dark, the assassin found the berth, or raised shelf, on which Aboro was sleeping, and struck at him with a hatchet. The blow, falling on a bamboo tie-beam, woke the Tahitian, who sprang up and grappled with the miscreant, not, however, without receiving deep wounds on his arm. In the dark the two men struggled, until Aboro put an end to the conflict, by stabbing the other in the breast with a long knife.

Fijians express their malice in strong terms. " My hatred of thee begins at the heels of my feet, and extends to the hairs of my head." An angry Chief sent the following message to the object of his displeasure. " Let the shell of the *vasua* " (the giant oyster) " perish by reason of years, and to these add a thousand more ; still my hatred of thee shall be hot !" This relentless animosity will pursue its object to the grave, and gratify itself by abusing a putrid carcass. I have seen a large stake hammered through a poor fellow's head, to please his enemy's malice ; to which motive must also be attributed the practice of the Chief's eating the tongue, heart, and liver of a foe.

Many instances have already been given of the treachery of the Fijians, and many more might be adduced ; but one only is here added, as displaying, to their utmost extent, some of the darkest qualities of the native character, and presenting scenes full of savage romance.

Tambai-valu, a former King of Rewa, was excited by Randi Ndreketi, his Queen, to hate Koroi Tamana, his son by another wife of high rank. The animosity of the Queen, who was a wicked and artful woman, was roused by a consciousness that Koroi Tamana was exceedingly popular, and a fear lest he should prevent her own children from succeeding to the government. The father, yielding at last to her influence, resolved to kill his son, who fled again and again from his unjust anger. After being hunted about for some time, and becoming tired of being the object of groundless suspicion, he listened to the suggestion of certain malcontent Chiefs, and determined to accomplish his father's destruction, and assume the supreme power, his treacherous advisers pledging themselves to stand by him. One night, Koroi Tamana set the King's canoe-house on fire, and then went to arouse the King, telling him that Rewa was in flames. On hearing the alarm, Tambai-valu ran out, and was suddenly struck dead by the club of his own son. Thus the Queen's evil schemes seemed frustrated; but her cunning, stimulated with fresh malice, showed itself equal to the emergency. Seeing that the death-wound of her husband was scarcely apparent, she cried out, "He lives! He lives!" Then, assisted by a Tongan woman, she carried the body into the *loqi*, or private part of the house, and announced that the King was recovering, but that, being very weak, he desired that no one should approach him. She then went to the Chiefs, professing to bring Tambai-valu's command that his son should be put to death. For some time, none seemed disposed to attend to the message; and the Queen, fearing lest her plan should, after all, fall through, went to the Chiefs again, carrying with her a present of large whales' teeth, stating that they were sent by the King's hand to purchase the death of Koroi Tamana. Adding all her own eloquence and female persuasion, this determined woman prevailed, and the Chiefs went to the doomed man, informed him of the King's order, and killed him. They immediately went into the presence of the King to report his son's execution, when the putrid smell of the corpse told them the truth. But it was now too late. Tambai-valu and Koroi Tamana were both dead; and, after burying the former, nothing was left to the Chiefs but to elect, as successor, Mathanawai, the Queen's son, and thus complete the triumph of his designing and unscrupulous mother, who, contrary to custom, did not die with her husband. These particulars, in the form of a *meke*, I heard at Lakemba.

Another deformity which disfigures the Fijian, is his cowardice. This, too, has been mentioned before. Many examples might be given of most dastardly cruelty, where women and even unoffending children were abominably slain; but such details would prove to be neither pleasing nor interesting. The boasting of which so much has been said, cannot exist with true bravery. *A qaqa ni cau solevaki*—"A brave man, when not surrounded by enemies"

—is descriptive of nine out of ten instances of Fijian valour. Few are found who will walk alone at night or in the dusk ; and, on their visits to strange places, suspicious fear prevents enjoyment. The approach of a canoe makes every one uneasy, until they ascertain the character and disposition of those on board. Should a house take fire, the fear of the flames is overcome by a dread of imaginary enemies lurking about to kill those who may escape. Nearly every feast is a season of misgiving, because of reports that some particular person is selected to be slain during its celebration. I have seen women disperse, like frightened doves, at the appearance of a solitary man, and youngsters of various ages scamper pell-mell at the uplifting of a spy-glass. A Fijian cannot be comfortable with a stranger at his heels. It has so happened, several times, that when I have had a room full of visitors, the door has suddenly slammed with the wind, and, in an instant, the affrighted natives would rush out at the windows, like bees from a disturbed hive. In dragging a canoe that was only roughed out, from the forest, it received a jar, so as to cause a split near a hole cut to receive one of the ropes. The man who first perceived this, whispered his discovery to the one next him, he to the third; and so the news went round, until, in a few minutes, all were flying in every direction, each fearing lest he should be clubbed, as a caution to survivors to be more careful.

Such a feeling of suspicious fear must necessarily accompany the lawless cruelty, treachery, and utter disregard of the value of human life, which are so prominently characteristic of the inhabitants of Fiji. To multiply most terrible proofs of these would be easy. But such details are unnecessary, and only serve to awaken feelings of horror and disgust. Atrocities of the most fearful kind have come to my knowledge, which I *dare* not record here. And it must not be forgotten that, in the case of murder, the act is not a simple one, ending in the first bloodshed. The blow which falls fatally on one man, may be said to kill several more; for, if the victim is married, his wife or wives will be strangled as soon as the husband's death becomes known, and often the man's mother will die at the same time. Then again, if the deed is such. as to justify the perpetrator's claim to receiving "a new name," other murders will be necessary to complete the ceremony. He and his friends must *silima*— "wash"—his club, if possible, within a few weeks of the first crime; that is, the club must spill more blood. Murder is not an occasional thing in Fiji; but habitual, systematic, and classed among ordinary transactions.

All the evils of the most licentious sensuality are found among this people. In the case of the Chiefs, these are fully carried out, and the vulgar follow as far as their means will allow. But here, even at the risk of making the picture incomplete, there may not be given a faithful representation.

After so dark a portraiture as the above, the reader will scarcely expect to find affection much developed in the Fijian heart, at any rate beyond the mere animal attachments, such as are manifested by the lower orders of creatures, for instance, towards their young. But something higher than this is really to be found, although not reaching the loftier standard of more enlightened nations. In the case of this people, however, allowance must be made for the manner in which custom and training have directed the expression of their affections, or we shall be in danger of denying the existence of the principle, because developed in a manner different from that to which we are accustomed. To murder a wife, that she may be the companion of her deceased husband in Hades, or a mother, that her son may not be buried alone, would be repugnant to every Christian heart; but not so to the Fijian. I do not doubt that misdirected affection influences some sons to destroy her who bore them, and some daughters to weep when Christian charity has rescued their mothers from the fatal noose. But the exhibition of parental love is sometimes such as to be worthy of admiration. The most remarkable case of this kind with which I am acquainted, was that of a Lakemba woman, whose child a friend was taking away to Tonga, to rear as his own. The mother had given a reluctant assent to the plan, and went on board the canoe, which was just starting, with her boy. Her affection kept her there until the canoe had passed the sea-reef, and yet she could not tear herself from her child. Being partly compelled to do so, she plunged into the sea, and faintly swam towards land. But her strokes grew feebler and feebler as she was further parted from her idol, until, in her great sorrow, she began to sink. The Mission canoe had followed the other, and the crew, seeing something dark afloat, steered for it, and rescued the drowning woman. When the mother was restored to consciousness, she upbraided her deliverers with unkindness in not permitting her to end her grief in the deep sea.

I have been astonished to see the broad breast of a most ferocious savage heave and swell with strong emotion on bidding his aged father a temporary farewell. I have listened with interest to a man of milder mould, as he told me about his " eldest son—his head, his face, his mien —the admiration of all who saw him." Yet this father assisted to strangle his son; and the son first named buried his old father alive !

Generally speaking, and with but few exceptions, suspicion, reserve, and distrust pervade the domestic relationships, and a happy and united household is most rare.

CHAPTER VI.

MANNERS AND CUSTOMS.

THE habits, manners, and customs of a savage people must always prove interesting, and, to a certain extent, instructive. In the present instance, the people described are but little known, and there are very few who have had the opportunity of long and intimate acquaintance with them, and who, at the same time, have been either able or disposed to give a fair and unprejudiced statement of what they have witnessed. Hence, to the other attractions belonging to a description of Fijian life, private and public, will be added much of the charm of novelty. Any portraiture, too, of a people living, for many generations, under the uninterrupted power of influences different from any which we daily feel, and strangers to those motives and forces which have, more than anything else, modified the development of our own individual and social character, must convey instruction, imparting, as it does, revelations which shed new light on the difficult study—man.

Although domestic habits are found to a great extent among the Fijians, yet, as was intimated at the close of the last chapter, there is too much reserve to allow the social element full influence. A general kindness of manner is prevalent, but the high attachments which constitute friendship are known to very few. A free flow of the affections between members of the same family is further prevented by the strict observance of national or religious customs, imposing a most unnatural restraint. Brothers and sisters, first cousins, fathers and sons-in-law, mothers and daughters-in-law, and brothers and sisters-in-law, are thus severally forbidden to speak to each other, or to eat from the same

dish. The latter embargo extends to husbands and wives
—an arrangement not likely to foster domestic joy. Husbands are as frequently away from their wives as with
them, since it is thought not well for a man to sleep regularly at home. Among other similar practices may be mentioned the forbidding of wives, when pregnant, to wait on
their husbands. In native opinion, it is common for a
woman to hate her husband, but rare for a man to hate his
wife, and very rare for a woman to hate a man by whom
she had children before her marriage with her present lord.
Full-grown men, it is true, will walk about together,
hand in hand, with boyish kindliness, or meet with hugs
and embraces; but their love, though specious, is hardly
real. Violent quarrels are not frequent; nor need they be,
if those I have seen were specimens, ending, as they did,
with the axe and club, wounded heads, or broken arms.
Too much has been said about the cleanliness of the
natives. The lower classes are often very dirty; a fact
which becomes more evident when they wear calico, to
which no soap is applied, and which presents a larger
surface to the eye than the ordinary *masi*. They sit and
often sleep on the ground, and seldom hesitate to sink
both cleanliness and dignity in what they call comfort.

To the description which has been given of the interior
of a Fijian house, there may be added here a notice of its
furniture and contents, which are few and simple. Where
part of the floor is raised, forming a dais which, by day, is
the divan, and, by night, the bed of a Chief, it is covered
with mats, varying in number from two to ten, and spread
over a thick layer of dried grass and elastic ferns, while
on them are placed two or three neat wooden or bamboo
pillows. Over this hangs the mosquito curtain, which is
generally large enough to hang across the house, thus giving
to one end of it an air of comfort. Chequered baskets,
gourds, and bottles for scented oil are hung about the
walls; and, in a conspicuous place, stands or hangs the
yaqona bowl, with a strainer and cup. In various parts
are suspended fans, a sunshade made of the leaf of the

cabbage palm, an oil dish of dark wood, and several food dishes of wood or wicker-work. On a slight frame behind the curtain stand a chest or two, with a musket hanging above, and, perhaps, an axe and spade beneath. Along the foot of the wall rest oblong wooden bowls with four feet, or round earthen pans with none. If there is any arrow-root, it is preserved in coarse wide-mouthed jars ; and one or more glazed water-vessels have a place near the hearth or bed, set in a nest of dry grass. The other domestic apparatus is found near the hearth, and comprises nets, a bone knife for cutting bread from the pit, and another of foreign make for cutting up yams, etc.; a concave board, four or six feet long, on which to work up the bread, and round stones for mashing the same; coarse baskets for vegetables, cocoa-nut and bamboo vessels for salt and fresh water, and soup dishes and a ladle made of the nut shell. On the hearth, each set on three stones, are several pots, capable of holding from a quart to five gallons. Near these are a cord for binding fuel, a skewer for trying cooked food, and, in the better houses, a wooden fork—a luxury which, probably, the Fijian enjoyed when our worthy ancestors were wont to take hot food in their practised fingers.

The large oval cooking-pots stand slanting, the angle being altered to suit the quantity of food contained in them. Should there be very little, the pot lies on its side. The small pots, which answer to our saucepans, stand upright. These facilities for boiling food and making hot drinks form one of the advantages almost peculiar to the Fijian, as contrasted with the other islanders. His domestic comforts have been stated to be inferior to those of the Tongans; but the comparison has been unfairly instituted between Christian Tongans and heathen Fijians. If the state of the former before their reformation were taken as the standard, the above erroneous judgment would be reversed ; and even now the Tongan owes many of his greatest comforts to Fijian ingenuity. Voyagers notice the superior fare of the Fijians in their daily use of hot boiled food, and various soups—luxuries which have recently been introduced from them among those with whom they have been contrasted. They also have the peculiar distinction of using mosquito curtains, of separate sleeping rooms for the young men, and a better style of houses. The use of oil for anointing the body has been stated as a point in which the Tongans are superior. But almost all the Christians of Fiji have now adopted the practice.

The natives usually take two meals in the day; the principal one being in the afternoon or evening. Where ovens are chiefly used, they cook but once a day, but twice where boiling is most in vogue. Their general food is light and plain, fish being highly esteemed. Contrary, to the taste of civilized gourmands, these people will have all their meat quite fresh, and some small kinds of fish are eaten alive as a relish. The Fijian bill of fare for usual consumption is somewhat lengthy, and contains many different vegetables, and shell and other fish in perhaps unequalled variety. Almost everything found living on the sea-reef, whether molluscous, articulate, or radiate, is eaten and enjoyed. To these are added a dozen varieties of bread, nearly thirty kinds of puddings, and twelve sorts of broths or soups, including—though the distinctions calipash and calipee are unknown—turtle-soup. Several kinds of warm infusions are made from aromatic grasses and leaves. These, however, they sometimes macerate, and eat with the liquid in which they are prepared. Some of the native dishes recommend themselves at once to European taste, and some strongly remind the English visitor of what he has been accustomed to see at home. A rich sort of gruel is made from the milk and pulp of the young cocoa-nut. Shrimps are used to make an elegant and delicious sandwich, being arranged between two thicknesses of taro leaves. Fish is sometimes served up with a relishing sauce; and sweet sauces are made for the richer sorts of pudding by expressing the juices of the nut, the ti-root, and the sugar-cane. Roasting and frying are added to the other methods of cookery.

The refreshing milk of the nut is much used by the Fijian; but his general beverage is water. In drinking without a cup, the head is thrown back with the mouth opened, the water-vessel held several inches above the lips, and a stream allowed to run down the throat—a process whereby a novice is more likely to be choked than refreshed. This method of drinking is adopted to avoid touching the vessel with their lips—a practice to which they strongly object. To drink from the long bamboos sometimes used is no easy task. These vessels are from two to ten feet long. One of the longest will hold two gallons; and to slake one's thirst from its open end, while a native gradually elevates the other, requires care, or a cold bath will be the unsought result.

On opening the oven of the Somosomo King, the *tui rara*, or master of the feast, names aloud the parties who are fed from it, that their several portions may be fetched away. The priests and the principal Mata-ni-vanua have the precedence. The King's Mata is served first; then the priests, whose portions are given in the name of their gods, accompanied by a short prayer; it being a rule in heathenism, never to do a god a small favour without asking a larger in return. If a chief lady receives a portion from the oven, it is distinguished by the cry *A magiti-i-i-i !** followed by clapping of hands.

The meal of a Chief only differs from that of a common man in that the food is of better quality, more frequently served, and received with greater form. Clean mats answer for both chair and table. The food is brought on an oblong dish lined with fresh leaves, while other leaves serve for a cover. If the Chief is not *liga tabu*—tabu as to the hands—he may feed himself or not, as he chooses; but if *liga tabu*, he must be fed by another, generally his chief wife, or a Mata. While he is eating, everybody present retains a sitting position—the attitude of respect; when he has done, he pushes the dish a little way from him, and each person claps his hands several times. Water is next

* "Cooked food."

brought to the Chief, who washes his hands and rinses his mouth, after which, in some parts, hands are again clapped by every one in the house. While eating, the Chief converses familiarly with those round him, and all are perfectly at their ease, but very orderly. In many parts of the group the day is commenced by taking a cup of yaqona, the preparation of which is attended with much ceremony.

Like the inhabitants of the groups eastward, the Fijians drink an infusion of the *piper methysticum,* generally called *ava* or *kava*—its name in the Tongan and other languages. In Fiji, however, it is termed *yaqona.* This beverage is not so commonly in use on Vanua Levu and some parts of Viti Levu, as it is on other islands, where it is frequently the case that the Chiefs drink it as regularly as we do coffee. Some old men assert that the true Fijian mode of preparing the root is by grating, as is still the practice in two or three places; but, in this degenerate age, the Tongan custom of chewing is almost universal, the operation nearly always being performed by young men.

More form attends the use of this narcotic on Somosomo than elsewhere. Early in the morning the King's herald stands in front of the royal abode, and shouts at the top of his voice, "Yaqona!" Hereupon, all within hearing respond, in a sort of scream, "*Mama!*"—"Chew it!" At this signal the Chiefs, priests, and leading men gather round the well known bowl, and talk over public affairs, or state the work assigned for the day, while their favourite draught is being prepared. When the young men have finished the chewing, each deposits his portion, in the form of a round dry ball, in the bowl, the inside of which thus becomes studded over with a large number of these separate little masses. The man who has to make the grog, takes the bowl by the edge and tilts it towards the King, or, in his absence, to the Chief appointed to preside. A herald calls the King's attention to the slanting bowl, saying, "Sir, with respects, the yaqona is collected." If the King thinks it enough, he replies, in a low tone, "*Loba,*" "Wring it;" an order which the herald communicates to the man at the bowl in a louder voice. The water is then called for, and gradually poured in, a little at first, and then more, until the bowl is full, or the master of the ceremonies says, "Stop!" the operator, in the meantime, gathering up and compressing the chewed root. Now follows the *science* of the process, which Mariner describes so accurately, that I cannot do better than transcribe his account. The strainer is composed of a quantity of the fine fibrous *vau*, (hibiscus,) which is spread over the surface of the infusion, on which it floats, and "the man who manages the bowl now begins his difficult operation. In the first place, he extends his left hand to the farther side of the bowl, with his fingers pointing downwards, and the palm towards himself; he sinks that hand carefully down the side of the bowl, carrying with it the edge of the *vau ;* at the same time, his right hand is performing a similar operation at the side next to him, the finger pointing downwards, and the palm presenting outwards. He does this slowly, from side to side, gradually descending deeper and deeper, till his fingers meet each other at the bottom, so that nearly the whole of the fibres of the root are by these means enclosed in the *vau*, forming as it were a roll of above two feet in length, lying along the bottom from side to side, the edges of the *vau* meeting each other underneath. He now carefully rolls it over, so that the edges overlapping each other, or rather intermingling, come uppermost. He next doubles in the two ends, and rolls it carefully over again, endeavouring to reduce it to a narrower and firmer compass. He now brings it cautiously out of the fluid, taking firm hold of it by the two ends, one in each hand, (the back of the hands being upwards,) and, raising it breast high, with his arms considerably extended, he brings his right hand towards his breast, moving it gradually onwards; and, whilst his left hand is coming round towards his right shoulder, his right hand partially twisting the *vau*, lays the end which it holds upon the left elbow, so that the *vau* lies thus extended upon that arm, one end being still grasped by the left hand. The right hand, being now at liberty, is brought under the left fore-arm, (which still remains in the same situation,) and carried outwardly towards the left elbow, that it may again seize, in that situation, the end of the *vau*. The right hand then describes a bold curve outwardly from the chest, whilst the left comes across the chest, describing a curve nearer to him, and in the opposite direction, till, at length, the left hand is extended from him, and the right approaches to the left shoulder, gradually twisting the *vau* by the turn and flexures principally of that wrist: this double motion is then retraced, but in such a way (the left wrist now principally acting) that the *vau*, instead of being untwisted, is still more twisted, and is at length again placed on the left arm, while he takes a new and less constrained hold. Thus the hands and arms perform a variety of curves of the most graceful description : the muscles, both of the arms and chest, are seen rising as they are called into action, displaying what would be a fine and uncommon subject of study for the painter ; for no combinations of animal action can develope the swell and play of the muscles with more grace or with better effect. The degree of strength which he exerts, when there is a large quantity, is very great, and the dexterity with which he accomplishes the whole never fails to excite the attention and admiration of all present......Sometimes the fibres of the *vau* are heard to crack with the increasing tension, yet the mass is seen whole and entire, becoming more thin as it becomes more twisted, while the infusion drains from it in a regularly decreasing quantity, till at length it denies a single drop." The man now tosses the dregs behind him, or, with a new lot of *vau*, repeats the operation, until the liquid is clear and fit for use.

When an adept has been manipulating, I have seen the various curves described by him watched, with mute attention, by interested hundreds, whose countenances indicated a pleasure which I could not but share. Regular attenders provide their own cups, formed of the half of a cocoa-nut, which, after long use, takes a fine polish and a

purplish hue. When cups are few, an elegant substitute is
made of the banana leaf. As the water is poured in, the
chief herald repeats the following prayer : "The water ;
ay. Prepare the libation! Prepare the libation to the
Tavasara ; a libation to Oroi rupe ; to the Veidoti ; to the
Loaloa ;* to the Chieftains of the Sokula,† who have died
on the water, or died on the land ! Be gracious, ye lords, the
gods ! that the rain may cease, and the sun shine forth ! A libation to my Lady of Weilangi, etc. Be gracious, ye lords, the
gods ! that the rain may cease!" Here all in the ring join
with him to chant, "*Ei Ma-nai di-na : se-di-na-li !*" finishing
with three or four sharp claps of the hands from all present.

The yaqona being ready for use, a person approaches,
in a sitting posture, with a cup, or frequently with two,
one holding water to be drunk after the infusion ; the *vau*
is laid over the cup, and the liquor poured through until it
is full, when the herald, addressing the cup-bearer, says,
"*A woi—ceri caki !*" "Stand up!" While the man
obeys, the herald offers prayer thus :—

> "*Me loma viuaka na kalou
> A lutu mada na tokalau.*"‡

The cup-bearer, in a stooping attitude, presents the cup
to the King, who pours out a few drops—the libation—and
then drinks, while the whole company chant, "*Ma-nai di-na.
La-ba-si-ye : a-ta-mai-ye : ai-na-ce-a-toka : Wo-ya! yi!
yi! yi!*" All now clap their hands together, producing a
quick and merry measure, finishing abruptly. The triple
yi ! is uttered in a high key, and followed by a shout, in
which the people round the house join ; those who are more
distant catch and repeat the sound, until it is carried far
beyond the boundaries of the town. Not to shout would
be considered disloyal.

After the King, the herald names the next in rank, who
notifies his position by slowly clapping his hands twice or
thrice ; and the cup-bearer carries him his draught, which,
whether it measure one half-pint or three, is drained with-

---

* Names of temples.   † The Somosomo people.
    Let the gods be of a gracious mind, and send a wind from the east."

out pausing. Other individuals are named in the same
way, until all have had their morning cup.

To be served next to the King is a high honour. A
Tongan once piloted the King of Lakemba and his suite
through a very dangerous opening in the reef during a
storm. The King, after eulogizing the man's services,
nobly bade him name his own reward. After a short
pause, the Tongan said, "Let my name be announced in
the yaqona-circle after the King's, as long as I live."
This great honour was granted, and enjoyed to the end of
the man's life.

In more social parties, the straining process is accompanied by vocal music. Those present join in singing
short songs, while they sometimes imitate the varied pos-
tures of the chief operator. Each snatch of song is finished
by clapping.

In addition to the water taken after yaqona, most
Fijians eat a small piece of old cocoa-nut, or other food;
some say, to add more potency to the stupifying dose. Few
of the women partake of this drink. I have heard it said,
however, that the females of Waya, on the west coast of
Viti Levu, like the Tongan women, have drinking-parties
among themselves.

A few variations of custom may be noted. At Mbau,
when the herald shouts, "Yaqona!" the people, instead of
answering, "Mama!" strike upon any sonorous substance
that may be near, thus calling silence for the uninterrupted
performance of the following ceremonies. At Lauthala,
the prayer is uttered by the herald in the open air, the
populace joining in the final shout. At Mbouma, the
libation is poured into a dish devoted to that purpose,
which, when I saw it, was filthy from long service. Here
also the gods had a share of water apportioned to them,
taken in a leaf by the priest, and transferred to the bowl
with some ceremonious rubbings. At Vuna, directly the
Chief takes the cup to his lips, the company begin a
measured clapping, which they continue all the while he
is drinking the yaqona and the water which follows.

A very remarkable feature associated with Fijian drinking customs, is the *Vakacivo*, a kind of toast or wish announced after the draught is swallowed. A man blows away the moisture that may remain about his mouth, with a hissing noise, and then shouts aloud his toast, which is sometimes common-place, sometimes humourous, and sometimes sentimental. Some of these wishes allude to the cannibal practices of the people; *e. g.*, a skull! a man's heart! or a human ham! Others indicate the profession of the drinker: thus the fisherman asks for a report from the reef, a husbandman for propitious seasons, and the sailor for a brisk wind. The ruling passion is thus frequently manifested: the covetous man calls for wealth, plenty of tortoise-shell, or a whale's tooth; the epicure, for broiled fish, rich puddings, or turtle soup. A kind neighbour of mine used to ask for pleasant conversation. A treacherous Chief was accustomed to say, "There yet is, that is kept back." An ill-looking doctor was ever crying out for a "good god," and a little priest always said of the gods, "They pull, and I pull." Many drinking-wishes are expressed enigmatically: "a red string," means sinnet; "a path that resounds," a canoe; "a bamboo basket," food from Somosomo; "a long pig," a human body (to be eaten): sugar-cane is asked for as "water in dams," and the milk of the nut as "water that trembles in the breeze." The origin of this custom may perhaps be traceable to the common practice of ending a report and many business transactions by a short wish or prayer.

Very few Fijians drink to excess; the intemperate are easily distinguished by their inflamed eyes and a scaly appearance of the skin. By one or two ordinary draughts a stupor is produced, from which the drinker manifests an unwillingness to be aroused.

The yaqona-ring is often the prelude to a feast, for which, when on a large scale, preparations commence months beforehand. Yams and taro are planted with special reference to it, a *tabu* is put upon pigs and nuts, and the turtle-fishers are sent to set their nets. As the time approaches, messengers are sent far and near to announce the day appointed. This announcement, which is a respectful way of inviting the guests, is made to the several Chiefs, and through them to their people. The invitations are liberal, including all the male population of the town or district to which the Mata is sent.

On the part of the entertainers, there is a vigorous effort at display. Every member of the community has an interest in the affair, and anticipates, as his own, a large portion of the praise elicited by a liberal feast. A day or two beforehand, every one is full of activity; the King issuing orders, the Matas communicating them to the people, and the people carrying them out. The ovens are prepared during the previous night, when the chopping of fuel and squealing of pigs is heard in every direction, while the flames from the ovens yield a light greatly helping the labours of the cooks. The name of *cook*, among the natives, is an eminently derisive epithet, and considerable amusement arises from the fact that, at these times of preparation, all persons, from Princes downwards, feed the oven, or stir the pot. The baking of all kinds of food, and the making of all kinds of puddings, are intrusted to the men. The ovens, which are holes or pits sunk in the ground, are sometimes eight or ten feet deep, and fifty feet in circumference; and in one of these several pigs and turtles and a large quantity of vegetables can be cooked. English roasters of an entire ox or sheep might learn some useful philosophy from the Fijian cook, whose method insures the thorough and equal baking of the whole carcass. The oven is filled with firewood, on which large stones are placed, and the fire introduced. As soon as the fuel is burnt out, the food is placed on the hot stones, some of which are put inside the animals to be cooked whole. A thick coat of leaves is now rapidly spread over all, and on these a layer of earth about four inches thick. When the steam penetrates this covering, it is time to remove the food; whereupon the lull that followed the closing of the oven gives place to renewed activity, as the men, besides having rested, have also regaled themselves on the hearts, livers, kidneys, etc., of the pigs they have killed, and which tit-bits they ate *ex officio*. Thus refreshed, they proceed to plait green baskets, beat up the taro paste with ponderous pestles, prepare the large beautiful leaves to receive the paste and sauce, tie them up, count, report, and carry them away with as much alacrity as though they had lost sight of the characteristic counsel of their forefathers, to "go gently, that they may live long."

The food prepared by each tribe and family is presented for inspection, and in some cases collected and piled before the house of the King, to whom a specimen of each kind is always sent. The usual custom is, after all has been thus seen, counted, and reported by the Tui-rara—"Master of the feast;" literally, "Master of the area," viz., where the feast is held—and the Matas, to remove it to the public area in front of the chief temple, where are heaped together the contributions of several tribes. A floor of clean leaves is laid, eight or twelve feet in diameter; on this, where they abound, is placed a layer of cocoa nuts, on which are heaped up the baked taro and yams, to the amount of several tons. The next tier is formed of *vaka-lolo*, the generic name of native puddings, the fresh green envelopes of which glisten with the sweet nut-oil. Surmounting this pedestal of food are two or three hogs, baked whole, and lying on their bellies. As the natives, in killing these, generally break the snout across, they do not present the quiet appearance of dead pigs, but look as though they snarled defiance on those assembled to eat them. When every thing is ready, all is publicly offered to the gods, to whom a share is voted, the rest being reserved for the visitors.

On these occasions profusion is always aimed at: waste is the consequence, and want follows. At one public feast, I saw two hundred men employed for nearly six hours in collecting and piling cooked food. There were six mounds of yams, taro, *vakalolo*, pigs, and turtles: these contained about fifty tons of cooked yams and taro, fifteen tons of sweet pudding, seventy turtles, five cart-loads of yaqona, and about two hundred tons of uncooked yams. One pudding, at a Lakemba feast, measured twenty-one feet in circumference.

The head-men of the visitors sit to receive the food, as it is brought and piled before them, expressing their approval by saying aloud, " *Vinaka! Vinaka!* " "Good! Good!" Having finished, the carriers sit down near the heap, and clap their hands several times, and then retire. An officer from among the strangers now walks up to the food, extends his hands over it, and, inclining his head towards his Chief, says, "The food, Sir." "Thanks! thanks!" He then stoops down and gently claps his hands, to which the Chief and his followers answer by a similar clapping, while they repeat, "It is good! it is good! Thanks! thanks!" Certain officials then proceed to share out the food; a duty which, on account of the extreme punctili-ousness of the people about rank, is attended with consider-able difficulty. A Chief is honoured or slighted, according to the quantity or quality of the food set before him: and nothing of this kind can escape notice, as every eye eagerly watches the proceedings. When there are several Chiefs in the party, an accurate knowledge of the grade of each is necessary to avoid error. The food having been divided into as many portions as there are tribes, the Tui-rara, beginning with the first in rank, shouts out, "The share of Lakemba!" or whichever may take precedence. This is met by a reply from that party: "Good! good!" or "Thanks! thanks!" and a number of young men are sent to fetch the allotted portion. The Tui-rara goes on, calling the names in succession, until his list is exhausted. If a foreigner should be observed among the spectators, he is sure not to be passed by, but a portion—very likely enough for twenty men—will be given to him. When each tribe has received its share, a re-division takes place, answering to the number of its towns; these, again, sub-

divide it among the head families, who, in their turn, share
what they get with their dependents, and these with the
individual members of their household, until no one is
left without a portion, the food disappearing forthwith,
with a rapidity which baffles calculation. The males eat
in the open air, sending the women's share to their houses.
Should some wayfarer pass by, he is pressingly invited to
partake of the entertainment, and allowed to dip in the
same dish with those who bid him.

Indeed, while witnessing such a scene, it is only by an
effort of the mind that one can believe that a people so
blithe and benevolent are capable of the atrocities with
which they are charged. But beneath all that apparent
pleasantness and repose, there lurk strong elements of
disquiet. A misarrangement or impropriety would cause
a hundred bright eyes to flash with anger, which, though
suppressed then, would burst forth with a deadlier effect
on a future day.

It would be regarded as extremely wrong for even a high
Chief to ask to taste food from the common stock before it
had been formally presented to him. The memory of a
Vanua Levu Chief is execrated to this day, for having been
guilty of this breach of etiquette.

The most admirable order is observed at these feasts.
Gentlemen of the United States navy who witnessed the
ceremonies of a Fijian entertainment record their opinion
thus: " Their feasts are attended with much ceremony
and form, and evince a degree of politeness and good
breeding that was unexpected, and cannot but surprise all
who witness it."

That there is sufficient reason for caution in the
observance of established routine, the following facts, given
by an unquestionable authority, will show.

A Naitasiri Chief was on a visit at Makongai, attended
by some of his Mbatis. Before one of these he ate part of
an old cocoa-nut, which, in the estimation of the Mbati,
was a luxury, and, as a piece was not given to him, he
deemed himself insulted. Intent on revenge, he shortly

joined the enemies of his master; and a victory which they subsequently achieved, gave the offended Mbati the opportunity he desired. He intercepted his former Chief, who was fleeing for life, and who, on seeing him, reckoned on his help, asking to be spared; but the unforgiving vassal replied, "It is in my mind to spare you; but, Sir, the nut! Do you not remember the nut? For that you must die." The word was followed by a death-blow.

Another case concerned a Chief of Tai Vungalei. He sat down to eat with his father-in-law, and a cooked guana was provided for each. In passing the one intended for his father, the young man broke off part of its tail. A dark scowl covered his relation's face at this, and, at an early opportunity, he slew his son, having first told him that he could not brook the insult put upon him by the breaking of the guana's tail!

I have often been struck by the promptness with which a party of natives, while eating, have transferred their meal to others passing by; and, so long as I was a tyro in native matters, I liked to regard this as a sign of the people's hospitality. But the assurance of many among themselves compelled me to believe that this act of seeming liberality was the result of fear; lest by withholding any part, or by something in their manner of eating, they should give offence.

Besides the forms observed on public occasions and towards persons of rank, there are others which affect ordinary life. Foreign visitors, who have only a ship-deck intercourse with them, cannot estimate them fairly. Some such have supposed them ill-behaved; and it is true that many natives, from what they have seen and heard on board ordinary vessels, have come to the conclusion that the observance of good manners would not be appreciated *there*. Among themselves the rules of politeness are minute, and receive scrupulous attention. They affect the language, and are seen in forms of salutation, in attention to strangers, at meals, in dress, and, indeed, influence their manners in-doors and out. None but the very lowest

are ill-behaved, and their confusion on committing themselves shows that they are not impudently so. The forms
of salutation used towards Chiefs have been noticed. Equals,
on meeting each other early in the day, say, " *Sa yadra,*"
" Awake," or, "You are awake;" in the evening, "*Sa moce,*"
or, " *La'ki moce,*" " Sleep," or, " Go to sleep." On Vanua
Levu the person addressed replies, "*Roaroa,*" " The morning
of to-morrow," meaning, " We will meet again to-morrow."
From some who have been told to sleep while the sun was
yet high, I have heard the smart rejoinder, "Let that be
for the owls!" A husband ought not to address the
morning salutation to his wife. I knew one who did so,
and the wife took it as a dismissal. Persons meeting
about mid-day, generally ask each other whence they have
come, and whither they are going. Bandied remarks on the
weather, or inquiries about health,—so common in England,—are here unheard. Certainly the Fijian methods of
salutation are confirmatory of the observation, that such
forms indicate the character of the people using them:
they are civil, inquisitive, and heartless.

On a visit of a person from a distance, as soon as he is
seated, the master of the house gently claps his hands three
or four times, and says, very much in eastern style, " Come
with peace!" The name of the place whence the visitor
has come is generally added, or the name of the house,
should he reside in the same town. Thus a wife of the
King of Somosomo would be welcomed with, " Come with
peace, the lady from Nasima,"—the name of the King's
house. If the visitor should be a person of rank, the
formula is either the former, or, " Good is the coming in
peace of the Chief." On a person leaving the house, those
within say, "*Sa lako,*" or, "*Sa lako tale,*" "You go," or, "You
return;" to which the answer is, " I go; you remain"
(literally, *sit*). Any one going on a voyage parts from his
friends by saying, " You stay and watch;" to which they
reply, "Yes, and you voyage." The parting kiss of the
Fijians is peculiar, one *smelling* the other with a strong
sniff. Equals do this on each other's faces. A Chief of

lower grade will thus salute a superior's hand, and inferiors will embrace the knees and smell the feet of a Chief. Shaking hands has been introduced by the Missionaries, and is in high repute. *" Sa loloma,"* " My love to you," owes its origin to the same source, and is used by all the Christians.

When a canoe or canoes arrive at a place,—Somosomo, for example,—those on board shout, " *O, aa !*" and put a messenger on shore, who goes direct to the King's house, to report their arrival. Having arrived, the messenger again shouts, " *O aa !*" and ascends the steps with his hands clasped, entering at a bidding from within. As soon as he is seated, the King's Mata welcomes him with the usual clapping, and says, " Good is your coming from Vuna," or another place, as the case may be. The messenger replies by clapping, and saying, " Good, with respect, is your sitting in a lordly style at Somosomo." Several voices will then exclaim, " Report ! What is the report ?" The orator is not allowed to stand, and the disadvantages of sitting are increased by his having to bow his head and body towards the Chief, and either clasp his hands or hold his beard. When fairly fixed, he begins by stating that his party were in their own land, and the thought of their Chiefs turned towards the Chiefs of this land ; and they said, " Here are these pigs or yams ; why are they not taken, that the King may eat them ? Let a canoe be launched at once, that they may be taken." The messenger then proceeds, " We therefore were sent off, and we set sail, and the wind was northerly, and, not long after, the clouds gathered and we had a squall, and then we had fine weather, and at last we got here, and found you Chiefs sitting together, and the gods ; and this is the end of my report, and that it may be accepted only." This kind of detail is generally wearisomely minute, and delivered in a tedious, slovenly, and irregular style. At one time, the speaker talks very rapidly ; then suddenly changes into a protracted drawl, sucking the air through his teeth, at intervals, with a hissing noise. As he warms, he gets his hands at liberty, but it is only to play with a straw, or, if out of doors, to pull up the grass near him. The final sentence of this wonderful speech is accompanied by clapping his hands. The Mata, whose business it is to answer, often does so by saying, " Seven !" to which the reporter responds, " Eight !" The Mata proceeds, " Let your report be favourably received, and peace prevail in the land." He then claps, being joined by those sitting round, who also accompany him in repeating, " *Mana dina li,*" " So let it be, truly." Unless the report is one of unusual interest, it receives little attention from the hearers. " Good, good !" is repeated now and then ; but the King often talks most of the time to sóme one else. At Vata-vulu, it is said, the messenger has to sit with his back towards the Chief to whom he speaks.

Pitiable as are their attempts at speechifying, the Fijians talk about eloquence, and point out one man as " a master of words," and another as " the salt of language." Perhaps the dignity of a court daunts the orator, forbidding his eloquence and wit to shine forth ; at any rate, he never rises above dry detail, and a little trite adulation.

Should a canoe carry a great Chief, or belong to strangers, a proper person is sent on board to inquire who the visitors are, and why they have come. Whenever one Chief purposes to pay a visit to another, a messenger is always sent beforehand, to give at least a few days' notice of his intention, to prevent surprise, and allow time for preparation. The herald on such occa-sions is generally of a superior sort. If the visitor is of higher rank than those to whom he comes, a company of the leading men of the place, headed by a Mata, are sent ten miles or more on the way to meet and welcome him, when sometimes they present a nut or a whale's tooth, to indicate good will. When equals meet, they are free from servility.

The Fijian, on such occasions, is careful to avoid remarks which might give offence, or the claiming of a station that does not belong to him. He will pass no one until he has intimated his purpose by a well-known word, or by asking permission,—a form observed also if he should wish to remove any thing from above or near to any person.

The existence of expressions equivalent to our "Mr.," "Sir," and "Madam," does much towards polishing the intercourse of this people ; and it is remarkable that they only in the South Seas have these terms in regular use. The flattery of the natives is often gross, and sometimes thoroughly oriental. Soon after my location in Lakemba, the Mission family visited the house of the King's brother; and as we were about to retire, the lady of the house requested a servant to bring food, that "the Chiefs from the eye of the sun might eat."

Some of their forms connected with giving and receiving deserve notice. I have several times received valuable presents of food; but the donor declared the gift worthless, saying, "I have nothing fit to offer you; but these fowls are an expression of my love for your children." Another, on presenting some fish, named my servants ; and a valuable lot of yams was, if the giver spoke truly, "a matter of little importance, but given to help in fattening my hogs." All this, however, is quite insincere. Presents, which generally consist of "changes of raiment," or mats, or oil, are almost always offered, whether to men or gods, in a set form. Thanks are always expressed aloud, and generally with a kind wish for the giver, as, "I take this, and may ——— have good health," or "live long." Sometimes the wish is more general, as, "Let Christianity spread throughout the land!" But such forms are plastic and fitted to circumstances. It is not uncommon for a man, on receiving a gift which he values, to lift it up to his head, or, sometimes, kiss it. One man to whom I gave a plane-iron, laid it on the floor, and then stooped down to kiss it.

Guests who are about to leave by water, are always accompanied by their entertainers to the canoe; and often a few friends will go a short distance with them, although they have to regain the shore by swimming. Such as go by land are attended beyond the skirts of the town, and for some little distance. This is a fitting close to a visit which, if the road was dirty and no water at hand, began by the offering of water for the feet, and oil to anoint the face and body.

In their dress, scanty as it is, the Fijians display great care and pride. In judging of this matter, it is very difficult for a civilized stranger to form a right opinion, influenced, as he must be, by the conventionalities of costume to which he is accustomed. Hence the natives are frequently spoken of as naked; but they only seem so when compared with other nations. It must be borne in mind that the character of the climate and the quality of their skin both render dress, as far as mere utility is concerned, unnecessary: the people, therefore, ought to receive full credit for modesty in the partial covering which they adopt, and about the use of which they are scrupulously particular. Vanity adds ornament to the simple dress, and decorates or defaces, according to prevailing custom, different parts of the body.

The dress of the men is a kind of sash of white, brown, or figured *masi*, varying in length from three to a hundred yards. Six or ten yards, however, is the usual measure. This sash is passed between the legs, and wound two or three times round the loins, securing one end in front, so as to fall over to the knees like a curtain; the end behind is fastened in a bunch, or left to trail on the ground. When a Chief is dressed in style, a few folds are taken higher up round his body, like a sword belt, and both ends of the sash form long trains.

The women are not allowed to use *masi*, but wear the *liku*, or fringed band, which has been already described. It is tied on the right side with bass, which, on high days, is long enough to form a train.

The turban, consisting of a gauze-like scarf of very fine white *masi*, from four to six feet long, is worn by all Fijians who can lay claim to respectability, except such as are forbidden its use. The apparent size is entirely regulated by the quantity of hair underneath, which is generally considerable. This head-dress may be fastened by a neat bow in front, or tied in a tassel-knot on the top of the head, or arranged so as to hang in lappets on one side. By some it is worn as a band or cord at the root of the hair, the greater part being allowed to fall down the back. In most cases it is ornamental and graceful.

It is the heads, however, rather than their covering, which excite wonder, and on no other part of his person does the Fijian expend so much time, pains, and skill. Most of the Chiefs have a hairdresser, to whose care his master's head is intrusted, often demanding daily attention, and, at certain stages of progress, requiring several hours' labour each day. During all this time the operator's hands are *tabu* from touching his food, but not from working in his garden. The hair is strong and often quite wiry, and so dressed that it will retain the position in which it is placed, even when projecting from the head to a distance of six or eight inches. One stranger, on seeing their performances in this department, exclaims, "What astonishing wigs!" another, "Surely the beau-ideal of hairdressing must reside in Fiji:" a third, "Their heads surpass imagination." No wonder, then, that they defy description. A few modes of adorning or disfiguring the head are given in the engraving; but they might be greatly multiplied without including all the vagaries of Fijian fancy in this particular; for if in anything the natives have a claim to originality and versatility of genius, it is in hairdressing. Whatever may be said about the appearance being unnatural, the best *coiffures* have a surprising and almost geometrical accuracy of outline, combined with a round softness of surface, and uniformity of dye, which display extraordinary care, and merit some praise. They seem to be carved out of some solid substance, and are variously coloured. Jet black, blue black, ashy white, and several shades of red prevail. Among young people bright red and flaxen are in favour. Sometimes two or more colours meet on the same head. Some heads are finished, both as to shape and colour, nearly like an English counsellor's wig. In some the head is a spherical mass of jet black hair with a white roll in front, as broad as the hand; or, in lieu of this, a white oblong occupies the length of the forehead, the black passing down on either side. In each case the black projects farther than the white hair. Some heads have all the ornamentation behind, consisting of a crowd of twisted cords ending in tassels. In others the cords give place to a large red roll, or a sandy projection falling on the neck. On one head, all the hair is of a uniform height; but one-third in front is ashy or sandy, and the rest black, a sharply defined separation dividing the two colours. Not a few are so ingeniously grotesque, as to appear as if done purposely to excite laughter. One has a large knot of fiery hair on his crown, all the rest of the head being bald. Another has the most of his hair cut away, leaving three or four rows of small clusters, as if his head were planted with small paint-brushes. A third has his head bare, except where a large patch projects over each temple. One, two, or three cords of twisted hair often fall from the right temple, a foot or eighteen inches long. Some men wear a number of these braids so as to form a curtain at the back of the neck, reaching from one ear to the other. A mode that requires great care, has the hair wrought into distinct locks, radiating from the head. Each lock is a perfect cone, about seven inches long, having the base outwards; so that the surface of the hair is marked out into a great number of small circles, the ends being turned in, in each lock, towards the centre of the cone. In another kindred style, the locks are pyramidal, the sides and angles of each being as regular as though formed of wood. All round the head, they look like square black blocks, the upper tier projecting horizontally from the crown, and a flat space being left at the top of the head. When the hair, however, is not more than four inches long, this flat does not exist, but the surface consists of a regular succession of squares or circles. The violent motions of the dance do not disturb these elaborate preparations, but great care is taken to preserve them from the effects of the dew or rain.

Married women often wear their hair in the same style as the men, but not projecting to quite the same extent. A large woollen mop, of a reddish hue, falling over the eyes, will represent the hair as worn by the younger women.

I have often girted men's heads which were three feet ten inches, and one nearly five feet, in circumference. A coating of jet-black powder is considered superlatively ornamental; but its use is forbidden to the women, who, however, in common with the men, paint themselves with vermilion, applied in spots, stripes, and patches. White and pink armlets, and others made of a black wiry root or white cowries, ivory and shell finger-rings, knee and ankle bands with a rose-shaped knot, are much worn. Ivory, tortoiseshell, dogs' teeth, bats' jaws, snake vertebræ, native beads ground out of shells, and foreign beads of glass, are formed into necklaces, the latter being generally braided into neat bands. Breast ornaments are, pearl-shells as large as a dessert-plate, plain or edged with ivory, orange and white cowries, and crescents or circles formed by a boar's tusk. Chiefs and priests sometimes wear across the forehead a frontlet of small scarlet feathers fixed on palm-leaf, while a long black comb or tortoiseshell hair-pin—alias, "scratcher"—projects several inches beyond the right temple. Ear ornaments are used by both sexes, not pendent, but passing through the lobe of the ear, and varying in size from the thickness of the finger to that of the wrist. Some insert a white cowry, and a few have the opening so distended as to admit a ring ten inches in circumference.

The Fijian procures many ornamental articles of his toilette from the forest, the vines and flowers of which are wrought into chaplets, necklaces, and wreaths: the latter are thrown over one shoulder, so as to cross the body and fall gracefully on the opposite hip. Fillets of dried leaves are worn on the limbs, and enduring but unsightly scars are cut in the skin, sometimes in concentric circles; rows of wart-like spots are burned along the arms and backs of the women, which they and their admirers call ornamental. Genuine tattooing is only found on the women; but not much of it is seen, as it is covered by the *liku*. Young women have barbed lines on their hands and fingers; and the middle-aged, patches of blue at the corners of the mouth. The custom of tattooing is said to be in conformity with the appointment of Ndengei, and its neglect punished after death. The native name is *qia*, and, as it is confined to women, so the operators are always of the same sex. An instrument called a "tooth," consisting of four or five fine bone teeth fixed to a light handle six inches long, is dipped in a pigment made of charcoal and candle-nut oil; the pattern having been previously marked on the body, the lines are rendered permanent by the blackened comb, which is driven through the skin in the same manner as a fleam, though with less violence. Months are often occupied in the process, which is painful, and only submitted to from motives of pride and fear. Feasts are held also in connexion with this. The command of the god affects but one part of the body, and the fingers are only marked to excite the admiration of the Chief, who sees them in the act of presenting his food. The spots at the corners of the mouth notify, on some islands, that the woman has borne children, but oftener are for the concealment of the wrinkles of age.

Fijians account humorously for the Tongan practice of tattooing being confined to the men instead of the women. They say that the Tongan who first reported the custom to his countrymen, being anxious to state it correctly, repeated, in a sing-song tone, as he went along, "Tattoo the women, but not the men; tattoo the women, but not the men." By ill luck, he struck his foot violently against a stump in the path, and, in the confusion which followed, reversed the order of his message, singing, for the rest of his journey, "Tattoo the men, but not the women." And thus the Tongan Chiefs heard the report; and thus it came to pass that the smart of the *qia* tooth was inflicted on the Tonga men, instead of their wives.

Sleep and tobacco are among the leading comforts of the Fijian. He follows activity with slumber, from which he hates to be aroused. Tobacco, though known only for about thirty years, is in such high favour, that its use is all but universal, children as well as adults indulging in it freely. The native method of smoking is decidedly social. A small cigarette, formed by folding leaf tobacco in a strip of dead banana leaf, is lit, and passed to four or six persons in succession. Having to swim across a river does not interrupt this transfer; for the same cigar may be conveyed from one bank to the other in several different mouths. The habit of smoking is strengthened by much leisure, to which may be attributed the filthy practice of eating the vermin with which their heads are often largely stocked. Even this custom is put by the natives to the score of revenge, and many spare moments are devoted to it, the produce being shared between the capturer of the game and the owner of the preserve.

Many of their vacant hours are filled up by the Fijians in sports, some of which closely resemble the innocent games of English children; such as "hide and seek," "blind-man's buff," making "ducks and drakes," etc. Others are more boisterous; as the *veiyama*, a sham fight among children; the *veimoli*, pelting each other with bitter oranges; wrestling, and the *cere*, or race, the runners being persons who have been employed in digging a garden, the owner of which offers the prize—generally *masi*—for their competition. Mock battles are also fought, which sometimes become too real, and loss of life is the result.

The swing supplies a favourite amusement to children and young people. It consists of a single cord, either a rope or a strong vine, suspended from a tree, and having at its lower end a loop in which to insert one foot, as in a stirrup, or a knot, on which both feet rest. Grasping at a convenient height the cord, which varies in length from

M

thirty to fifty feet, the swinger is set in motion, and rejoices to dash through the air, describing an arc that would terrify a European.

A very great favourite is the game of *veiteqi vutu*, which consists in throwing the fruit of the *vutu* (*Barringtonia speciosa*). This fruit is also used as floats for their nets.

Veikalawanasari is a species of "hop, skip, and jump."

Lavo, a game at pitching the fruit of the *walai* (*Mimosa scandens*). The fruit is flat and circular, and, from its resemblance in form to money, money is also called *ai lavo*.

A more athletic sport is the *tiqa* or *ulutoa*. This game is played by throwing from the forefinger a reed of three or four feet long, armed with a six-inch oval point of heavy wood. This weapon is made to skim along the ground to a distance of a hundred yards or more. Nearly every village has near it a long level space kept clear of grass for the practice of this favourite exercise.

A kind of skittles, played with stones, is not uncommon; and skilful players will throw the stone with their back towards the skittles. Canoe racing is somewhat frequent.

The *veisaga* is practised on a large scale in some parts of the group. Upon the top of a hill men and women assemble to sport and wrestle. If a man closes with a woman, he attempts to throw her, and, on succeeding, they both roll together down the hill. Sometimes a sprain is the consequence; but the sufferer takes care to conceal the accident, lest the taunts and ridicule of the crowded spectators should be added to his misfortune.

The *veisolo* is another rough sport. In the cases which I saw, the attack was made by women on a number of male visitors. They waited until food was brought to the men, and then rushed on their guests, endeavouring to disperse them, and take away the food. The men, either from custom or gallantry, merely retaliate by taking the women captives, or throwing them gently on the ground. The women, however, were not so mild; and I was acquainted with instances of men dying from the violence of their blows. One Amazon engaged in this sport shot a man dead with an arrow.

The *kalou rere*, described in the following chapter, is also considered a pastime.

Veivasa ni moli is a game which consists in suspending a *moli* (orange, lemon, &c.) by a string, and trying to pierce it with the *vasa*, (a pointed stick,) while it is swinging about.

Several amusements belong to the water, such as chasing each other, wrestling, and diving. Shoals of men or of women are seen, on a calm day, striking away from the shore, with gleeful notes, or that hearty abandonment of broad-mouthed mirth for which they are so famous. In the game of *ririka*, an upright post is fixed at the edge of a reef, and the upper end of a long cocoa-nut tree rested on it, so as to form an easy ascent, with the point projecting beyond the post, and raised about fifteen or twenty feet above the surface of the water. The natives run up this incline in a continuous single file, and their rapidly succeeding plunges keep the water all round white with foam. Youngsters use the surf-boards which are so often found in Polynesia.

Nocturnal serenading is practised by companies of men or women.

Although most of the Fijians are fond of music, yet their own attempts in that direction are very rude. Their musical instruments are the conch-shell, the nose-flute, the

GIRL PLAYING ON THE NOSE-FLUTE.

M 2

Pandean pipes, a Jew's harp made of a strip of bamboo, a long stick, large and small drums, made of a log hollowed like a trough, and having cross pieces left near the ends, and bamboos used for the same purpose. The shell is the favourite instrument of the fishermen. The long stick belongs to the dance. Clapping of hands always accompanies singing, which is invariably in a major key.

DRUMS AND MUSICAL INSTRUMENTS.

The dance is undoubtedly the most popular pastime of Fiji. The song by which it is regulated is often very dull, and the movements slow and heavy, consisting of stepping and jumping, mingled with many inflections of the body and gesticulations with the hands. There is always a conductor, and, in one or two of their dances, a buffoon is introduced, whose grotesque movements elicit immense applause. In a regular dress or feast dance, two companies are always engaged,—the musicians and the dancers. Twenty or thirty persons constitute the "orchestral force," while the dancers often number one or two hundred. The performance of the musicians "is on one note, the bass alternating with the air: they then sound one of the common chords in the bass clef, without the alternation." Several of them elicit clear notes from the long stick by hitting it with a shorter one; others produce a sort of tambourine sound by striking their bamboos on the ground; the rest clap their hands, and all give vocal help. They keep excellent time, and the words sung refer either to the occasion, or to some event in their past history.

The dancers are gaily dressed; and as all bear clubs or spears, and perform a series of marchings, steppings, halts, and varied evolutions, a stranger would rather suppose them to be engaged in a military review than in a dance. As the performance approaches the close, the speed quickens, and the actions steadily increase in violence, accompanied by a heavy tramping on the ground, until the excited dancers, almost out of breath, shout, at the top of their voices, "*Wa-oo!*" and the dance is ended.

Persons who know a new dance are paid for teaching it, the fee being called *votua*. The following short song contains the complaint of an ill-rewarded teacher:—

> "The mother of Thangi-limba is vexed.
> How can we teach, unrewarded, the dance?
> Here is the basket for the fees—and empty!
> Truly this is an illiberal world."

Some few of the islanders are acquainted with sleight-of-hand tricks, which they exhibit among their friends. The Chiefs occasionally amuse themselves by *vakaribamalamala*, punning, and playing upon words. Thus, as the word *ulaula* means either to thatch a house, or to throw *ulas*—short clubs—at one another, the Mbau people sometimes order the Tailevu people to come to Mbau to *ulaula*. They come, expecting to thatch a house, and find themselves pelted with clubs. On fine nights, or rainy days, story-telling, including all kinds of traditions, histories, and fictions, often of the most extravagant kind, is a favourite amusement.

Such children as are allowed to live are treated with a

foolish fondness; but, in some parts, the father may not speak to his son after his fifteenth year. Family discipline is unreal, and its apparent restraints easily set aside. Children stray away at pleasure, and very soon become independent of their parents, by whom they are taught to dance, to plant, and to fight. Insults or injuries endured by their friends are impressed on their susceptible minds; and the parties who inflicted them are pointed out as the objects of present hatred, and the victims of future revenge.

The hair of the boys is kept short, but that of the girls is allowed to grow long, and fall in all directions from the crown of the head, in twisted locks of a brown, red, or flaxen colour, so as often entirely to hide the eyes. The countenances of the children show signs of that restless observance which is so fully developed in the faces of their parents. They ascend the hill of life with rapid strides, and, having reached the summit, run into their graves. "You English," said a fine young man to me, "grow slowly, like the nut, and abide: we Fijians grow with the rapidity of the plantain, and, like it, decay and are not in a few days." Both sexes go unclad until the tenth year, and some beyond that. Chiefs' children are kept longest without dress.

Males are circumcised when from seven to twelve years old. The cutting instrument is a piece of split bamboo, and the recovery is rapid. The operation is generally performed on a company of ten or twenty at a time, who, for several days afterwards, live together in some public building, their food being taken to them by women, who in some places, as they carry the meal, generally a dish of cooked greens, sing,—

> "*Memu wai o qori ka Kula;*
> *Au solia mai loaloa;*
> *Au solia na drau ni cevuga:*
> *Memu wai o qori ka Kula.*"

> "This is your broth, Sirs the Circumcised;
> I give it from the wilderness;
> I give the leaf of the cevuga:
> This is your broth, Sirs the Circumcised."

Kula is one of the names by which those who are newly circumcised may be spoken of by or before women, *teve*, the proper word, being *tabu* if a woman is present. *Kula* is also the name of a strip of cloth which receives the blood, and, on Vanua Levu, is afterwards hung from the roof of the temple or Chief's house. The proper time for performing this rite is after the death of a Chief, and many rude games attend it. Blindfolded youths strike at thin vessels of water hung from the branch of a tree. At Lakemba, the men arm themselves with branches of the cocoa-nut, and carry on a sham fight. At Ono, they wrestle. At Mbau, they fillip small stones from the end of a bamboo with sufficient force to make the person they hit wince again. On Vanua Levu, there is a mock siege.

On the fifth day after a Chief's death, a hole is dug in the floor of a *bure*, and one of the circumcised youths is secreted in it, whereupon his companions fasten the doors of the house securely, and run away. When the one within blows a shell, the friends of the deceased surround the house, and thrust their spears at him through the fence.

The ceremony may be followed by the assumption of the man's dress; but this is not invariable, as some wear it long before, and others not till some time after. When a Chief's son first puts on the *masi*, a feast is made, followed by dancing. Youths, while uncircumcised, are regarded as unclean, and are not permitted to carry food to the Chiefs. Young men, as was intimated before, have separate sleeping apartments, and are forbidden to eat of food left by women, and to unroll and lie on their mats.

Girls are betrothed at a very early age, and often to men past the prime of life. Although, when old enough to think for themselves, women express their dislike of this system, yet it certainly gives them one advantage,— that of a more careful guardianship. Not that the future husband takes the girl under his immediate care; but the fear of him or his friends causes her parents to keep a strict watch over her, and his influence would be exerted to punish any one who might insult her. An imprudent

step on her part sometimes costs her life. In the case
of a young girl near Mbua, her friends, on perceiving
the result of her infidelity, assembled, and strangled her,
and then sent word to her intended husband, asking for
forgiveness. About the middle of 1852, Ritova, the
Mathuata Chief, on finding that his sister, or cousin, had
been guilty of a similar offence, sent a messenger to the
tribe to which her secret lover belonged, demanding that
he should be given up to punishment. This, however, his
friends refused. But Ritova, fixed in purpose, commanded
his relation to be strangled and buried. Stern justice
appears in both cases; but it is in appearance only.
Fear, in the first instance, and mortified pride, in the
other, was the real motive.

When betrothed in infancy, as the daughters of Chiefs
usually are, the mother of the girl, in some cases, takes
a small *liku* to the future husband, as a pledge that her
child shall hereafter be his wife. If he is grown up, he
observes a form of asking the parents to give him their
daughter, presenting, at the same time, one or more
whales' teeth. Most improper matches are made. I have
seen an old man of sixty living with two wives both under
fifteen years of age. Women, indeed, are regarded as a
sort of property, in which a regular exchange is carried
on; but there is no truth in the assertion that the natives
sell their women among themselves. Whatever there has
been like this, has been taught them by white men. The
low estimate in which, on some islands, women are held,
may be judged from the following fact. A Chief of
Nandy, Viti Levu, was very desirous to have a musket
which an American Captain had shown him. The price
of the coveted piece was two hogs. The Chief had only one;
but he sent on board with it a young woman as an equivalent. I afterwards saw the girl, and was acquainted with
her purchaser, by whose wife she was kept as a servant.

The natives have gravely asked the Missionaries whether
they bought their wives, and what they cost, supposing
that such was the custom in the white man's land.

Nevertheless, although not an article of trade among themselves, woman is fearfully degraded in Fiji. In many parts of the group she is as a beast of burden, not exempt from any kind of labour, and forbidden to enter any temple : certain kinds of food she may eat only by sufferance, and that after her husband has finished. In youth, she is the victim of lust, and in old age, of brutality. Such of the young women as are acquainted with the way in which a wife is secured in England, regard it with strong admiration, and envy the favoured women who wed "the man to whom their spirit flies."

It sometimes happens, however, that persons are thus privileged in Fiji, and permitted to choose for themselves. When such is the case, affection progresses to possession by certain steps, which vary slightly in different parts of the group. When the female is betrothed, the obser-vances are nearly the same.

The *veidomoni,* or "mutual attachment," is the first step. In this the young man asks the girl of her parents, taking a present or not, as he judges best. When anything is given, it is not considered in the light of a price paid, but merely as a matter of form. Should the request meet with a favourable reply, the girl's friends *veimei,* "nurse," or take her to the house of her intended husband's parents, presenting, at the same time, property—teeth, cloth, or mats. A custom, which is certainly pretty, is then observed. Not even a heathen can leave the scenes of childhood and careless joy without tears, and the "nursed" girl often weeps freely. The friends of the bridegroom endeavour to solace her, by presenting trinkets as expressions of their regard. This is called the *vakamamaca,* or "drying-up-of-the-tears." Then follows the *vakatakata,* or "warming." This is food made by the man, and taken to the friends of the bride, who still remains where her friends left her. In some parts, she enjoys a holiday for four days, sitting in her new home, oiled, and covered with turmeric powder. At the end of four days she bathes, accompanied by a number of women—generally married women—who help her to fish.

On returning home, the fish is cooked, and, when ready, an intimation to that effect is sent to the young man, who dresses himself in style, and, accompanied by a number of his companions, oiled and dressed, directs his steps to the house in which his betrothed waits his arrival. The bridegroom and his companions take off their new dresses, which are given to the relatives of the bride. . The fish-soup is then served up with good yam, the prospective wife commencing her duties by pouring out and handing to her future lord a dish of soup, which he drinks, eating yam with it. A part of the yam he gives to the bride, who eats with him. Probably they never were so near or spoke to each other before, and very likely this their first meal passes in silence. This ceremony is named *na sili*, " the bathing." In the leeward islands, this generally concludes the form of marriage. To windward such is not the case ; but the girl goes back to her parents, and the friends on both sides make cloth and mats to present with the young people on the wedding-day. Meantime the young man is expected to build a house to which to take his wife, who undergoes now the painful process of tattooing, if it has not already been done. Some chief ladies, however, defer the performance of this operation until they have become mothers. During this period the bride is *tabu siga*, kept from the sun, to improve her complexion. These preliminaries over, the grand feast takes place, when the friends of each party try to outdo the others in the food and property presented. As in other native feasts, so here it is easier to specify the good cheer by yards and hundred-weights, than by dishes. When Tanoa gave his daughter to Ngavindi, the Lasakau Chief, there was provided for the entertainment of the friends assembled, a wall of fish five feet high, and twenty yards in length, beside turtles and pigs, and vegetables in proportion. One *dish* at the same feast was ten feet long, four feet wide, and three deep, spread over with green leaves, on which were placed roast pigs and turtles. Whatever is prepared by the friends of the woman is given to those of the man, and *vice versâ*. The conclusion of this day is the *vaqasea*, when the marriage is complete, the announcement of which, in some tribes, is by tremendous shoutings; and arrangements are made for the *veitasi*, or "clipping," which, to windward, consists in cutting off a bunch of long hair worn over the temples by the woman while a spinster. To leeward, however, the woman is deprived of all her hair, and thus made sufficiently ugly to startle the most ardent admirer. This act has its feast, food being prepared, and often taken as the breakfast of the newly married couple. In some places the great feast follows the *clipping*. Priests are never in requisition officially on marriage occasions. Matrimony, in Fiji, is a social or civil contract only. Every presentation of property or food is associated with good wishes or prayers for the long life and happiness of the young couple; but no priest is needed in this, as it is only the observance of a custom used on every occasion that will admit of such forms. Commodore Wilkes's account of Fijian marriages seems to be compounded of oriental notions and Ovalau yarns. A change in the form of *liku* always takes place. Young unmarried women wear a *liku* little more than a handsbreadth in depth, which does not meet on the hip by several inches. On marrying, they put on a broader dress, which entirely surrounds the body, and the depth of which is increased as the wearer grows older. An owl flying about a house is considered by the natives as a sign that things are in a fair way for the master becoming a father. When such a hope is proved to be well established, certain matrons and the newly-made wife get up a sort of pic-nic, which they call *vakata kakana*. For this they choose some sylvan retreat, where embowering trees, with their thick foliage interwoven with various creepers, afford a cool and secluded shade. Here the women feast together, and indulge in the "wide-mouthed mirth" of which they are so fond, unmindful of future care. After this comes the *vakavotu*, the "becoming visible," and with it another feast; when friends eat and rejoice together, and a bartering of property takes place between them. The next step is the *tátavu*, the "broiling." This is much quieter, and not so commonly observed, and consists in feeding the expectant mother with fish just before her confinement.

Voluntary breach of the marriage contract is rare in comparison with that which is enforced, as, for instance, when a Chief gives up the women of a town to a company of visitors or warriors. Compliance with this mandate is compulsory; but should the woman conceal it from her husband, she would be severely punished. Fear prevents unfaithfulness more than affection, though I believe that instances of the latter are numerous.

. Too commonly there is no *express* feeling of connubial bliss. Men speak of "our women," and women of "our men," without any distinctive preference being apparent. If a man does not approve of his betrothed, he quietly neglects the usual advance. If a woman rejects the suit of a man, after being promised to him, property must be taken to him or his friends, by whom the *vakalutu*, the "letting drop," is generally accepted.

This, however, does not apply to persons of high rank, marriages among whom are so interwoven with the civil and political interests of the country, that no deviation from form is allowed, out of regard to the wishes of the female concerned, who, in these matters, may have no will of her own. I saw a daughter of the King of Lakemba leave for Mbau. She was a fine girl, of very amiable manners, and a general favourite. Her intended husband was Tanoa, a man quite old enough to be her great-grandfather. There was something really affecting about the separation from the companions of her girlhood; and how she managed to bear such a weight of grief, aggravated by the hugs and embraces of a dozen persons at once, for so long a time, and in such hot weather, I could not understand. Such ladies are under the care of a duenna, who accompanies them, together with the servants given by the bride's father. A Princess of first rank had ten female servants from her father, and five from her husband. One, two, or three, is more commonly the number. These attendants are sometimes called the *tauvaki*, a word which combines the meaning of " menial " and " pet."

I saw a young girl of good family, who was given to the daughter of Tuikilakila, brought in form to that Chief. As she was presented in the way usually observed in giving a bride, I will describe the ceremony. She was brought in at the principal entrance by the King's aunt and a few matrons, and then, led only by the old lady, approached the King. She was an interesting girl of fifteen, glistening with oil, wearing a new *liku*, and a necklace of carved ivory points, radiating from her neck, and turning upwards. The King then received from his aunt the girl, with two whales' teeth, which she carried in her hand. When she was seated at his feet, his Majesty repeated a list of their gods, and finished by praying that " the girl might live, and bring forth male children." To her friends—two men who had come in at the back door—he gave a musket, begging them not to think hardly of his having taken their child, as the step was connected with the good of the land, in which their interests, as well as his own, were involved. The musket, which was about equivalent to the necklace, the men received with bent heads, muttering a short prayer, the close of which was exactly the same as they had offered for years, " Death to Natawa!" Tuikilakila then took off the girl's necklace, and kissed her. The gayest moment of her life, as far as dress was concerned, was past; and I felt that the untying of that polished ornament from her neck was the first downward step to a dreary future. Perhaps her forebodings were like mine, for she wept; and the tears which glanced off her bosom and rested in distinct drops on her oily legs, were seen by the King, who said, " Do not weep. Are you going to leave your own land? You are but going a voyage, soon to return. Do not think it a hardship to go to Mbau. Here you have to work hard; there you will rest. Here you fare indifferently; there you will eat the best of food. Only do not weep to spoil yourself." As he thus spoke, he played with her curly locks, complimenting her on her face and figure.

She reminded him of a sister of hers who had been taken to Mbau in years past, and the mention of whose name seemed to have a talismanic effect on the aged aunt. "Ay!" she exclaimed, "that *was* a woman! Her face!" (placing a hand edgeways on either side of her own shrunk phiz,) "O what a face!" Then followed several other exclamations of admiring remembrance, more pointed than delicate, when, happily, the King interrupted the old lady before her admiration led her still farther beyond the bounds of propriety. Just then the King's women appeared with their nets, and he ordered the poor girl to go and "try her hand at fishing."

On the large islands is often found the custom, prevalent among many savage tribes, of seizing upon a woman by apparent or actual force, in order to make her a wife. On reaching the home of her abductor, should she not approve of the match, she runs to some one who can protect her: if, however, she is satisfied, the matter is settled forthwith, a feast is given to her friends the next morning, and the couple are thenceforward considered as man and wife.

"Writing to a woman" is of recent date, and generally done without pen, ink, or paper. It is the "popping the question" of English life, and though for the most part done by the men, yet the women do not hesitate to adopt the same course when so inclined. The man, however, takes a present to help his suit; the woman trusts only to her charms. Wonderfully artless are some of the appeals made by the men. Thivalala, whose legs were disfigured with elephantiasis, addressed a smart young widow thus: "You know my circumstances; I am poor; I am afflicted; I am far away from my friends: I need some one to care for me, love me, and become my wife." She, sympathizing, consented. Plain speaking in these affairs is not uncommon. Simioni Wangkavou, wishing to bring the object of his affection to decision, addressed these homely remarks to her, in the hearing of several other persons: "I do not wish to have you because you are a good-looking woman; that you are not. But a woman is like a necklace of flowers,—pleasant to the eye and grateful to the smell: but such a necklace does not long continue attractive; beautiful as it is one day, the next it fades and loses its scent. Yet a pretty necklace tempts one to ask for it, but, if refused, no one will often repeat his request. If you love me, I love you; but if not, neither do I love you: only let it be a settled thing."

But to return to the wife whom we left being fed with fish. Generally the women suffer little in parturition, and the aid of a native midwife is rarely needed, and, when given, is rather injurious than otherwise. A wide difference exists between the observances of Tongan and Fijian women at this time. The Tongan mother, on the birth of a child, gets up directly, and bathes in some pond or river, and, on her return, eats freely of food: if fish, poultry, or pork is provided, so much the better. Fijians profess to keep the house a few days, and some lie at their ease a full month. They are forbidden the free use of animal food and fish for a long time, being well supplied with vegetables; unripe bananas and greens being esteemed excellent for women at this time. A Tongan babe is anointed with oil and turmeric, and fed with old cocoa-nut chewed, the juice being passed from the mouth of the nurse into that of the child. This continues until the mother is fit to nurse. The Fijian infant is kept from the mother three days, and is suckled by another woman, or fed with sugar-cane juice, administered in the way just described. It also receives a coating of oil and turmeric. It is an ill omen if a child does not cry soon after it is born; and the male child born in the day-time is expected to prove a great warrior.

The Fijian father must celebrate the birth of a child by making a feast; and, if it is the first-born, sports follow, in one of which the men imitate on each other's bodies the tattooing of the women. The name of this feast is *a tunudra*, and seems to regard the woman rather than the child. Friends seek the place where the babe lies, and present love-tokens, receiving some presents in return. On Vanua Levu, the woman's friends plait small mats, measuring about two feet by one, for the mother to nurse her babe upon. The name of the visit imports that the women will take the child in their arms; and those who do so always kiss it. Next in order is the feast given at the falling off of the umbilical cord, which is sometimes buried, together with a cocoa-nut, to grow for the future use of the little stranger. A tribe on Viti Levu take the food prepared on this occasion to the priest, who notifies the event to their god thus: "This is the food of the little child; take knowledge of it, ye gods! Be kind to him. Do not pelt him, or spit upon him, or seize him, but let him live to plant sugar-cane." Food is again made ready on the first bathing of the child, and there is another little feast on the event of its first turning over without help. The women seem fond of their offspring; but an English mother finds it difficult to reconcile the thought of much affection, with so much dirt as is often allowed to collect on the child.

The naming of the infant takes place very early, sometimes before birth, but generally within two or three days after. Longer delay might endanger the child's life, by leading the mother to suspect that her offspring was uncared for. It is a common practice to name the first child after the man's father, and the second after the mother's father. In the first case, the friends of the man make the wife a present; and in the other, her friends offer the gift to the husband. The above practice, however, is very variable; and the naming of children is often left to accident, caprice, or malice. Some peculiarity in the infant, or in the time or circumstances of its birth, often decides the name. Or, in the absence of more durable monuments, the epithet is made a record of the family triumphs, or the weakness, folly, and disgrace of their enemies. Such instances abound, and names worse than these, of the lowest and filthiest kind, such as ought to be rejected from the language.

Natives nurse in eastern style, the child sitting, quite naked, astride the mother's hip, where it is kept from falling by her arm passed round its body. Children who have the *coko*—an ulcerous disease, like the yaws of the West Indies—stand at the back of their mother, whose hands are clasped behind, forming a soft standing-place for the feet of the little sufferer, who holds on by the parent's shoulders. Most native children have this disease, and those who escape are said to grow up sickly and feeble, and incapable of much exertion,—an opinion which, I believe, is well founded.

Women who regard the health of their child generally abstain from the pleasures of fishing during the time of nursing. One of the first lessons taught the infant is to strike its mother, a neglect of which would beget a fear lest the child should grow up to be a coward. Thus these people are nurtured "without natural affection," and trained to be "implacable, unmerciful." Several proofs of this I witnessed at Somosomo; mothers leading their children to kick and tread upon the dead bodies of enemies. The violent passions of revenge and anger are fostered in the native children, so that, when offended, they give full vent to their fury; and it is not surprising that their riper years exhibit such fearful developments of rage. Visiting, on the same island, a family who were mourning the recent slaughter of six of their friends, one of the first objects I saw was a good *malo*—a man's dress—much torn, by which sat a child of about four years old, cutting and chopping it with a large butcher's knife, while his own hand was covered with blood, which flowed from the stump where, shortly before, his little finger had been cut off, as a token of affection for his deceased father. The *malo* had been stripped from one of the party who had attacked the friends of that child, and was placed before him to excite and gratify a revengeful disposition.

Grim, immodest representations of the human figure, about eighteen inches long, are used on the larger islands to terrify the children into quietness.

When at Lakemba, I was told by Mosese Vakaloloma that, in their heathen state, they did not address their little ones as children, but would say, "Come here, you *rats!*"

Beside attending to the children, it is the duty of the
women to fetch salt and fresh water, collect fuel, and attend
to the boiled food. If a woman, when putting bananas into
a pot, let one fall on the outside, or if the bread-fruit burst
in roasting, she will wring her hands in dismay, or cry
aloud, fearing the ill luck betokened by the accident. On
Vanua Levu, the women are treated with a little consideration, and more as equals, by the men ; a kindness which
they repay by dealing largely in scandal, which thus grows
with tropical rapidity. Fishing with hand-nets is their
duty and delight. Women of all ranks engage in this
employment with a kind of passion, and use the time for
the unbridled indulgence of slander and gossip.

Polygamy is looked upon as a principal source of a
Chief's power and wealth. It certainly is the source of
female degradation, domestic misery, and personal suffering. One day, the Missionary's wife asked a woman who
was *minus* her nose, "How is it that so many of you
women are without a nose?" A native wife replied,
"It grows out of a plurality of wives. Jealousy causes
hatred, and then the stronger tries to cut or bite off the
nose of the one she hates."

The lady wife of the Mbua Chief had a rival more powerful than was agreeable to her, in an interesting young
woman, who engrossed most of her lord's attention. Not
having a club at hand with which to take vengeance on
the object of her angry jealousy, the enraged wife pounced
on her, and tore her sadly with nails and teeth, and injured
her mouth by attempting to slit it open. The young
woman was placed under my care, her shoulders being
severely lacerated. A few months after, a young girl—
the second wife of a man whose former spouse was getting
old—was brought to me, in a very emaciated condition,
through the cruel treatment of her rival. The man was
fond of his young wife, but could not shield her from the
fury of the elder, who added to much rough treatment the
employment of witchcraft. A severe illness was the result
of this double attack ; the body sinking under cruelty, and

the mind under superstitious fears. Thus we find that bites, scratches, and rent ears are among the smaller evils of polygamy. The following dialogue between Mrs. Williams and a native woman will further illustrate these evils.

" Where is Ratu Lingalingani ? "

" He is at Vuna, Madam. He is angry with Andi Lasangka," (a favourite wife,) "who is ill at that place."

" Is she not likely to become a mother ? "

" Yes : and it is on that account that she has gone to Vuna. The other wives of the Chief are displeased at it; and, rather than endure their anger, she has gone to destroy the child, that it may be still-born."

The treatment of a fine girl, the daughter of the mate of an American vessel, and inferior wife of a Mbau Chief, is too horrid to narrate.

The herd of women brought together by polygamy under the will of one man, are robbed of the domestic pleasures springing from reciprocated affection, and are thus led literally " to bite and devour one another." The testimony of a woman who lived two years in my family, after having been one among several of a Chief's wives, is, that they know nothing of comfort. Contentions among them are endless, the bitterest hatred common, and mutual cursing and recrimination of daily occurrence. When their quarters become untenable, they generally run. Indeed, I was told by a chief lady that it was a settled point, that an offensive under-wife must be made to fly by abundant scolding and abuse. When a woman happens to be under the displeasure of her master as well as that of his lady wives, they irritate the Chief by detailing her misdemeanours, until permission is gained to punish the delinquent, when the women of the house—high and low—fall upon her, cuffing, kicking, scratching, and even trampling on the poor creature, so unmercifully as to leave her half dead.

Another and most heavy curse of polygamy falls on the children, since it is an institution which virtually dissolves

N 2

the ties of relationship, and makes optional the discharge
of duties which nature, reason, and religion render imperative. Hence there are multitudes of children in Fiji
who are wholly uncared for by their parents; and I have
noticed cases beyond number, where natural affection was
wanting on both sides. The Fijian child is utterly deprived
of that wholesome and necessary discipline which consists
of regular and ever repeated acts of correction and teaching. Fitful attempts to gain the mastery are made by the
parent, coming in the form of a furious outburst of passion,
to which the child opposes a due proportion of obstinacy,
and, in the end, is triumphant. Thus the children grow
up without knowledge, without good morals or habits,
without amiability or worth, fitted, by the way in which
they are reared, to develope the worst features of heathen
life. And this hapless condition they owe to polygamy,
which robs the parent of the comforts and endearments of
married life, and gives the child but a slight advantage
over the whelp of the brute.

Murder, in various forms, is the result of this vicious
system. Great numbers produce sterility by drinking
medicated waters prepared for that purpose, and many
more kill their unborn children by mechanical means;
while, in the case of others, death follows immediately on
birth. Scarcity and war, when they prevail, are often
urged in excuse for these crimes. Perhaps the parents
belong to two tribes which are at enmity, in which case the
mother, rather than multiply the foes of her tribe, will
destroy her progeny. In 1850, the Mbua Chief took a
principal wife to his home, whereupon another of his wives,
in a fit of jealousy, disappointed him by destroying the
child which she expected shortly to be born. Nandi, one
of whose wives was pregnant, left her to dwell with a
second. The forsaken one awaited his return some months,
and at last the child disappeared. This practice seemed to
be universal on Vanua Levu,—quite a matter of course,—
so that few women could be found who had not, in some
way, been murderers. The extent of infanticide in some

parts of this island reaches nearer to two-thirds than half. Abominable as it is, it is reduced to a system, the professors of which are to be found in every village. I know of no case after the child is one or two days old; and all destroyed after birth are females, because they are useless in war, or, as some say, because they give so much trouble. But that the former is the prevailing opinion appears from such questions as these, put to persons who may plead for the little one's life: "Why live?. Will she wield a club? Will she poise a spear?" When a professed murderess is not near, the mother does not hesitate to kill her own babe. With two fingers she compresses its nostrils, while, with the thumb, she keeps the jaw up close; a few convulsive struggles follow, and the cruel hand of the mother is unloosed, to dig a grave close by where she lies, in which the dead child is placed. Unlike the infanticide of the Hindus, that of Fiji is done from motives in which there is no admixture of anything like religious feeling or fear, but merely whim, expediency, anger, or indolence.

In connexion with this subject, another proof may be given of the assertion already made, that the Fijians are made up of contradictions. They often adopt orphans, for whom they display far more love than for their own offspring. I should hesitate to give the following illustration, were I not well acquainted with most of the parties concerned. Tokanaua was slain in the last Mbua war, in 1844, leaving a son and infant daughter, who were thrown on the care of their friends, the mother having been strangled, and buried with her husband. The orphans were taken to the house of Tokanaua's elder brother, who provided wet-nurses for the babe. He became, however, dissatisfied with this arrangement; and as his wife was just then confined, he arranged with her to murder their own child, that the adopted one might take its place and receive her care.

The wives sometimes become unruly. Near to the King of Lakemba, and, afterwards, to the King of Mbua, I saw lying a stick of heavy wood, about the size of a broom-

handle.   On inquiry, I found that the free use of this
truncheon was very effective in subduing the wayward wills
of the women when they became disorderly.   Tanoa's staff,
used for this purpose, was inlaid with ivory, but did not, on
that account, cause less pain.   This is employed in cases
not grave enough to demand the club, as, for instance, the
dredre kaci—the call by laughing—the way in which
women are supposed to call their gallants.   These swains,
to make themselves increasingly agreeable, sweeten their
breath by eating a greyish clay, until nausea is produced.
But unhappy is the woman whose amours come to light!
The sweet words and pleasant breath of the lover are succeeded by the rough abuse of her lord, and by such a beating as leaves the difference between it and being clubbed
very small indeed.

The aged King, Tuithakau II., visited me one day in
evident trouble.   After sitting silent awhile, he said,
"Have you a spy-glass?"   Finding that I had one, he
proceeded, "Do look, and see if my woman has gone to
Weilangi only, or right away to Wainikeli."   Weilangi
was a village about six miles off, and Wainikeli about six
miles further, with high hills interposed.   It appeared that
the old gentleman had found it necessary to use severe discipline with one of his wives, who, after being beaten, ran
away; and he now felt anxious about her, and came to
solicit the help of my glass to ascertain her whereabouts.
I assured him that, in this case, the spy-glass was of no
use, as the woman had been gone several hours, and was
now, no doubt, in some house with her friends.   "Look,"
he rejoined, "if you can see her footsteps on the road from
Weilangi to Wainikeli."   It was with difficulty that I
persuaded him that it was impossible to see, at such a
distance, a path which was narrow and irregular, and,
moreover, hidden with forest and brushwood.

That which bears the name of swearing among the South
Sea Islanders, though bad enough, is different in its kind
from English swearing, and not so great an evil.   The
natives never blindly invoke the wrath of a god, or con-

demn themselves or each other to endless destruction ; but
they use filthy, irritating, and malevolent language, not
uncommonly having reference to their cannibal practices.
Like the Easterns, they speak abusively of the parents of
the persons with whom they are angry. I have heard
individuals, when protesting strongly, swear by the King.
It is *tabu* for those to swear at each other who are prohibited from conversing together ; but those who are
worshippers of the same god may swear at one another to
their heart's content.

To the aged and infirm, the kindnesses of the Fijians are
cruel. Bald heads and grey hairs excite contempt instead
of honour ; and, on this account, the aged, when they find
themselves likely to become troublesome, beg of their
children to strangle them. If the parents should be slow
to make the proposal, they are anticipated by the children.
The heathen notion is, that, as they die, such will their
condition be in another world ; hence their desire to
escape extreme infirmity. I have never known a case of
self-destruction which had personal defect or deformity for
its motive ; but a repugnance on the part of the sound,
the healthy, and the young, to associate with the maimed,
the sick, and the aged, is the main cause of the
sacrifice.

It could answer no good purpose to record many of the
frequent instances of abominable cruelty towards the aged
and infirm, which are precisely similar to those practised
by some other heathen nations. Exposure, burying alive,
and the rope, are the means generally used for dispatching
these unfortunates. One case, peculiarly Fijian, may be
narrated. Wangka i Vuki told me that his brother was
drowned at sea with Rambithi, a Somosomo Prince.
"Then," said I, " he went from you well, and you saw
him no more." Wangka i replied, " Well, not exactly so ;
we saw him again ; for, when the canoe on which he
sailed went down, he swam about until one of the fleet
came near him, and he got on board, resting some time, it
being night." As day broke, he was discovered by his

companions in trouble, and, since he had fared worse than they, it was at once decided that he ought to be clubbed. Just then, some one recognised him as a skilful sailor: this turned the scale in his favour, as it was agreed that he should live, and at once take the helm. Weak and unfit as he necessarily was for a post which wearies the most energetic, he took the great steer-oar; nor was he allowed to leave it until, after a tedious voyage, they reached Vuna. One heart there was among the crew that pitied that death-like being who grasped the helm, and, seeing that he was unable to move from the canoe, carried him ashore, and shared a piece of water-melon with him. His friends at Somosomo, on hearing of his two-fold escape, rejoiced greatly, brought him home, attended him for nearly two months, and had the satisfaction of witnessing his recovery. Soon after, through eating a piece of fowl, he suffered a relapse, so that his body became swollen, and his friends said that his breath smelt bad. They had received orders to go on a voyage the next day, and, as no one could be spared to look after the invalid, and to take him on the canoe might give him pain, and inconvenience his friends, they concluded that it would be best to strangle him; which purpose, with his own consent, they carried out. His relatives kissed and wept over him; strangled, buried, and mourned for him; and the next day set out on their voyage.

In the destruction of their decrepit parents, the Fijians sometimes plead affection, urging that it is a kindness to shorten the miserable period of second childhood. In their estimation, the use of a rope instead of the club is a mark of love so strong, that they wonder when a stronger is demanded. In many cases, however, no attempt is made to disguise the cruelty of the deed. It is a startling, but incontestable fact, that in Fiji there exists a general system of parricide, which ranks too, in all respects, as a social institution.

The ill-concealed cruelty of the people is further shown in their treatment of the sick. Unless the afflicted one is of high rank, or valued for his services, the patience of his friends will be exhausted in a few days.

Great effort was made on behalf of a Lakemba Princess who was sick, during my second year's residence on that island. The aid of the best native doctors was called in, and large offerings made to the gods, and a new temple begun, to secure their divine favour, but all in vain. Rich puddings, from sixteen to twenty-one feet in circumference, proved insufficient to attract the benignant notice of the gods; and, when all hope from that quarter was gone, the "lotu" was tried. The sick woman made a profession of Christianity, and, being placed under the kind care of Mr. and Mrs. Calvert, by God's blessing recovered. But very far different is the treatment of common people. Mr. Lyth found a woman in Somosomo who was in a very abject state through the protracted absence of her husband. For five weeks, although two women lived in the same house, she lay uncared for, becoming reduced to a mere skeleton. After this, she had food and medicine from the Mission Station, and improved. One morning, a servant of mine was taking her breakfast, but was met by her friends as they returned from her interment, who told him to take the food back. On reaching home he said that, on the previous day, he had found an old woman in the house, who made no secret of her errand. " I came," said she, " to see my friend, and inquire whether she was ready to be strangled; but, as she is strong, we shall not strangle her yet." Soon after, her friends changed their minds, and deprived her of life to hasten her funeral.

If sick persons have no friends, they are simply left to perish. Should they be among friends, they are cared for until they become troublesome, or, through weakness, offensive; whereupon they are generally put out of the way. The people near to Vatukali decide the question of a sick person's recovery by a visit to a famous *mulamula* tree, which is the index of death. If they find a branch of the tree newly broken off, they suppose that the person on whose account they pay the visit must die. If no

branch is broken, recovery is expected. When a warrior
meditates a daring deed, he says, "I shall come near to
breaking a branch of the *mulamula* to-day." The death
of the patient being once determined, any appeal on his
part is useless. Ratu Varani spoke of one among many
whom he had caused to be buried alive. She had been
weakly for a long time, and the Chief, thinking her likely
to remain so, had a grave dug. The curiosity of the poor
girl was excited by loud exclamations, as though something
extraordinary had appeared, and, on stepping out of the
house, she was seized, and thrown into her grave. In vain
she shrieked with horror, and cried out, "Do not bury
me! I am quite well now!" Two men kept her down by
standing on her, while others threw the soil in upon her,
until she was heard no more.

On Kandavu, sick persons are often thrown into a cave,
where the dead are also deposited.

It makes one sad to think that there is truth in what
the people allege, as one reason for their anxiety to get rid
of their sick. The malignity of the afflicted ones does not
seem to be diminished by their bodily weakness; for, when
left alone, they will lie on the mats of their friends, and
leave saliva on their drinking vessels, or even in their food,
that they may thus communicate the disease to the healthy
members of the household.

When the hour of death is allowed to approach naturally, and the dying one is respectable, or the head of a
family, the scene is certainly affecting. The patriarch calls
his children round him, that he may say farewell, and give
his parting advice. This is generally commenced in the
same way: "I am going. You will remain." He then
states any alteration he may wish in family affairs, or
expresses his satisfaction with them as they are. At that
hour of death he never forgets an enemy, and at that time
be never forgives one. The dying man mentions his foe,
that his children may perpetuate his hatred,—it may be
against his own son,—and kill him at the first opportunity.
The name of the hated one is uttered aloud, if not as the

object of immediate vengeance, yet of gloomy and disastrous predictions, which never fail to reach the ears
where they are least welcome. Deep concern is often
excited by these dying words, and the impression made on
the minds of those to whom the carrying out of their dark
purport is intrusted, is indelible. Thus, with the deep
marks of a murderous, unforgiving spirit upon him, does
the heathen pass away to his account.

When a Chief is either dead or dying, the fact is
announced to his various connexions ; and should he be
of supreme power, the principal persons in his dominions
come to pay their respects, and offer a present to him.
If he is merely the head of a tribe, the chief members of that
tribe assemble for the same purpose. The death of a male
is announced by the firing of muskets, or by dolorous blasts
on the trumpet-shell. On Vanua Levu, this is the signal
for plunder, the nearest relatives rushing to the house to
appropriate all they can seize belonging to those who lived
there with the deceased. Valuables are therefore removed,
and hidden in time. The general custom, however, takes
the form of an eastern mourning. The people nearest at
hand bewail the dead in a sudden outburst of grief—
uncurbed, excessive, and outrageous. Their cries are heard
far away, and render needless the solemn tones of the
passing bell. Numbers, from all parts, run together to
the place where the deceased lies, and from each is required
an extravagant demonstration of sorrow, but of short continuance. Some of the women accompany their cry with
gesticulations indicative of great anguish. " War ! War !
Precious ! Valiant ! " and similar exclamations, rend the air
on all sides. I have heard the dead questioned in the
style which has prevailed among every people where
similar modes of lamentation have been observed. " Why
did you die ? Were you weary of us ? We are around
you now. Why do you close your eyes upon us ? "
Sometimes these wailings continue through the night, and
their dreary, dismal effect cannot be imagined by any one
who has not heard them. The tones are those of hope-

less despair, and thrill through "nerve, and vein, and bone."

The process of laying out is often commenced several hours before the person is actually dead. I have known one take food afterwards; and another who lived eighteen hours after. All this time, in the opinion of a Fijian, the man was dead. Eating, drinking, and talking, he says, are the involuntary actions of the body,—of the "empty shell," as he calls it,—the soul having taken its departure. Laying out consists in removing any old clothes which may be about the sick man, washing him, if needful, oiling his body, and covering the upper part with black paint, so as to give him the appearance of a warrior. A large new *masi* is thrown loosely round his loins, a clean head-dress put on, and his lower extremities are covered with a kind of sheet. Ornaments on the arms and forehead are often added. When these decorations are complete, the surrounding friends think of nothing but the man's death, acting as though his recovery would disconcert their plans, and therefore be by no means desirable. When really dead, a ponderous club, newly oiled, is laid by his right side, and the lifeless hand holds one or more whales' teeth. This custom is analogous to that of the ancient Greeks, in placing an *obolus* on the lips of the corpse; but, instead of the sweet cake taken to propitiate Cerberus, the Fijians dispatch a strong man to secure the infernal guard until the chiefly ghost has passed by.

The next step is the preparation of the *loloku*. This word expresses anything done out of respect for the dead, but especially the strangling of friends. This custom may have had a religious origin, but at present the victims are not sacrificed as offerings to the gods, but merely to propitiate and honour the manes of the departed. It is strengthened by misdirected affection, joined with wrong notions of a future life. The idea of a Chieftain going into the world of spirits unattended, is most repugnant to the native mind. So strong is the feeling in favour of the *loloku*, that Christianity is disliked because it rigorously discountenances the cherished custom. When the Christian Chief of Dama fell by the concealed musketry of the Nawa-thans, a stray shot entered the forehead of a young man at some distance from him, and killed him. The event was regarded by many of the nominal Christians as most fortunate, since it provided a companion for the spirit of the slain Chief.

Ordinarily, the first victim for the *loloku* is the man's wife, and more than one, if he has several. I have known the mother to be strangled too. In the case of a Chief who has a confidential companion, this his right-hand man, in order to prevent a disruption of their intimacy, ought to die with his superior; and a neglect of this duty would lower him in public opinion. I knew one who escaped; but the associate of Ra Mbombo, the Chief of Weilea, was, together with the head wife of the deceased, murdered, to accompany him into the regions of the dead. The bodies of these victims are called "grass" for bedding the Chief's grave. When Mbithi, who was a Chief of high rank and greatly esteemed in Mathuata, died, (1840,) in addition to his own wife, five men and their wives were strangled, to form the floor of his grave. They were laid on a layer of mats, and the Chief was placed on them. Mbule-i-Navave, a Chief of limited influence, was buried on four poor women, one quite a girl. Six were to have been killed; but one was bold enough to object, and was spared; the other owed her life to missionary interposition. The usual victims on these occasions are two women, or a man and a woman. After the women are strangled, they are well oiled, their heads dressed and ornamented, new *likus* put on them, and vermilion or turmeric powder spread on their faces and bosoms. I have seen this done on some women before death. When prepared, they are placed by the side of the warlike dead, and together form one of the strangest and saddest of groups. The young Chief of Lasakau, Ngavindi, was laid out with a wife at his side, his mother at his feet, and a servant a short way off. After this, visits are received from companies of ten or twenty—men and

women—who weep in the way already described; and if
tears may be taken as evidence, their sorrow is sincere.
These visits are styled *ai reguregu,* a name which is also
applied to presents given at the same time. The word
comes from *regu,* to "kiss," since the visitors kiss as well
as bewail the dead. After this, I have seen the heads of
tribes who had maintained a friendly intercourse with him
whom they mourn, present a whale's tooth or a mat to the
man who has succeeded him as the head of the house, and,
pointing to the deceased, mention the friendship which
existed between him and them, saying, that the object of
their visit was not only to show their regard for the dead,
but also to put the living in mind of their friendly relationship, lest, forgetting it, they should break up a long
cherished union. The person addressed receives what is
offered, and expresses a wish that the friendship of the
two tribes may remain unbroken. On Vanua Levu, the
visitors turn from this form to kiss and weep over the
corpse.

If a person dies towards evening, the body is kept in the
house, and a sort of wake follows; persons sit and watch
with the corpse, the tedium of their duty being relieved by
companies of young men who, either indoors or outside,
sing a succession of dirges. The climate makes speedy
burial necessary, and the grave is dug the next morning.
Certain persons do this work, while another party prepares
the oven for the feast. At some funerals priests attend, and
superintend the ceremonies. The two diggers, seated
opposite each other, make three feints with their digging
sticks, which are then struck into the earth, and a grave,
rarely more than three feet deep, is prepared. Either the
grave-diggers, or some one near, repeats twice the words,
"Fiji, Tonga." The earth first thrown up is laid aside
apart from the rest. When the grave is finished, mats are
laid at the bottom, and the body or bodies, wrapped in
other mats and native cloth, are placed thereon, the edges
of the under mats folding over all: the earth is then
thrown in. Many yards of the man's *masi* are often left

out of the grave, and carried in festoons over the branches of a neighbouring tree. The sextons go away forthwith and wash themselves, using, during their ablutions, the leaves of the *ciuciu* or the *uci* for purification; after which they return, and share the food which has been prepared for them.

In the native funeral ceremonies there is an effort to exhibit sympathy and kindness. Articles prized by the dead are either buried with them, or laid on the grave. Friends withhold nothing needed for the obsequies. Poor people who, when alive, could scarcely procure a mat to lie upon, I have seen buried in four or even six. A decent burial is much coveted. The King of Lakemba used to ask of the Missionaries, as the greatest favour, a wooden coffin, that his body might not be trampled upon. The Chief of Mbau sent for Tongans to cut him a stone tomb. In Lakemba I recollect seeing the graves of children at the best end of the houses of several Chiefs; "That the wind," they said, "might not disturb, nor the rain fall upon them." On certain parts of Viti Levu, the same reason is assigned for burying their dead in the temples; also that the living may have the satisfaction of lying near their departed friends, and thus prevent their graves from being defiled; for a Fijian burial-ground is generally a very filthy place.

A faithful old servant of mine was constantly alluding to his death, and giving me directions about his interment. Lotu, a recent convert, asked me with concern whether she might be anointed with oil and turmeric after death; and, although dying, her eyes brightened as she told me the size of the cake of turmeric which she had in reserve for the occasion. A woman at Na Volivoli would not allow her babe to be buried at all, but kept it on a shelf in the house. Some have carried this out further. A child of rank died under the care of Marama, the Queen of Somosomo. The body was placed in a box, and hung from the tie-beam of the chief temple, and, for some months, the best of food was taken to it daily, the bearers approaching with the greatest respect, and, after having waited as long as a person would be in taking a meal, clapping their hands, as when a Chief has done eating, and then retiring. If tortoise-shell or mats were divided, Tui Vanuavou—the child—always had his share.

Over some of the graves a small roof is built, three or six feet high, the gables of which are filled in with sinnet, wrought into different-sized squares, arranged diagonally. Common graves are only edged round with stones, or have nothing more than one set at the head and another at the foot. The lady named above was greatly beloved by Tui-thakau, and he buried her in costly style. A good double canoe, forty feet long, was placed on a large mound cast up for that purpose, and faced with stones. It was then imbedded in earth, and the decks covered over with fine shingle, on which mats were spread to receive the body, which was covered with sand, and upon it were placed the remains of the boy of whom the Queen had been so fond. The body was further protected with a large roof, made of a kind of mahogany, and ornamented with pure white cowries. On some graves I have seen large cairns of stones, which are sometimes set up also to mark the spot where a man has died. On some few graves I have observed a basket of sundry ornaments which used once to please the deceased who lay below. Only the burial-places of Chiefs are *tabu*, and those only to natives. A general unwillingness is shown to disturb the dead.

On my first going to Somosomo, I entertained a hope that the aged King would be allowed to die a natural death, although such an event would be without precedent. The usage of the land had been to intimate that the King's end was near by cleaning round about the house, after which his eldest son, when bathing with his father, took a favourable opportunity and dispatched him with a club. On inquiry made on the spot, I found that this, according to the account of the Chiefs of Somosomo, was the practice of their neighbours at Vuna. This statement relieved my mind; for the kind old Chief was a general favourite, and it was painful to think that so cruel an end awaited him.

Commodore Wilkes justly describes him as "a fine specimen of a Fiji Islander ; and he bore no slight resemblance to our ideas of an old Roman. His figure was particularly tall and manly, and he had a head fit for a Monarch." Speaking of him afterwards, the American Commodore says, " He looks as if he were totally distinct from the scenes of horror that are daily taking place around him, and his whole countenance has the air and expression of benevolence." This is all true ; yet there was never a more besotted heathen, or a more inveterate cannibal, than the man thus ortra , and whose last hours may fitly be described here. yed

The venerable Chieftain grew feeble towards the middle of 1845, but not so as to prevent his taking an occasional walk. About August, however, he was obliged to keep his mat, and I often called, and endeavoured to instruct without irritating him. I visited him on the 21st, and was surprised to find him much better than he had been two days before. We talked a little, and he was perfectly collected. On being told, therefore, on the morning of the 24th, that the King was dead, and that preparations were being made for his interment, I could scarcely credit the report. The ominous word *preparing* urged me to hasten without delay to the scene of action ; but my utmost speed failed to bring me to Nasima—the King's house—in time. The moment I entered, it was evident that, as far as concerned two of the women, I was *too late* to save their lives. The effect of that scene was overwhelming. Scores of deliberate murderers, in the very act, surrounded me : yet there was no confusion, and, except a word from him who presided, no noise, but only an unearthly, horrid stillness. Nature seemed to lend her aid to deepen the dread effect : there was not a breath stirring in the air, and the half subdued light in that hall of death showed every object with unusual distinctness. All was motionless as sculpture, and a strange feeling came upon me, as though I was myself becoming a statue. To speak was impossible ; I was unconscious that I breathed ; and involuntarily, or,

o

rather, against my will, I sank to the floor, assuming the cowering posture of those who were not actually engaged in murder. My arrival was during a hush, just at the crisis of death, and to that strange silence must be attributed my emotion; for I was but too familiar with murders of this kind, neither was there anything novel in the apparatus employed. Occupying the centre of that large room were two groups, the business of which could not be mistaken. All sat on the floor; the middle figure of each group being held in a sitting posture by several females, and hidden by a large veil. On either side of each veiled figure was a company of eight or ten strong men, one company hauling against the other on a white cord, which was passed twice round the neck of the doomed one, who thus, in a few minutes, ceased to live. As my self-command was returning, the group furthest from me began to move; the men slackened their hold, and the attendant women removed the large covering, making it into a couch for the victim. As that veil was lifted, some of the men beheld the distorted features of a mother, whom they had helped to murder, and smiled with satisfaction as the corpse was laid out for decoration. Convulsive struggles on the part of the poor creature near me showed that she still lived. She was a stout woman, and some of the executioners jocosely invited those who sat near to have pity, and help them. At length the women said, " She is cold." The fatal cord fell; and, as the covering was raised, I saw dead the obedient wife and unwearied attendant of the old King. Leaving the women to adjust her hair, oil her body, cover the face with vermilion, and adorn her with flowers, I passed on to see the remains of the deceased Tuithakau. To my astonishment I found him alive! He was weak, but quite conscious, and, whenever he coughed, placed his hand on his side, as though in pain. Yet his chief wife and a male attendant were covering him with a thick coat of black powder, and tying round his arms and legs a number of white scarfs, fastened in rosettes, with the long ends hanging down his sides. His head was turbaned in a scarlet handkerchief, secured by a chaplet of small white cowries, and he wore armlets of the same shells. On his neck was the ivory necklace, formed in long curved points. To complete his royal attire, according to Fijian idea, he had on a very large new *masi*, the train being wrapped in a number of loose folds at his feet. No one seemed to display real grief, which gave way to show and ceremony. The whole tragedy had an air of cruel mockery. It was a masquerading of grim death, a decking, as for the dance, of bodies which were meant for the grave.

The conflicting emotions which passed through my mind at that moment cannot be described. I had gone there to beg that the old man might be buried alone; but he was not dead. I had hoped to have prevented murder; but two victims lay dead at my feet. I came to the young King to ask for the life of women; but now it seemed my duty to demand that of his father. Yet, should my plea be successful, it would cause other murders on a future day. Perplexed in thought, with a deep gloom on my mind, feeling my blood curdle, and "the hair of my flesh stand up," I approached the young King, whom I could only regard with abhorrence. He seemed greatly moved, put his arm round and embraced me, saying, before I could speak, "See! the father of us two is dead." "Dead!" I exclaimed, in a tone of surprise: "Dead! No." "Yes," he answered; "his spirit is gone. You see his body move; but that it does unconsciously." Knowing that it would be useless to dispute the point, I ceased to care for the father, and went on to say, that the chief object of myself and my colleague was to beg him to "love us, and prevent any more women from being strangled, as he could not, by multiplying the dead, render any benefit to his father." He replied, "There are only two; but they shall suffice. Were not you Missionaries here, we would make an end of all the women sitting around." The Queen, with pretended grief, cried, "Why is it that 1 am not to be strangled?" The King gave as a reason, that there was no one present of sufficiently high rank to suffocate her. Two other

women sat near the executioners, one of whom I had heard
mentioned previously as part of "the grass" for the King's
grave; and their gloomy aspect made me doubt the King's
sincerity, so that we resolved to stay. While waiting in
the midst of these murderers and their victims, and lost in
sad thoughts of the tyranny exercised by the devil over
those who were so entirely under his control, our reverie
was disturbed by the long, dull blast of two conch shells
blown by priests standing outside. It was as the passing
bell, announcing the demise of the old King. After several
blasts, Ratu Lewe-ni-lovo turned towards the King elect, and
greeted him: "Peace, Sir,"—a congratulation to which
his false heart gave the lie. The chief priest, as the voice
of the people, then repeated the salutation: "Peace, Sir.
Sit in peace, Sir. True, the sun of one King has set, but
our King yet lives. Peace, Sir; there are none here evil-
minded." Tuikilakila made no reply, but sat with his
head bent down to his breast. After a few moments of
silence he spoke. Gazing on the corpse of his father's
faithful attendant, he exclaimed, "Alas! Moalevu!" Several others having repeated the exclamation, he added,
"There lies a woman truly wearied: not only in the day,
but in the night also, the fire consumed the fuel gathered
by her hands. If we awoke in the still night, the sound
of her feet reached our ears; and, if spoken to harshly, she
continued to labour only. Moalevu! Alas! Moalevu!"
A priest continued the lament: "We used not to hear
Moalevu called twice." Similar remarks, with others on
the recent struggles of the dead women, the skill of the
stranglers, the quantity of cloth on which the corpses lay,
and the premonitory symptoms of the old King's decease,
occupied the remainder of the time.

Preparations being made for removing the bodies, we,
having no further cause for staying, retired from "the
large house." In doing so, I noticed an interesting female,
oiled and dressed in a new *liku*, carrying a long bamboo,
the top of which contained about a pint of water, which, as
the bodies were carried out at one door, she poured on the

threshold of another, and then retired by the way she came. The words of the widow of Tekoah were thus
. brought, with peculiar force, to my mind: "For we must needs die, and are as water spilt on the ground, which cannot be gathered up again." My inquiry into the origin and meaning of this act resulted in nothing satisfactory. Neither could I learn why the side of the house was broken down, to make a passage for the aged King to be carried through, when there were sufficient doorways close at hand. The bodies of the strangled women, having been secured in mats, were carried on biers to the sea-side. They were placed one on either end of a canoe, with the old King on the front deck, attended by the Queen and the Mata, who with a fan kept the insects off him. Thus was Tuithakau carried to Weilangi, to the sepulchre of the Kings.

Tongans were appointed to bury the King. The grave had been dug by the people of the place, and lined with mats, on which the Tongans laid the bodies of the women, and on them the once powerful Chief. The shell ornaments were taken off his person, which was then covered with cloth and mats, and the earth heaped upon him. He was heard to cough after a considerable quantity of soil had been thrown in the grave. These latter particulars I received from those who buried him, as I could not, by my presence, seem to sanction the unnatural deed.

On the death of the Tuithakau, it is customary to strangle his herald: the present one, however, escaped, since he only officiated as deputy for the proper one. A family on the opposite coast—Vanua Levu—enjoys the privilege of supplying a hale man to be buried with the King, that he may go before, and hold the Fijian Cerberus. On the present occasion, no such man could be found, and the old Chief was even sent to meet the dangers of the gloomy path without a club.

Next day, the *kana-bogi*, or fasting till evening, commenced. This is observed during ten or twenty days. Many made themselves "bald for the dead;" some by shearing the head only, others by cutting off whiskers and beard as well. Females burnt their bodies, and orders were issued that one hundred fingers should be cut off; but only sixty were amputated, one woman losing her life in consequence. The fingers, being each inserted in a slit reed, were stuck along the eaves of the King's house. Toes are never taken off for this purpose. Some, to express their grief, merely make bare the crown of the head.

The following ceremonies were confused and boisterous. Companies of young men danced, shouted, and made perfect uproar for several successive nights. The blindfolded lads tried to hit the hanging water-vessel, and, if successful, were to become great warriors. The common women, at this time, are not allowed to eat flesh or fish; and the chief wife, for three months following, may not touch her own food with her hands. The coast for four miles was made *tabu,* so that no one might fish there; and the nuts, for at least six miles, were made sacred.

Real sorrow, among these people, is sometimes indicated by abstinence from fruit, fish, or other pleasant food, for several months together, or by the use of leaves for dress, instead of any manufactured clothing. Denying themselves the luxury of oil on their bodies, or a mat to lie on, and lying whole nights on the grave of their friend, are other modes of expressing grief. The native word for "widow" refers to the practice of women neglecting to dress their heads for some time after the husband's death. The manifestations of mourning just described are optional: the following are exacted by custom. *Vakavidiulo,* "jumping-of-maggots," is a bitter lamentation for the dead, to which friends assemble on the fourth day after the funeral, and which consists in picturing to themselves the corruption which has taken place in the dead body of the departed. In strongest contrast with this custom is one observed on the fifth night, called the *vakadredre,* "causing-to-laugh." On this occasion companies gather together, and entertain the friends of the dead with comic games, in which decency is not always regarded, for the purpose of helping them to forget their grief. About the tenth day, or earlier, the women arm themselves with cords, switches, and whips, and fall upon any men below the highest Chiefs, plying their weapons unsparingly. I have seen grave personages, not accustomed to move quickly, flying with all possible speed before a company of such women. Sometimes the men retaliate by bespattering their assailants with mud; but they use no violence, as it seems to be a day on which they are bound to succumb.

Funeral banquets are made out of respect to the dead, and to comfort the surviving friends. This is not only done by those near at hand, but by those at a distance. If these should not hear of the death for a year, a feast of the dead is prepared directly the news reaches them. *Bogi drau,* "hundred nights," whatever it meant originally, is now the name of a feast at which the mourners return to their usual mode of life, after having abstained for ten or more days.

Every canoe arriving at a place for the first time after the death of a great Chief, must show the *loloku* of the sail. A long *masi,* fixed to the mast-head or yard, is sometimes the *loloku,* or a whale's tooth is thrown from the mast-head so as to fall into the water, when it is scrambled for by people from the shore. When the canoe gets nearer in, the sail and *masi* are both thrown into the water.

The *lawa ni mate* is, perhaps, the final ceremony, and signifies the accomplishing of some unusually large or good work, as the building of a canoe, or the making of an immense ball of sinnet, bale of cloth, or roll of matting, in memory of the dead, whose name the production thus completed bears. Thus the *Ra Marama* was built in memory of the Queen of Thakaundrovi. When the *lawa ni mate* is a canoe, it is, while in progress, regularly "awoke" every morning before the carpenters begin their day's work, and "put to sleep" again when they have finished. This is done at each time by a merry beat of drums.

One custom I observed only on Lakemba. A long line of women, each bearing on her shoulder or hip a green basket of white sand, to cover over the grave, went singing in a clear tone, *"E-ui-e,"* while another party answered *"E yara;"* thus producing a solemn and agreeable effect on the mind of a stranger. While still ignorant of Fijian manners, I approached such a company as I should a funeral procession at home; but a loud burst of laughter told me that it was mere ceremony without feeling.

In the case of a Chief drowned at sea, or slain and eaten in war, the *loloku* is carefully observed, as well as if the deceased has died naturally, and been buried in a strange land. But in these instances the grief of the survivors is more impassioned, and their desire to manifest it by dying, more enthusiastic.

When Ra Mbithi, the pride of Somosomo, was lost at sea, seventeen of his wives were destroyed. After the news of the massacre of the Namena people at Viwa in 1839, eighty women were strangled to accompany the spirits of their murdered husbands.

Before leaving this dark subject, it demands more full and explicit examination. It has been said that most of the women thus destroyed are sacrificed at their own instance. There is truth in this statement; but, unless other facts are taken into account, it produces an untruthful impression. Many are importunate to be killed, because they know that life would thenceforth be to them prolonged insult, neglect, and want. Very often, too, their resolution is grounded upon knowing that their friends or children have determined that they shall die. Some women have been known to carry to the grave the mats in which they and their dead husbands were to be shrouded, and, on their arrival, have helped to dig their own tomb. They then took farewell of their friends. Some have submitted their neck to the cord, or seated themselves in the grave, in silence. Others have spent their last breath in wishing for their friends success in war, plentiful crops, and whatever might make them happy. Generally such courage is forced, or the result of despair. Death offers an escape from the suffering and wrong which await the woman who survives her husband; and the dark grave is an asylum into which she hastens from "the bitterness and sting of taunting tongues."

If the friends of the woman are not the most clamorous for her death, their indifference is construed into disrespect either for her late husband or his friends, and would be accordingly resented. Thus the friends and children of the woman are prompted to urge her death, more by self-interest than affection for her, and by fear of the survivors rather than respect for the dead. Another motive is to secure landed property belonging to the husband, to obtain which they are ready to sacrifice a daughter, a sister, or a mother. Many a poor widow has been urged by the force of such motives as these, more than by her own apparent ambition to become the favourite wife in the abode of spirits.

The husbands of two Na Sau women were shot in war, and they were doomed to be strangled. They had a slight acquaintance with the truths of Christianity, and feared the future; beside this, one of them was with child. A Native Teacher begged their lives on these considerations. The women wished to live, and said, "Our case is one to cause pity; but we dare not live; our friends dare not save us." Very few escape through a failure on the part of the executioners. It is said that one such case occurred on Ovalau. While the people sung their mournful dirges over a man and his wife, they were surprised by the latter showing signs of life. A messenger was at once sent to the Chief of the place, to inquire what was to be done. As he had already experienced some trouble in the case through foreign intervention on behalf of the woman's life, he returned the following answer: "If any of you so love the woman as to die with her, strangle her again; for I have made up my mind that those who kill her shall be buried with her." No one was found to insist upon her death, either for affection or interest.

Some women, it is said, submit to be strangled, that they may prove thereby the legitimacy of their children. This particularly refers to such children as are Vasus.

Cases in which women *would* not be saved have sometimes come under my notice. When Mbati Namu was killed, the relatives of Sa Ndrungu, his chief wife, brought and offered her to his friends. I presented my *soro* for her life, but it was neutralized by her friends presenting one to " press it down." I made another offering, gained my point, and sent the disappointed murderers about their business,—one holding a bottle of oil, another turmeric powder, and a third the instrument of death,—all sad at heart that these were not to be used. A short time after, in consequence of the dissatisfaction of her friends, the woman left the Christian village, crossed the river, and entered the house of the man who was most anxious to destroy her, taking her stand in the midst, so as to intimate that she gave herself up to his will. I followed, and got permission from the dead Chief's brother to take her back with me, and, by taking my proffered hand, she might have lived. She intimated her sense of my kind intention, but declined to accompany me. Next morning she was strangled.

Many, however, were saved through our efforts, and some were thankful for the deliverance. A Somosomo woman received a reprieve which we had obtained from the King, just as she was being oiled and dressed for death. It was evidently not unwelcome; but it would have been at the risk of her reputation to have said or done anything indicative of gratitude. A vexatious circumstance took place on Taviuni. A Chief of that island was slain on Vanua Levu, in war. On receiving information of this, the principal women soon assembled in his house to prepare for the murder of his wives; but an interdict from the King prevented them, and the prey was rescued. But they were not to be defeated. The prohibition did not include the Chief's mother, whom they at once surrounded, and, before we could get authority to check them, dispatched with their own hands. Often, on that island, have I been compelled to acknowledge the truth of the couplet,—

" O woman! woman! when to ill thy mind
Is bent, all hell contains no fouler fiend."

The advancing light of a merciful religion is daily exposing the horrors of this practice, and preparing the way for its abandonment. Na Thilathila, a heathen whose children were Christians, was visited by them on the death of her husband. They admonished her that she was dying without preparation for so solemn a change. She replied, " I know it. I know it. As certainly as I die, I shall go to the flaming fire; but there is no remedy, there is no one to procure my reprieve." One case I knew, in which a Christian man tore the cord from the neck of his heathen cousin, and rescued her, amidst the cuffs and execrations of those who had commenced the work of death. One heathen woman saved herself by stratagem. Having directed a man how he might obtain her deliverance, she gave herself up, and was outrageously determined to die. The friend pursued the plan she had advised, and they retired together to laugh over its success.

As it affects the children, this dreadful custom is fearfully cruel, depriving them of the mother when, by ordinary or violent means, they have become fatherless. Natural deaths are reduced to a small number among the heathen Fijians, by the prevalence of war and the various systems of murder which custom demands. A proper examination of this subject would, I am persuaded, educe appalling facts. Minute inquiries of this kind have never yet been instituted; but one or two made by myself on Vanua Levu will show what results might be expected. Of nine boys presented for baptism, three were brothers, and the parents of the whole would therefore number fourteen. Of these only four were living; and, of the rest, one half had come to a violent death. In a class of seventeen children under twelve years of age, I found nine orphans. None of these were related; so that the parents were eighteen. Of these, two mothers were rescued by Christian interposition; the

remaining sixteen persons were all either killed in war or
strangled!

Among the dark mysteries of death and the grave, superstition traces her wildest and most terrible imaginings; for
herein ignorance, credulity, and fear work and develope un-
hindered.   In Fiji, as well as England, the howling of a
dog at night is believed to betoken death, and the grim
dread is near indeed to the man round whose feet a cat
purrs and rubs itself, though frequently repulsed.   If rats
scratch the mound of a woman's grave, it decides that she
was unchaste.   Popular superstition dooms that warrior to
certain death whose face looks but indifferently after great
pains have been taken to make it a jet black.   Large
" shooting-stars" are said to be gods; smaller ones, the
departing souls of men.   Being on the sea one night, off
the east coast of Vanua Levu, we heard, at midnight, a
single loud report like a clap of thunder; the sky, however,
was so clear, that all on board agreed it must be something
else.   Heathen natives, with whom we conversed next
morning, assured me that it was "the noise of a spirit, we
being near the place in which spirits plunge to enter the
other world, and a Chief in the neighbourhood having just
died."

The following tradition professes to account for the universal spread of death.   When the first man, the father of
the human race, was being buried, a god passed by this
first grave, and asked what it meant.   On being informed
by those standing by, that they had just buried their father,
he said, " Do not inter him.   Dig the body up again."
" No," was the reply, " we cannot do that; he has been
dead four days, and stinks."   " Not so," said the god;
" disinter him, and I promise you he shall live again."
Heedless, however, of the promise of the god, these original
sextons persisted in leaving their father's remains in the
earth.   Perceiving their perverseness, the god said, " By
refusing compliance with my commands, you have sealed
your own destinies.   Had you dug up your ancestor, you
would have found him alive, and yourselves also, as you passed

from this world, should have been buried, as bananas are, for
the space of four days, after which you should have been dug
up, not rotten, but ripe. But now, as a punishment for
your disobedience, you shall die and rot." "O," say
the Fijians after hearing this recounted, "O that those
children had dug up that body!"

Another tradition relates a contest between two gods as
to how man should die. Ra Vula (the moon) contended
that man should be like himself,—disappear awhile, and
then live again. Ra Kalavo (the rat) would not listen to
this kind proposal, but said, "Let man die as a rat dies."
And he prevailed.

The following contains the native reason why "death
takes us before we are ready or old." Between Kasavu
and Nanutha, off the south-east coast of Vanua Levu, is a
small island, which, in the people's imagination, bears resemblance to a canoe, and on this the souls in those parts
pass over the river of death. The island lies parallel with
the main, the reason assigned for which is as follows.
When first brought there, the commander ordered it to be
run with its bows on the shore, that the passengers might
board it in good order,—the aged first, and so on down to
the children. This arrangement was set aside by others,
who said that it should rather lie "broadside on," that all
ages might come on board indiscriminately. And so it
was.

Leaving the notions of Fijians about the soul and a
future state to be stated in connexion with their religion,
the subject which next demands notice is one of painful and
revolting interest, viz., their cannibalism.

Until recently, there were many who refused to believe in
the existence of this horrible practice in modern times;
but such incredulity has been forced to yield to indisputable
and repeated evidence, of which Fiji alone can supply
enough to convince a universe, that man can fall so low as
habitually to feed upon his fellow-men. Cannibalism
among this people is one of their institutions; it is
interwoven in the elements of society; it forms one

of their pursuits, and is regarded by the mass as a re-
finement.

Human bodies are sometimes eaten in connexion with
the building of a temple or canoe; or on launching a large
canoe; or on taking down the mast of one which has
brought some Chief on a visit; or for the feasting of such
as take tribute to a principal place. A Chief has been
known to kill several men for rollers, to facilitate the
launching of his canoes, the "rollers" being afterwards
cooked and eaten. Formerly a Chief would kill a man or
men on laying down a keel for a new canoe, and try to add
one for each fresh plank. These were always eaten as
" food for the carpenters." I believe that this is never
done now; neither is it now common to murder men in
order to wash the deck of a new canoe with blood. This
is sometimes the case, and would, without doubt, have been
done on a large scale when a first-rate canoe was completed
at Somosomo, had it not been for the exertion of the Missionaries then stationed there. Vexed that the noble vessel
had reached Mbau unstained with blood, the Mbau Chiefs
attacked a town, and killed fourteen or fifteen men to eat
on taking down the mast for the first time. It was owing
to Christian influence that men were not killed at every
place where the canoe called for the first time. If a Chief
should not lower his mast within a day or two of his arrival
at a place, some poor creature is killed and taken to him as
the "lowering of the mast." In every case an enemy is
preferred; but when this is impracticable, the first common
man at hand is taken. It is not unusual to find "black-
list" men on every island, and these are taken first. Names
of villages or islands are sometimes placed on the black
list. Vakambua, Chief of Mba, thus doomed Tavua, and
gave a whale's tooth to the Nggara Chief, that he might, at
a fitting time, punish that place. Years passed away, and
a reconciliation took place between Mba and Tavua. Un-
happily the Mba Chief failed to neutralize the engagement
made with Nggara. A day came when human bodies were
wanted, and the thoughts of those who held the tooth were

turned towards Tavua. They invited the people of that place to a friendly exchange of food, and slew twenty-three of their unsuspecting victims. When the treacherous Nggarans had gratified their own appetites by pieces of the flesh cut off and roasted on the spot, the bodies were taken to Vakambua, who was greatly astonished, expressed much regret that such a slaughter should have grown out of his carelessness, and then shared the bodies to be eaten.

Captives are sometimes reserved for special occasions. I have never been able, either by inquiry or observation, to find any truth in the assertion that in some parts of the group no bodies are buried, but all eaten. Those who die a natural death are always interred. Those slain in war are not invariably eaten; for persons of high rank are sometimes spared this ignominy. Occasionally, however, as once at Mbouma, the supply is too great to be all consumed. The bodies of the slain were piled up between two cocoa-nut trees, and the cutting up and cooking occupied two days. The *valekarusa,* or trunk of the bodies, was thrown away. This native word is a creation of cannibalism, and alludes to the practice of eating the trunk first, as it will not keep.

When the slain are few, and fall into the hands of the victors, it is the rule to eat them. Late in 1851, fifty bodies were cooked at one time on Namena. In such cases of plenty, the head, hands, and intestines are thrown away; but when a large party can get but one or two bodies, as at Natewa in 1845, every part is consumed. Native warriors carry their revenge beyond death, so that bodies slain in battle are often mutilated in a frightful manner, a treatment which is considered neither mean nor brutal.

When the bodies of enemies are procured for the oven, the event is published by a peculiar beating of the drum, which alarmed me even before I was informed of its import. Soon after hearing it, I saw two canoes steering for the island, while some one on board struck the water, at intervals, with a long pole, to denote that they had killed

some one.   When sufficiently near, they began their
fiendish war-dance, which was answered by the indecent
dance of the women.   On the boxed end of one of the
canoes was a human corpse, which was cut adrift and
·tumbled into the water soon after the canoe touched land,
when it was tossed to and fro by the rising and falling
waves until the men had reported their exploit, when it was
dragged ashore by a vine tied to the left hand.   A crowd,
chiefly females, surrounded the dead man, who was above
the ordinary size, and expressed most unfeelingly their
surprise and delight.   " A man truly! a ship! a land!"
The warriors, having rested, put a vine round the other
wrist of the *bakolo*—dead body designed for eating—and
two of them dragged it, face downwards, to the town, the
rest going before and performing the war-dance, which
consists in jumping, brandishing of weapons, and two or
three, in advance of the main body, running towards the
town, throwing their clubs aloft, or firing muskets, while
they assure those within of their capability to defend them.
The following song was uttered in a wild monotone, finished
with shrill yells :—

> " *Yari au malua.   Yari au malua.*
>   *Oi au na saro ni nomu vanua.*
>   *Yi mudokia !   Yi mudokia !   Yi mudokia !*
>   *Ki Dama le !*
>   *Yi ! u-woa-ai-e !*" *

On reaching the middle of the town, the body was thrown
down before the Chief, who directed the priest to offer it
in due form to the war-god.   Fire had been placed in the
great oven, and the smoke rose above the old temple, as the
body was again drawn to the shore to be cut up.   The
carver was a young man ; but he seemed skilful.   He used
a piece of slit bamboo, with which, after having washed the
body in the sea, he cut off the several members, joint by
joint.   He first made a long, deep gash down the abdomen,

---

* " Drag me gently.   Drag me gently.
    For I am the champion of thy land.
          Give thanks! Give thanks! Give thanks!" etc.

and then cut all round the neck down to the bone, and rapidly twisted off the head from the axis. The several parts were then folded in leaves and placed in the oven. According to a popular rhyme, it is only the courageous who are thus treated, while life is the reward of cowardice:—

> *" Sa vei ko Qaqa ?*
> *Sa yara ki rara.*
> *Sa vei ko Dadatuvu ?*
> *Sa la'ki tukutuku."* *

These details will answer to the most of such scenes; except that, on the larger islands, the bodies have often to be carried to a distance inland, when a strong stick is lashed down the back at the arms, knees, and sometimes the trunk, and the burden borne on the shoulders of two men. When the cooking is done on the field of battle, the dancing is dispensed with. I never saw a body baked whole, but have most satisfactory testimony that, on the island of Ngau, and one or two others, this is really done. The body is first placed in a sitting posture, and, when taken from the oven, is covered with black powder, surmounted with a wig, and paraded about as if possessed of life. When *bakolo* is to be boiled, the flesh is first cut from the bones.

Revenge is undoubtedly the main cause of cannibalism in Fiji, but by no means invariably so. I have known many cases in which such a motive could not have been present. Sometimes, however, this principle is horribly manifested. A woman taken from a town besieged by Ra Undreundre, and where one of his friends had been killed, was placed in a large wooden dish and cut up alive, that none of the blood might be lost. In 1850, Tuikilakila inflicted a severe blow on his old enemies the Natewans, when nearly one hundred of them were slain, among whom was found the body of Ratu Rakesa, the King's own cousin. The Chiefs of the victorious side endeavoured to obtain permission to

---

* " Where is the courageous ?
  Gone to be dragged (into the town to be cooked).
  Where is the coward ?
  Gone to report."

bury him, since he held the high rank of Rakesa, and
because there was such a great abundance of *bakolo*.
"Bring him here," said Tuikilakila, "that I may see
him." He looked on the corpse with unfeigned delight.
"This," said he, "is a most fitting offering to Na Tavasara (the war-god). Present it to him: let it then be
cooked, and reserved for my own consumption. None shall
share with me. Had I fallen into his hands, he would
have eaten me: now that he has fallen into my hands, I
will eat him." And it is said that he fulfilled his word in
a few days, the body being lightly baked at first, and then
preserved by repeated cooking.

When I first knew Loti, he was living at Na Ruwai.
A few years before, he killed his only wife and ate her.
She accompanied him to plant taro, and when the work
was done, he sent her to fetch wood, with which he made a
fire, while she, at his bidding, collected leaves and grass to
line the oven, and procured a bamboo to cut up what was
to be cooked. When she had cheerfully obeyed his commands, the monster seized his wife, deliberately dismembered her, and cooked and ate her, calling some to
help him in consuming the unnatural feast. The woman
was his equal, one with whom he lived comfortably; he
had no quarrel with her or cause of complaint. Twice
he might have defended his conduct to me, had he been so
disposed, but he only assented to the truth of what I here
record. The only motives could have been a fondness for
human flesh, and a hope that he should be spoken of and
pointed out as a terrific fellow.

Those who escape from shipwreck are supposed to be
saved that they may be eaten, and very rarely are they
allowed to live. Recently, at Wakaya, fourteen or sixteen
persons, who lost their canoe at sea, were cooked and eaten.

So far as I can learn, this abominable food is never eaten
raw, although the victim is often presented in full life and
vigour. Thus young women have been placed alive beside
a pile of food given by the Kandavuans to the Chiefs of
Rewa. I knew also of a man being taken alive to a Chief

on Vanua Levu, and given him to eat. In such cases they would be killed first.

Some of the heathen Chiefs hate cannibalism, and I know several who could never be induced to taste human flesh. These, however, are rare exceptions to the rule. No one who is thoroughly acquainted with the Fijians, can say that this vitiated taste is not widely spread, or that there is not a large number who esteem such food a delicacy, giving it a decided preference above all other. The practice of kidnapping persons, on purpose to be eaten, proves that this flesh is in high repute. I have conversed with those who had escaped, severely wounded, from an attempt to steal them, as a supply for a forthcoming feast; and one of the last bodies which I saw offered to a Chief was thus obtained for the special entertainment of the distinguished visitor.

Cannibalism does not confine its selection to one sex, or a particular age. I have seen the grey-headed and children of both sexes devoted to the oven. I have laboured to make the murderers of females ashamed of themselves; and have heard their cowardly cruelty defended by the assertion that such victims were doubly good—because they ate well, and because of the distress it caused their husbands and friends. The heart, the thigh, and the arm above the elbow are considered the greatest dainties. The head is the least esteemed, so that the favourite wife of Tuikilakila used to say it was "the portion for the priests of religion."

Women seldom eat of *bakolo*, and it is forbidden to some of the priests. On the island of Moala, graves were not unfrequently opened for the purpose of obtaining the occupant for food. Chiefs say that this has also been done on Vanua Levu. Part of an unburied body was stolen and eaten in 1852. When there are several bodies, the Chief sends one or more to his friends; when only one, it is shared among those nearest to him; and if this one has been a man of distinction, and much hated, parts of him are sent to other Chiefs fifty or a hundred miles off. It is most certainly true that, while the Fijian turns with disgust from pork, or his favourite fish, if at all tainted, he will eat *bakolo* when fast approaching putrescence.

Human bodies are generally cooked alone. I know of but one exception, when a man and a boar were baked in the same oven. Generally, however, ovens and pots in which human flesh is cooked, and dishes or forks used in eating it, are strictly *tabu* for any other purpose. The cannibal fork seems to be used for taking up morsels of the flesh when cooked as a hash, in which form the old people prefer it. It seems strange that men-eaters should be afraid to eat the porpoise, because it had ribs like a man; yet many old heathens have assured me that they used to have such fears.

CANNIBAL FORKS.

CANNIBAL FORKS.

Rare cases are known in which a Chief has wished to have part of the skull of an enemy for a soup-dish or drinking-cup, when orders are accordingly given to his followers not to strike that man in the head. The shin-bones of all *bakolos* are valued, as sail-needles are made from them. If these bones are short, and not claimed by a Chief, there is a scramble for them among the inferiors, who sometimes almost quarrel about them.

Would that this horrible record could be finished here! but the *vakatotoga*, the "torture," must be noticed. Nothing short of the most fiendish cruelty could dictate some of these forms of torment, the worst of which consists in cutting off parts and even limbs of the victim while still living, and cooking and eating them before his eyes, sometimes finishing the brutality by offering him his own cooked flesh to eat.

I could cite well authenticated instances of such horrors, but their narration would be far more revolting than profitable.

The names of Tampakauthoro, Tanoa, Tuiveikoso, Tuikilakila, and others, are famous in Fiji for the quantity of human flesh which they have individually eaten. But these are but insignificant cannibals in comparison with Ra Undreundre of Rakiraki. Even Fijians name him with wonder. Bodies procured for his consumption were designated *lewe ni bi*. The *bi* is a circular fence or pond made to receive turtles when caught, which then becomes its *lewena*, "contents." Ra Undreundre was compared to such a receptacle, standing ever ready to receive human flesh. The fork used by this monster was honoured with a distinctive epithet. It was named *Undro-undro;* a word used to denote a small person or thing carrying a great burden. This fork was given by his son, Ra Vatu, to my respected friend, the Rev. R. B. Lyth, in 1849. Ra Vatu then spoke freely of his father's propensity, and took Mr. Lyth nearly a mile beyond the precincts of the town, and showed him the stones by which his father registered the number of bodies he had eaten " after his family had begun to grow up." Mr. Lyth found the line of stones to measure two hundred and thirty-two paces. A teacher who accompanied him counted the stones,—eight hundred and seventy-two. If those which had been removed were replaced, the whole would certainly have amounted to *nine hundred*. Ra Vatu asserted that his father ate all these persons himself, permitting no one to share them with him. A similar row of stones placed to mark the bodies eaten by Naungavuli contained forty-eight, when his becoming a Christian prevented any further addition. The whole family were cannibals extraordinary; but Ra Vatu wished to exempt himself.

It is somewhat remarkable that the only instance of cannibalism in Fiji witnessed by any gentleman of the United States Exploring Expedition, was the eating of a human eye,—a thing which those who have seen many bodies eaten never witnessed, the head, as has been stated already, being always thrown away.

One who had been but a very short time in Fiji wrote

thus to me : "I have been to Mbau thrice, and have witnessed something of Fijian horrors each time. First visit, I saw them opening an oven, and taking a cooked human body out of it: second visit, limbs of a body preparing for being baked : third visit, a woman of rank who had just had her nose cut off." Visitors, however, generally manifest considerable incredulity on this subject; though it would not require a long stay actually among the people, to place the matter beyond doubt. An English Lieutenant manifested a good deal of unbelief, until he found his head in pretty close contact with parts of several men which hung from a tree near the oven, where, a few days before, their bodies had been cooked.

Whatever may have been the origin of man-eating in Fiji—whether famine or superstition—there is not the slightest excuse for its continuance. Food of every kind abounds, and, with a little effort, might be vastly increased. The land gives large supply spontaneously, and, undoubtedly, is capable of supporting a hundred times the number of its present inhabitants.

In the foregoing details, all colouring has been avoided, and many facts, which might have been advanced, have been withheld. All the truth may not be told. But surely enough has been said to prove that the heathenism of Fiji has, by its own uninfluenced developement, reached the most appalling depth of abomination. The picture, without exaggerating, might have been far darker; but it is dark enough to awaken sympathy for a people so deplorably fallen, and to quicken an earnest longing that their full deliverance may be at hand.*

* It is but just to state, that much detail and illustrative incident furnished by the author on this subject, have been withheld, and some of the more horrible features of the rest repressed or softened.—EDITOR.

CHAPTER VII.

RELIGION.

BURE OF NA UTUTU.

An examination of the religious system of the Fijians is attended with considerable difficulty. Their traditional mythology is dark, vague, and perplexing. Each island has its own gods, each locality its own superstitions, and almost each individual his own modification of both. Yet, amidst all this confusion, there may be traced certain main tracks of belief, appearing again and again from among the undefined legends—wild, or puerile, or filthy—in which they are often lost. In these, without being over fanciful, there may be found some points of interest in the study of comparative mythology.

The idea of Deity is familiar to the Fijian; and the existence of an invisible superhuman power, controlling

or influencing all earthly things, is fully recognised by
him.   Idolatry—in the strict sense of the term—he seems
to have never known ; for he makes no attempt to fashion
material representations of his gods, or to pay actual
worship to the heavenly bodies, the elements, or any
natural objects.   It is extremely doubtful whether the
reverence with which some things, such as certain clubs
and stones, have been regarded, had in it anything of
religious homage.

The native word expressive of divinity is *kalou*, which,
while used to denote the people's highest notion of a god,
is also constantly heard as a qualificative of any thing
great   or   marvellous,   or,   according   to   Hazlewood's
Dictionary, "anything superlative, whether good or
bad." Unless—as seems probable—the root-meaning of
the term is that of wonder and astonishment, this latter
use of it presents an interesting analogy to the similar form
of speech in Hebrew.   Often the word sinks into a mere
exclamation, or becomes an expression of flattery.   "You
are a *kalou !* " or, "Your countrymen are gods !" is often
uttered by the natives, when hearing of the triumphs of art
among   civilized   nations.   In this case, however, it is a
courteous way of declaring unbelief, or their own dis-
inclination to attempt an imitation of what they admire.

It is remarkable that the gods of Eastern Polynesia
seem to be unknown to the Fijians, in whose polytheistic
mythology the objects of worship are divided into two
classes ; *kalou vu*, gods strictly so called, and *kalou yalo*,
deified mortals, like the dæmons of classic Greece.
The exalted individuals of the first grade are supposed
to be absolutely eternal ; but those of the second order,
though raised far above humanity, are subject to its
passions, wants, accidents, and even death.   These are
the spirits of Chiefs, heroes, and friends.   But monsters
and abortions are often ranked here ; and the list, already
countless, is capable of constant increase, every object that
is specially fearful, or vicious, or injurious, or novel, being
eligible for admission.   This seems further to support the

hypothesis advanced above as to the origin of the title *kalou.*

The god most generally known in Fiji is Ndengei, who seems to be an impersonation of the abstract idea of eternal existence. He is the subject of no emotion or sensation, nor of any appetite, except hunger. The serpent—the world-wide symbol of eternity—is his adopted shrine. Some traditions represent him with the head and part of the body of that reptile, the rest of his form being stone, emblematic of everlasting and unchangeable duration. He passes a monotonous existence in a gloomy cavern—the hollow of an inland rock near the N. E. end of Viti Levu—evincing no interest in any one but his attendant, Uto, and giving no signs of life beyond eating, answering his priest, and changing his position from one side to the other. There are points in this description which remind one of the Cronos of Grecian mythology. Although Ndengei ranks as supreme among the gods, yet he is less worshipped than most of his inferiors. Except about Rakiraki, he has scarcely a temple, and even there his worshippers do not always use him well. The natives suppose that Uto comes to attend every feast at Rakiraki, and, on his return, Ndengei inquires what portion of food has been allotted to him. The consequent mortification is made the subject of a humourous song, supposed to contain a dialogue between the god and his attendant.

NDENGEI.—" Have you been to the sharing of food to-day?"

UTO.—"Yes: and turtles formed a part; but only the under-shell was shared to us two."

ND.—" Indeed, Uto! This is very bad. How is it? We made them men, placed them on the earth, gave them food, and yet they share to us only the under-shell. Uto, how is this?"

The other gods are proud, envious, covetous, revengeful, and the subject of every basest passion. They are demonized heathen,—monster expressions of moral corruption. Some of them had a monster origin, and wear a monster shape. NDANDAVANUA was produced from the centre of a large stone. ROKOMOUTU was a son of Ndengei's sister, and insisted upon being born from her elbow. Soon after his birth, he assumed "a chief-like appearance," and showed the amiableness of his disposition by threatening to devour his mother and friends, unless they acknowledged him as a god.

THANGAWALU, his mother's first-born, came into the world a giant, two months after conception, and rapidly grew to the height of sixty feet. His remarkable forehead —eight spans high—gives him his name.

ROKO MBATI-NDUA, "the one-toothed lord," has the appearance of a man with wings instead of arms, and emits sparks of fire in his flight through the air. On his wings are claws with which to catch his victims, and his one tooth, fixed in the lower jaw, rises above his head. LIN-GAKAU is the wooden-handed. KOKOLA has eight arms, indicative of mechanical skill. MATAWALU has eight eyes, denoting wisdom. RA NAMBASANGA has two bodies— one male and the other female—united after the fashion of the Siamese twins. WALUVAKATINI, "ten times eight," has that number of stomachs.

Then there is KANUSIMANA, who "spits miracles," *i. e.,* does them easily. NAITONO is the leper. MBAKANDROTI is the name of a war-god worshipped at Na Vunindoaloa, and implies that, if he were to use nothing stronger than the pandanus leaf for fortification, it would be impregnable to human power.

The names of some gods indicate their habits. Thus, TUNAMBANGA is the adulterer. NDAUTHINA steals women of rank and beauty by night or torch-light. KUMBUNA-VANUA is the rioter; MBATIMONA, the brain-eater; RAVU-RAVU, the murderer; MAINATAVASARA, fresh from the cutting up or slaughter; and a host besides of the same sort.

Among the lower order of gods, imagination finds less scope. These are generally described as men of superior mould and carriage, and bear a close analogy to the *lares, lemures,* and *genii* of the Romans. Their influence is of the same limited kind; but they are never represented by images, and have not always shrines. Admission into their number is easy, and any one may secure his own apotheosis who can insure the services of some one as his representative and priest after his decease.

The rank of the gods below Ndengei is not easily ascertained, each district contending for the superiority of its own divinity. TOKAIRAMBE and TUI LAKEMBA RANDINANDINA seem to stand next to Ndengei, being his sons, and acting as mediators by transmitting the prayers of suppliants to their father. Ndengei's grand-children rank next, and, after them, more distant relations, and then "legion."

Some of the gods confine their attention to this earth, the higher presiding over districts and islands, and the rest over tribes and families, their influence never reaching beyond their own special jurisdiction. Others, as Ravuyalo, Lothia, and some few more, find employment in Hades.

Nearly every Chief has a god in whom he puts special trust; and a few are of opinion that their god follows them wherever they go. Different classes have their own tutelary deities. ROKOVA and ROKOLA are trusted in by the carpenters, and ROKO VOUA and VOSAVAKANDUA by the fishermen. The same deity is worshipped in different places by different names. RATU MAIMBULU of Mbau is known at Somosomo as RATU LEVU, and on Vanuambalavu and other places as MAI WAKOLOTU.

It has already been asserted that the Fijians are unacquainted with idols properly so called; but they reverence certain stones as shrines of the gods, and regard some clubs with superstitious respect, like the Scythians, who treated a scymitar as the symbol of their war-god. In addition to these, certain birds, fish, plants, and some men, are supposed to have deities closely connected with or residing in them. At Lakemba, Tui Lakemba, and on Vanua Levu, Ravuravu, claim the hawk as their abode;

Viavia, and other gods, the shark. One is supposed to inhabit the eel, and another the common fowl, and so on until nearly every animal becomes the shrine of some deity. He who worships the god dwelling in the eel, must never eat of that fish, and thus of the rest; so that some are *tabu* from eating human flesh, because the shrine of their god is a man. The people clearly maintain the Popish distinction between the material sign and the spiritual essence symbolized; but, in one case as in the other, the distinction seems sometimes to be practically lost. Thus the land-crab is the representative of ROKO SUKA, one of the gods formerly worshipped in Tiliva, where land-crabs are rarely seen, so that a visit from one became an important matter. Any person who saw one of these creatures, hastened to report to an old man, who acted as priest, that their god had favoured them with a call. Orders were forthwith given that new nuts should be gathered, and a string of them was formally presented to the crab, to prevent the deity from leaving with an impression that he was neglected, and visiting his remiss worshippers with drought, dearth, or death.

Rude consecrated stones are to be seen near Vuna, where offerings of food are sometimes made. Another

SACRED STONES.

stands on a reef near Naloa, to which the natives *tama ;* and one near Thokova, Na Viti Levu, named Lovekaveka, is regarded as the abode of a goddess, for whom food is prepared. This, as seen in the engraving, is like a round, black milestone, slightly inclined, and having a *liku* tied round the middle. The shrine of O Rewau is a large stone, which, like the one near Naloa, hates mosquitoes, and keeps them from collecting where he rules: he has also two large stones for his wives, one of whom came from Yandua, and the other from Yasawa. Although no one pretends to know the origin of Ndengei, it is said that his mother, in the form of two great stones, lies at the bottom of a moat. Stones are also used to denote the locality of some gods, and the occasional resting-places of others. On the southern beach of Vanua Levu, a large stone is seen which has fallen upon a smaller one. These, it is said, represent the gods of two towns on that coast fighting, and their quarrel has for years been adopted by those towns.

Nearly every town or village has one or more *bures,* or "temples ;" some have many, which are well built, no pains being spared in their erection and finish. The quantity of sinnet used in the decoration of some of these is immense ; for every timber is covered with it, in various patterns of black and red. Reeds wrapped with the same material are used for lining door and window openings, and between the rafters and other spars. Sinnet-work is seen in every part, and hangs in large cords from the eaves. Spears are often used for laths in thatching temples, as well as for fastening the thatch of the ridge-pole, on the projecting ends of which white cowries are fixed, or hang in long strings to the ground.

The spot on which a Chief has been killed is sometimes selected as the site of the *bure,* which is generally placed upon a raised foundation, thrown up to the height of from three to twenty feet, and faced with dry rubble-work of stone. The ascent is by a thick plank, having its upper face cut into notched steps.

BURE OF NA TAVASARA, TAVIUNI.

On setting up the pillars of a temple, and again when the building is complete, men are killed and eaten. On Vanua Levu, trumpet shells are blown, at intervals of one or two hours, during the whole progress of the erection.

The *bure* is a very useful place. It is the council-chamber, and town-hall; small parties of strangers are often entertained in it, and the head persons in the village even use it as a sleeping-place. Though built expressly for the purposes of religion, it is less devoted to them than any others. Around it, plantains and bread-fruit trees are often found, and yaqona is grown at the foot of the terrace, the produce of each being reserved for the priests and old men. Several spears set in the ground, or one transfixing an earthen pot, as well as one or more blanched human skulls, are not uncommonly arranged in the sacred precincts.

Votive offerings, comprising a streamer or two, with a few clubs and spears, decorate the interior, while a long piece of white *masi*, fixed to the top, and carried down the angle of the roof so as to hang before the corner-post and lie on the floor, forms the path down which the god passes to enter the priest, and marks the holy place which few but he dare approach. If the priest is also a doctor in good practice, a number of hand-clubs, turbans, necklaces of flowers, and other trifles paid as fees, are accumulated in the temple. A few pieces of withered sugar-cane are often seen resting over the wall-plate. In one *bure*, I saw a huge roll of sinnet; and in another, a model of a temple, made of the same material. In one at Mbau, parts of victims slain in war are often seen hung up in clusters. From some temples, the ashes may not be thrown out, however they may accumulate, until the end of the year. The clearing out takes place in November, and a feast is made on the occasion.

There are priestesses in Fiji; but few of sufficient importance to have a temple; and in the case of these, it merely serves as a place for sleeping, and the storing of offerings.

Bures are often unoccupied for months, and allowed to fall into ruin, until the Chief wants to make some request to the god, when the necessary repairs are first carried out. Nothing like regular worship or habitual reverence is found, and a principle of fear seems the only motive to religious observances; and this is fully practised upon by the priests, through whom alone the people have access to the gods, when they wish to present petitions affecting their social or individual interest. When matters of importance are involved, the *soro* or offering consists of large quantities of food, together with whales' teeth. In smaller affairs, a tooth, club, mat, or spear, is enough. Young nuts, covered with turmeric powder, formed the meanest offering I have known. On one occasion, when Tuikilakila asked the help of the Somosomo gods in war, he built the war-god a large new temple, and presented a great quantity of cooked food, with sixty turtles, besides whales' teeth.

Part of the offering—the *sigana*—is set apart for the deity, the rest forming a feast of which all may partake. The portion devoted to the god is eaten by his priest, and by old men; but to youths and women it is *tabu*.

Strang rs wishing to consult a god, cut a quantity of fire-wood efor the temple. Sometimes only a dish of yam or a whale's tooth is presented. It is not absolutely necessary for the transaction to take place at a temple. I have known priests to become inspired in a private house, or in the open air; indeed, in some parts of Fiji, the latter is usually the case.

One who intends to consult the oracle, dresses and oils himself, and, accompanied y a few others, goes to the priest, who, we will suppose,has been previously informed of the intended visit, and is lying near the sacred corner, getting ready his response. When the party enters, he rises, and sits so that his back is near to the white cloth by which the god visits him, while the others occupy the opposite side of the *bure*. The principal person presents a whale's tooth, states the purport of the visit, and expresses a hope that the god will regard him with favour. Sometimes there is placed before the priest a dish of scented oil, with which he anoints himself, and then receives the tooth, regarding it with deep and serious attention. Unbroken silence follows. The priest becomes absorbed in thought, and all eyes watch him with unblinking steadiness. In a few minutes he trembles; slight distortions are seen in his face, and twitching movements in his limbs. These increase to a violent muscular action, which spreads until the whole frame is strongly convulsed, and the man shivers as with a strong ague fit. In some instances this is accompanied with murmurs and sobs, the veins are greatly enlarged, and the circulation of the blood quickened. The priest is now possessed by his god, and all his words and actions are considered as no longer his own, but those of the deity who has entered into him. Shrill cries of "*Koi au! Koi au!*" "It is I! It is I!" fill the air, and the god is supposed thus to notify his approach. While giving the answer, the priest's eyes stand out and roll as in a frenzy; his voice is unnatural, his face pale, his lips livid, his breathing depressed, and his entire appearance like that of a furious madman. The sweat runs from every pore, and tears start from his strained eyes; after which the symptoms gradually disappear. The priest looks round with a vacant stare, and, as the god says, "I depart," announces his actual departure by violently flinging himself down on the mat, or by suddenly striking the ground with a club, when those at a distance are informed by blasts on the conch, or the firing of a musket, that the deity has returned into the world of spirits. The convulsive movements do not entirely disappear for some time; they are not, however, so violent as to prevent the priest from enjoying a hearty meal, or a draught of yaqona, or a whiff of tobacco, as either may happen to be at hand. Several words are used by the natives to express these priestly shakings. The most common are *sika* and *kundru*. *Sika* means "to appear," and is used chiefly of supernatural beings. *Kundru* means "to grunt or grumble." One word refers to the appearance, and the other to the sound, attendant upon these inspired shakings.

As whatever the *bete* or priest says during the paroxysm is supposed to be direct from the god, a specimen or two of these responses will be interesting. The occasion presents a favourable opportunity for boasting, and the response is often prefaced by lauding the god. A priest of Ndengei, speaking for that divinity, once said, "Great Fiji is my small club. Muaimbila is the head; Kamba is the handle. If I step on Muaimbila, I shall sink it into the sea, whilst Kamba shall rise to the sky. If I step on Kamba, it will be lost in the sea, whilst Muaimbila would rise into the skies. Yes, Viti Levu is my small war-club. I can turn it as I please. I can turn it upside down."

Complaints are also made at these times. A man who was inspired by Tanggirianima said, "I and Kumbunavanua only are gods. I preside over wars, and do as I please with sickness. But it is difficult for me to come here, as the foreign god fills the place. If I attempt to descend by that pillar, I find it pre-occupied by the foreign god. If I try another pillar, I find it the same. However, we two are fighting the foreign god; and if we are victorious, we

Q

will save the woman. I *will* save the woman. She will eat food to-day. Had I been sent for yesterday, she would have eaten then," etc. The woman, about whose case the god was consulted, died a few hours after these assurances of life.

A party who had been defeated in war, made a second application to their god, who replied, "My name is *Liu ka ca, ka muri ka vinaka,"*—"Evil first, and good afterwards."

Occasionally, the priest is the medium of communicating to a Chief the general opinion about some unpopular act. "The present famine eats us because you gave the large canoe to Tonga instead of Mbau." "This hurricane is in consequence of your refusing the Princess to the Rewa Chief. For that the gods are angry, and are punishing us." Generally, however, a good understanding exists between the Chief and the priest, and the latter takes care to make the god's utterances agree with the wishes of the former.

Once I saw a large offering made, and the priests were consulted as to whether the tribe ought then to go to battle, and whether they should have success. The interview was propitious, and the fleet was to sail without delay. In the long list of deities enumerated by the chief priest, Kanusimana had a place, and, among the rest, his favour was solicited. His priest, who was a neighbour of mine, sat by delighted, and looking with great satisfaction at the large fat turtles and ripe plantains which, with other food, were piled in the midst. When the division of the offering came, one poor pudding was all that fell to Kanusimana's share. Chagrined and mortified by losing the green fat and rich fruit which, in imagination, he had already tasted, the little priest started up and ran homewards, swinging his small club like a sling, and the ball-bell at his neck tinkling in the most excited manner as he hurried along. Creeping to his corner, his plan of revenge was soon marked out. In the night the divinity paid him a visit, and declared, on the authority of a god, that if Tuikilakila led his warriors to fight then, he should feel the effects of his godship's anger, punishing him for the recent slight.

At the morning yaqona party the priest made known the visit and the message from the god. A young man was directed to bear the important communication to the King forthwith. Tuikilakila listened, pondered, and, in a few minutes, the thoughts of fighting were given up for the present. The King knew that to pursue his own will in this case would lead to failure, as the threat of the neglected god had dispirited his warriors.

In another similar instance, matters took a very different turn. "Who are you?" angrily asked the Chief of the pri s who sought to turn his purpose: "Who is your god? If you make a stir, I will eat you!" And Oroi Rupe knew that this was no idle threat.

The priests exercise a powerful influence over the people, an influence which the Chiefs employ for the strengthening of their own, by securing the divine sanction for their plans. The sacerdotal caste has for some time been rapidly declining; but it still retains, in some parts, much of its old power.

The priesthood is generally, but not invariably, hereditary. A man who can shake well, and speculate shrewdly, may turn his abilities to account by becoming a priest. He must weigh probabilities with judgment, and take care that his maiden effort at divination is not too glaring a blunder. The rank of a priest is regulated by that of the god to whom he is a minister. When the chieftaincy and priesthood meet in the same person, both are of low order. Each god has a distinct order of priests, but not confined to one family. A *bete* can only officiate in the temple of the god whom he serves; and a worshipper of a particular god can have no access to him where he has neither temple nor priest. The sacred insignia are a long-toothed comb, and a long oval frontlet of scarlet feathers.

Wishing to hear from one of the fraternity an account of their inspiration by the god, and suspecting that any inquiries of my own would be

PRIEST'S COMB.

evaded, I got the well-known Tonga Chief, Tubou Toutai, to call into my house a famous Lakemba priest who was passing by, and question him in my hearing. The following dialogue took place :—

"Langgu, did you shake yesterday?"

" Yes."

" Did you think beforehand what to say?"

" No."

" Then you just say what you happen to think at the time, do you?"

" No. I do not know what I say. My own mind departs from me, and then, when it is truly gone, my god speaks by me."

This man had the most stubborn confidence in his deity, although his mistakes were such as to shake any ordinary trust. His inspired tremblings were of the most violent kind, bordering on fury. Gods are supposed to enter into some men while asleep, and their visit is made known by a peculiar snore.

There are various methods of divination used in Fiji. One is by a bunch of cocoa-nuts, pretty well dried. Having given the message of the god, the priest continues, " I shall shake these nuts: if all fall off, the child will recover; but if any remain on, it will die." He then shakes and jerks the nuts, generally with all his might. An easier mode is by spinning a nut on its side, and watching in which direction the eye points when again at rest. This method is not confined to priests. Some priests, when consulted, sit on the ground, with their legs stretched out, and a short club placed between them. They then watch to see which leg trembles first: if the right, the omen is good; if the left, it is evil. A Chief, wishing to ascertain how many of a certain number of towns would espouse his cause, consulted the *bete*, who took as many short reeds as there were places named, and gave each a name. When they were set in the ground, he held his right foot over each, and every one above which his foot trembled was de-clared disloyal, and all the rest true. Some chew a certain leaf, and let the fact of its tasting bitter or sweet determine the question at issue. Some pour a few drops of water on the front of the right arm, near the shoulder, and, the arm being gently inclined, the course of the water is watched; and if it find its way down to the wrist, the answer is favourable; but otherwise, if it run off, and fall on the floor. Some begin at the wrist, and let the water run towards the shoulder. Others decide by simply biting a leaf in two. The leaf is placed between the front teeth, and if cut clean through at once, all is well; but the reverse, if it still hang together. Some take an omen from the fact of a man's sneezing out of the right or left nostril while he holds a certain stick in his hand.

The seer also is known in Fiji. He sits listening to the applicant's wishes, and then, closing his eyes on earthly things, describes to the inquirer the scenes of the future which pass before his vision. These generally consist of burning houses, fleeing warriors, bloody plains, or death-stricken sick ones, as the case may require. A similar personage is the *taro*, "ask," who sits with his knee up and his foot resting on the heel, with a stick placed in a line with the middle of it. Without being told the object of the visit, he states whether his presentiment is good or evil, and then is informed of the matter inquired after, and proceeds to apply his impressions about it in detail. There is also the *dautadra*, or professional dreamer, who receives a present on communicating his revelations to the parties concerned, whether they tell of good or evil, and who seldom happens to dream about any one who cannot pay well. Some believe that a good present often averts the evil of a bad dream.

Besides these I have seen a man much prized by the Chief whom he attended, and whose valuable service consisted in placing a certain leaf of wondrous efficacy on either side of his master. If the leaf on the right side should sting the skin, the omen indicates the greatest safety and success to his friends; and no plot is so deep or scheme so suddenly planned as to escape the knowledge of the leaf on the left, which instantly communicates the lurking danger to its fortunate wearer by a sting on that side.

There used to be more mummery in invoking Ndengei than any other god. A credulous people willingly paid a high price to be deceived, to the extent—if report be true —of one or two hundred hogs and a hundred turtles at one time. On the day of offering a priest entered the sacred cave where Ndengei dwelt, taking with him what the occasion required. The offering being placed in order, several priests approached on their knees and elbows, and one, leaving the others behind, entered the cave's mouth and presented their request, perhaps for good yam crops. After a pause, he turned to the multitude, holding a piece of yam given him by the god as a pledge of plenty. If rain was wanted, the *bete* would return dripping with rain from Ndengei, and with a promise that he would thus bestow showers on all the district after two or four days. If they asked success in war, a fire-brand was darted from the cave ; a token that they should burn up their enemies. The splinter of burning wood must have been a mere trifle to his godship, if, as some assert, he has two vast logs always on fire on his hearth, the larger of which is thirty miles in circumference. In the event of the promised boon not being duly given, it was easy for the priests to discover some new offence or defect of offering on the part of the worshippers as the cause.

The worship of the gods of Fiji is not a regular and constant service, but merely suggested by circumstances, or dictated by emergency or fear. There are, however, certain superstitious ceremonies which are duly observed ; such as the *sevu*—presenting the first-fruits of yams ; *tadravu*— an offering made at the close of the year ; the keeping of silence when crossing sacred places ; the observance of tabus, and reverencing of shrines.

The people formed no idea of any voluntary kindness on the part of their gods, except the planting of wild yams, and the wrecking of strange canoes and foreign vessels on their coast. After successful fishing for turtle, or remarkable deliverance from danger in war or at sea, or recovery from sickness, a *madrali*—a kind of thank-offering—was sometimes presented. Clubs, spears, and other valuable articles are thus consecrated to the gods. I am told that many men, after killing an enemy, offer a spear to the priest, in order to insure protection from the spears of the enemy on future occasions.

Of the great offerings of food, native belief apportions merely the *soul* thereof to the gods, who are described as being enormous eaters; the substance is consumed by the worshippers.

Cannibalism is a part of the Fijian religion, and the gods are described as delighting in human flesh. Tuithakau once asked, in a fit of anger, " Is Jehovah the god of bodies killed to be eaten?" intimating that as Na Tavasara was so, he must be the superior deity. To maintain the exaltation of these false gods, the abominable practice referred to is continued, and pity for any age or sex has no influence with those who may have to prepare the offering.

At one time Ndengei would constantly have human bodies for his sacrifices; with each basket of roots a man's or woman's body was to be brought, and Chiefs sometimes killed their inferior wives in order to supply the horrible demand. This practice was checked in an unlooked for manner. The Chief, seeing the head and legs of a man, who had been cooked without being cut or tied up, hanging over the ends of a basket of food, was so disgusted at the spectacle, as to order that, in future, pigs and not *bakolo* should be offered. But human flesh is still the most valued offering, and " their drink-offerings of blood " are still the most acceptable in some parts of Fiji. I know that they consume the blood of turtles and pigs, and have heard that human blood is not excepted.

Some priests are *tabu* from eating human flesh. The priest of Ndau Thina has assured me that neither he nor those who worshipped his god might eat it, nor might the abomination be taken into his temple. Probably the shrine of Ndau Thina is a man, and hence the prohibition. To the priest of second rank in Somosomo, I know that no greater delicacy could be presented than hashed human flesh.

I had been in Fiji some years before I had good evidence of the existence of the practice of severe mortification among the people. Mbasonga, the Wailevu priest, after supplicating his god for rain in the usual way without success, slept for several successive nights exposed on the top of a rock, without mat or pillow, hoping thus to move the obdurate deity to send a shower.

When the Tiliva people found their land parched with drought, notwithstanding the presentation of the ordinary offerings, they repaired in companies to the bush, to dig up the *yaka*, which is a creeper with edible roots from two to three feet long, taking care not to detach the long vines springing from them. On returning, each man wound these round his neck, leaving the roots to hang beneath his chin, while the rest of the vines dragged after him on the ground. To this was added a large stone carried on the back of the neck. Thus equipped, the whole company performed a pilgrimage to the *bure* on their hands and knees, making a noise as though they were crying. At the end of this painful journey they found the priest waiting to receive them, and to him one of their number stated their distress, and begged him to accept their prayer and offering. "The *yaka* is for you to eat; the stones are for strengthening the base of your temple. Let our *soro* be accepted, and procure us rain." Some who took part in this humiliating scene gave me the above particulars.

The superstitious observances of Fiji are, however, mainly of a trivial kind. In one temple, it is *tabu* to eat food; in another, nothing may be broken; some may not be entered by strangers, and arms may not be carried over the threshold of others. Dogs are excluded from some, and women from all.

The gods allow only old men to eat certain kinds of plantains. In some houses, the turban may not be worn; in others, certain common words may not be spoken. The first fish caught in any creel may not be boiled, but must be broiled. To sit on the threshold of a temple is *tabu* to any but a Chief of the highest rank. All are careful not to tread on the threshold of a place set apart for the gods : persons of rank stride over ; others pass over on their hands and knees.* The same form is observed in crossing the threshold of a Chief's house. Indeed, there is very little difference between a Chief of high rank and one of the second order of deities. The former regards himself very much as a god, and is often spoken of as such by his people, and, on some occasions, claims for himself publicly the right of divinity.

It is believed that gods sometimes assume the human form, and are thus seen by men, generally in the likeness of some one particular person. Anybody who thus meets a god, must afterwards, on passing the same place, throw thereon a few leaves or blades of grass, to show that he keeps the event in mind.

In the eastern part of Fiji, if there is a god named after an island, it is *tabu* for its Chief to attach the name of the island to his official title. For this reason, the King of Lakemba is styled Tui Nayau, although Nayau is a very small island within his dominion. To the westward, this observance is disregarded.

Festivals, apparently of a religious character, are observed after the seed yams are in the earth, and again on the offering of the first-fruits. On both occasions plenty of noise is made. I have heard the natives of Mbua shout, blow the conch-shell, and fire muskets for an hour together at these feasts. Former times required one or more dead men to be placed on the top of the first-fruits ; but the influence of Christianity has already abolished this.

Frequent reference has already been made to that peculiar Polynesian institution known as the *tapu*, or *tabu*, or *tambu*, with which the civilized world is so familiar, and the name of which has, to some extent, become an adopted word in our own language, and is found as such in our modern dictionaries.

* See an interesting parallel in 1 Sam. v. 5.

The principle of the *tabu* seems to be exactly the same in every part of the South Seas, the only variety being in its application, and in the degree of severity with which its infringement is punished.

The institution, as it exists in Fiji, is the secret of power, and the strength of despotic rule. It affects things both great and small. Here it is seen tending a brood of chickens; and there it directs the energies of a kingdom. Its influence is wondrously diffused. Coasts, lands, rivers, and seas; animals, fish, fruit, and vegetables; houses, beds, pots, cups, and dishes; canoes, with all belonging to them and their management; dress, ornaments, and arms; things to eat, and things to drink; the members of the body; manners and customs; language, names, temples, and even the gods also, all come under the influence of the *tabu*. It is put into operation by religious, political, or selfish motives, and idleness lounges for months beneath its sanction. Many are thus forbidden to raise or extend their hands in any useful employment for a long time. In this district it is *tabu* to build canoes; on that island it is *tabu* to erect good houses. The custom is much in favour with Chiefs, who adjust it so as to sit easily on themselves, while they use it to gain influence over those who are nearly their equals: by it they supply many of their wants, and command at will all who are beneath them. In imposing a *tabu*, a Chief need only be checked by a care that he is countenanced by ancient precedents. Persons of small importance borrow the shadow of the system, and endeavour by its aid to place their yam-beds and plantain-plots within a sacred prohibition. The *tabu* secures to the priests of Mbakandroti all the one-eared pigs born in their neighbourhood. But as little profit would arise from a strict adherence to the letter of the charter, it is made to mean all swine which may have one ear shorter or narrower than the other.

When cocoa-nuts are to be *tabued* in any particular district, a mound of earth is thrown up by the side of the path leading thereto, and on this a stone or nut, covered with turmeric powder, is placed, and a reed fence built all round. Or a number of reeds are stuck in the mound in a circle, with their leafy tops tied together; or a piece of nut-leaf is plaited round several of the nuts at a few feet from the ground; or reeds are set a few rods apart through the district. In all cases, loud shouts of *" a tabu !"* are part

NUT TABUS.

of the ceremony. The length of time during which the embargo may be continued, is determined by the period at which the nuts ripen, or the arrival of a festival, or, simply, the will of a Chief, without whom the prohibition cannot be removed. This is generally done without form; but on removing the *tabu* from the Somosomo Straits, the King, priests, and a number of aged and influential men, assembled on board a first-rate canoe, which was moored at some distance from the shore. Yaqona was prepared, and part of the first cup poured into the sea as a libation, accompanied by a prayer to the gods for life, prosperity, and plenty of fish. The Straits were then open for the fishing parties.

Violations of the *tabu* are punished by robbing the transgressor, despoiling his gardens, and, in a few cases, by death.

Instances have come under my own observation, in which a King's son—quite a boy—was allowed to place a *tabu* on all kinds of food then in the gardens. About twenty lads, from eight to seventeen years of age, formed his suite, who passed the night under the same roof with him, and in the day-time were sent abroad as spies. When the party retired to rest, or rose from sleep, the fact was published by the noise of conch-shells. Persons who had to make any of the feasts belonging to the confinement of a wife, or other events, had first to lay their case before this juvenile court. Any who failed to do so, soon saw the Chief lad and his retinue running towards their house with little flags and native trumpets. A heavy blow on the house fence announced their arrival, and, in the space of another minute, they were on their way back to the rendezvous, each bearing a club, or spear, or mat, or any other article that came to hand, and all shouting amain over the mischief.

Fear of the gods is often alleged as a reason for observing the *tabu*; but it has already been shown that this fear is somewhat questionable. Sometimes the natives get angry with their deities, and abuse and even challenge them to fight.

The Malaki fishermen make offerings to their sea-gods to obtain success in catching turtles, which, when taken, they offer to the Rakiraki gods, who are more powerful than their own, and likely to be angry if these got the turtles.

One evening I walked with Tuikilakila to see a canoe which had been repaired, and was then to be launched. When she was fairly afloat, a shout was raised, and, each person present having picked up a good-sized stone, the house of the canoe was saluted with a smart shower of pebbles, to drive away the god of the carpenters, who had got possession of it while under repair.

Certain minerals and vegetables are dedicated to certain demons, but apparently in joke. A simple flower is called the hand-club of Raula. Red clay is given as a delicacy to another, and the blossom of the *boiboida*, which smells horribly, is named as the favourite nosegay of Ramba.

One remarkable religious observance remains to be noticed. Its practice is chiefly confined to youths of the male sex, and in it alone is observable a continuous attention to set forms. In some parts of the group it is known as *Kalou rèrè*, and in others as *Ndomindomi*. Retired places near the sea are preferred for the performance of the ceremonies of this peculiar observance. A small house is built, and enclosed with a rustic trellis fence, tied at the crossings with a small-leafed vine. Longer poles are set up, with streamers attached. Within the enclosure, a miniature temple of slight fabric is constructed, and in it a consecrated nut or other trifle is placed. The roof of the main building is hung with *masi* and scarfs of light texture. The wall is studded with the claws of crabs; and, after the gods have come together, span-long yams, ready cooked, with painted cocoa-nuts, are disposed at its base, that they may eat and drink. The party occupying this house number twenty or thirty, and, while kept together by the ceremonies, this is their home. To allure the expected gods, they drum with short bamboos, morning and evening, for several successive weeks. The "little gods" are called *luve-ni-wai*, "children of the waters." My list contains more than fifty of their names, and I believe it is incomplete. They are represented as wild or fearful, and as coming up from the sea. I knew one party who, to facilitate their ascent, built, for some distance into the sea, a jetty of loose stones. When it is believed that the *luve-ni-wai* have left their watery dwelling, little flags are placed at certain inland passes, to stop any who might wish to change for the woods their abode in the sea. On the high day, an enclosure is formed by twelve-feet poles laid on the ground, and piled up to the height of a

foot. These are wrapped with evergreens, and spears with
streamers at the top are fixed in the four angles. A company of lads, painted and attired in green leaves and scarfs,
bring from their house into this square the votive offerings,
consisting chiefly of small clubs and trumpet-shells. They
then seat themselves within the enclosure, and thump their
little drums right lustily.

While the *luve-ni-wai* have been thus occupied, the principal personages have not been idle. Each has been
decorating himself in character, and providing himself with
the apparatus needed for the performance of his part.
Presently their uncouth forms are seen in the distance, in
every variety of fantastic motion. Some run in one direction, and some in another; they nod their heads, gaze
upwards, dance ridiculously, and fill the air with groans,
grunts, and shrieks. One youth—the *Linga Viu*, or "shade-
holder"—runs round a circle which includes all the per-
formers, the drummers and the shakers; himself shaking
the while, and starting from his course as though unable
to command his limbs, and waving a sunshade which he
carries. *Vuninduvu*, "the chief man," was, on the particular occasion to which I have referred, armed with a
battle-axe, and exciting himself for his performances.
Mbovoro capered about with a cocoa-nut, which, when he
had summoned sufficient courage, was to be broken by a
violent blow on his bent knee. *Lingavatu* took the easier
method of pounding or pelting his nut with a stone.
These feats accomplished show that the gods are helping
them, and all are encouraged to call and whistle to the
deities to enter their votaries, each of whom becomes
excited into a frenzy. *Ai Vakathambe* calls amain for
his god, and *Matavutha* shoots at him, or at a nut he
holds under his right arm, while all shake like creatures
possessed. In some cases *Kau-ni-niu* holds the nut. The
others, as they persuade themselves that the god has
entered them, present themselves to the *Vuninduvu* to be
struck on the top of the abdomen, believing that if the god
is in them, they cannot be wounded by the axe, or spear, or

musket, whichever may happen to be used. These orgies are free from any pollution or licentiousness, but are, nevertheless, accompanied by their own evils. They encourage idleness, and injure the parties concerned by depriving them of proper food; while, if the *Vuninduvu* is over-simple or over-zealous, he is sure to kill some of the actors engaged.

Pilgrimages are sometimes made to Nai Thombothombo, the northern point of Mbua Bay, and the spot whence the spirits of the departed embark for the abode of Ndengei. I have known persons from a distance, who expected that they should see there both ghosts and gods. When contrasted with the bays between which it stands, this is a most beautiful spot. The shore gradually rises from high-water mark for a short distance, and then succeed abrupt, precipitous cliffs, about fifty feet high, having their rocky face richly draped with creeping plants. Further in, the land is wooded with large forest trees, the shade of whose foliage, with the softened gloom cast by the neighbouring rocks, gives to this scene an air of hallowed repose, well calculated to foster the native superstitions which crowd it with awful beings from the spirit-world, and to produce impressions of deep solemnity on the most enlightened minds.

The Fijian peoples with invisible beings every remarkable spot, especially the lonely dell, the gloomy cave, the desolate rock, and the deep forest. Many of these unseen spirits, he believes, are on the alert to do him harm, and hence he is kept in fear. When passing the territories of any of these, he piously casts a few leaves where many others have done so before him, and steps lightly along, hoping that he has propitiated the demon of the place. A path, part of the way to Nai Thombothombo, was one on which I had often to go. In one place it penetrated a shady defile, at the entrance of which, it is said, *Lewa-levu* —"the Great Woman"—watches to carry off such men as please her fancy; and, from the heap of leaves, I judge that few men pass that way without propitiating the Great

Woman, and leaving a proof that they consider themselves attractive enough to excite her affection.

Among the rincipal objects of Fijian superstition may be enumerated demons, ghosts, witches, wizards, wise-men, fairies, evil eyes, god-eyes, seers, and priests, all of whom he believes to be more or less possessed of super-natural power, and reverences accordingly. A very old Fijian used to talk to me of "those little gods" with as strong a faith as that of a Highlander in his fairies. And these "little gods" are the fairies of Fiji. "When living near the Kauvandra, I often used to hear them sing," said the old man ; and the recollection brightened his eye, as he went on to tell how they would assemble in troops on the top of the mountains, and sing unweariedly. "They were all little, like your sons : " (then six and five years old :) " I have often seen them, and this is the song I have heard them sing :—

> "' Ready for the digging are the *rukuruku* and the *raurau ;*
> And abundantly ready is my favourite *toarau ;*
> And ready at the same time is the yam of Nggalau.
>   The unwearied ones, ye !

> "' Bound, at one spring, to the top of the mountain ;
> Bound, at two springs, to the top of the mountain ;
> Let us gaze on the ocean returned to its fountain.
>   The low tides, ye !' " *

The *Ndrundru sambo* of Vanua Levu is a warlock in mischief, but not in invulnerability. He is thus described by the natives : In appearance, a man of high stature, of a grey colour, with a head *like an English dish ;* he breathes hard, and the noise of his going is like striking a hard shell with the back of a knife. He stands charged with stealing from fishermen the fish which they bring

---

* " *Bota rukuruku, boto raurau ;*
    Sa bini bota qou toarau ;
    Bota kaya na uvi ni Qalau ;
        Sa covi wai, ye !

  " *Teki vakadua ki ulu-ni-koro ;*
    Teki wakarua ki ulu-ni-koro ;
    Ta qoroya na taci ni meda boro.
        Na taci, ye !"

ashore at night, helping himself to reserved scraps of food, —and many such misdemeanours. I know a woman and her child whom he nearly frightened out of their wits, and whose screams brought me running to their assistance. Although he is a difficult mark, yet some skilful men have transfixed him; but, on being touched with a spear, he is instantly transformed into a rat.

Of apparitions the natives are very much afraid. They believe that the spirits of the dead appear frequently, and afflict mankind, especially when they are asleep. The spirits of slain men, unchaste women, and women who have died in childbed, they hold most in dread. I have known natives hide themselves for a few days, until they supposed the spirit of the dead was at rest. Spirits are supposed to assume the human form at will. Some tell us that they plant the tarawau, a tree bearing an acrid fruit. The notions of the people about the soul and its future state are very remarkable. While the Tongan restricted immortality to Chiefs, Matabules, and Muas, the Fijian has attributed spirits to animals, vegetables, stones, tools, and many other things, allowing that all may become immortal. Some speak of man as having two spirits. His shadow is called "the dark spirit," which, they say, goes to Hades. The other is his likeness reflected in water or a looking-glass, and is supposed to stay near the place in which a man dies. Probably this doctrine of shadows has to do with the notion of inanimate objects having spirits. I once placed a good-looking native suddenly before a mirror. He stood delighted. "Now," said he, softly, "I can see into the world of spirits." The *light spirit* of a murdered man is supposed to remain where the body fell. Hence such places are avoided, especially when it rains, because then the moans of the spirit are heard, as it sits up, endeavouring to relieve its pain by resting the head on the palms of its hands. Some say that these moans are caused by the soul of the murderer knocking down the soul of the slain, whenever it attempts to rise.

My informant on some of these points remarked rather

R

drily, "The old people were more apt to hear these moans than we of this day are." In one instance, at any rate, these dreaded sounds could be explained by natural causes. Na Saunimbua was slain in April, 1850. A few nights after his death, his wife visited the place where he fell, in order to *stroke* his spirit, as it was raining fast. On reaching the spot, she sat down and gave vent to her feelings in piercing cries. The slayers of her husband lived in a village close by, and, on hearing the noise of her lamentation, closed their houses securely, lest the spirit should come and injure them, saying, as they did so, "What a strong man Na Saunimbua must be ! Listen to his moans !"

It is believed, further, that the spirit of a man who still lives will leave the body to trouble other people when asleep. When any one faints or dies, their spirit, it is said, may sometimes be brought back by calling after it; and occasionally the ludicrous scene is witnessed of a stout man lying at full length, and bawling out lustily for the return of his own soul ! The visits of certain classic heroes to the lower world would at once be credited in Fiji; for some of its earlier inhabitants are said to have achieved a similar exploit while yet in the body.

The escape of the spirits of brutes and lifeless substances to Mbulu does not receive universal credit. Those who profess to have seen the souls of canoes, houses, plants, pots, or any artificial bodies, swimming, with other relics of this frail world, on the stream of the Kauvandra well, which bears them into the regions of immortality, believe this doctrine as a matter of course; and so do those who have seen the footmarks left about the same well by the ghosts of dogs, pigs, etc. On Vanua Levu it is admitted that such things evince a desire for immortality, and, when set free from their grosser parts, fly away for Mbulu by Nai Thombothombo, where a god named Mbolembole intercepts their flight, and appropriates them to his own use.

The native superstitions with regard to a future state go

far to explain the apparent indifference of the people about death; for, while believing in an eternal existence, they shut out from it the idea of any moral retribution in the shape either of reward or punishment. The first notion concerning death is that of simple rest, and is thus contained in one of their rhymes :—

"Death is easy :
Of what use is life ?
To die is rest." *

According to general opinion, the future world is to be much the same as the present. The Fijian Mbulu is the abode of departed spirits, where the good and the bad meet, and the road to which is long and difficult; for although we often hear the natives talk of going to Mbulu, as a plunge into the sea; and though every island, and nearly every town, has its Ndrakulu or Thimbathimba, yet these are but the portals where the spirit enters that mysterious path, the arrival at the termination of which is a precarious contingency.

Native traditions on this subject, which are variously modified in different localities, may be thus stated.

On the road to Nai Thombothombo, and about five miles from it, is a solitary hill of hard reddish clay, spotted with black boulders, having on its right a pretty grove, and on the left cheerless hills. Its name is Takiveleyawa. When near this spot, the disembodied spirit throws the spirit of the whale's tooth which was placed in the hand of the corpse at burial, at a spiritual pandanus; having succeeded in hitting this, he ascends the hill, and there waits until joined by the spirits of his strangled wife or wives. Should he miss the mark, he is still supposed to remain in this solitary resting-place, bemoaning the want of affection on the part of his wife and friends, who are depriving him of his expected companions. And this is the lone spirit's lament : " How is this ? For a long time I planted food

* "A mate na rawarawa:
Me bula—na ka ni cava ?
A mate na cegu."

R 2

TAKIVELEYAWA.

for my wife, and it was also of great use to her friends: why, then, is she not allowed to follow me? Do my friends love me no better than this, after so many years of toil? Will no one, in love to me, strangle my wife?"

If the ghost be that of a bachelor, he has to avoid the grasp of the Great Woman, who lurks near, and pass on to meet a more dreaded foe. Of all Fijian spirits, that of a bachelor is most hardly used. Nangganangga—the bitter hater of bachelors—undertakes to see after their souls; and so untiring is his watch that, it is said, no unwedded spirit has ever yet reached the Elysium of Fiji. These hapless ones know that it would be in vain to try to escape the avenging god at high tide, and therefore avail themselves of low water, to steal round to the edge of the reef opposite Nai Thombothombo, trusting to the Charon of that district to see, pity, and ferry them over. Nangganangga sits by the fatal stone, and, as he laughs at their vain efforts to escape, tauntingly asks them whether they suppose that the tide will never flow again, and how they will elude him if it does. And with these gloomy monitions in its ears, the poor ghost wanders, until the returning tide lessens his range, and at last drives him shivering to the beach, where he is pursued and seized by Nangganangga, and, for the unpardonable offence of bachelorhood, is dashed in pieces on the large black stone, just as one shatters rotten fire-wood.

We now return to the soliloquizing husband, who, blessed at last with the company of his wife or wives, who bear his train, or sad because of their absence, advances towards Nai Thombothombo, and, club in hand, boards the canoe which carries spirits to meet their examiner. Notice of his approach is given by a paroquet, which cries once, twice, and so on, according to the number of spirits in the canoe, announcing a great number by chattering. The highway to Mbulu lies through Nambanggatai, which, it seems, is at once a real and unreal town, the visible part being occupied by ordinary mortals, while in the unseen portion dwells the family who hold inquest on departed spirits. Thus the cry of the bird answers a two-fold purpose, warning the people to set open their doors that the spirit may have a free course, and preventing the ghostly inquisitors from being taken by surprise. The houses in this town are built with reference to a peculiarity in the locomotion of spirits, who are supposed at this stage to pass straight forward; hence all the doorways are opposite to each other, so that the shade may pass through without interruption. The inhabitants speak in low tones, and, if separated by a little distance, communicate their thoughts by signs.

Bygone generations had to meet Samu or Ravuyalo; but as he died in 1847 by a curious misfortune, his duties now devolve on his sons, who, having been long in partnership with their illustrious father, are quite competent to carry on his office. As it is probable that the elder son will shortly receive the paternal title or an equivalent, we will speak of him as Samuyalo, the "Killer of souls." On hearing the paroquet, Samu and his brothers hide them-

selves in some spiritual mangrove bushes, just beyond the
town, and alongside of the path, in which they stick a reed
as a prohibition to the spirit to pass that way. Should the
comer be courageous, he raises his club in defiance of the
tabu and those who placed it there; whereupon Samu
appears, to give him battle, first asking, "Who are you,
and whence do you come?" As many carry their inveterate habit of lying into another world, they make themselves out to be of vast importance, and to such Samu
gives the lie, and fells them to the ground. Should the
ghost conquer in the combat, he passes on to the judgment-
seat of Ndengei; but if wounded, he is disqualified for
appearing there, and is doomed to wander among the
mountains. If he be killed in the encounter, he is cooked
and eaten by Samu and his brethren.

Some traditions put the examination questions into the
mouth of Samu, and judge the spirit at this stage; but the
greater number refer the inquisition to Ndengei.

Those who escape the club of the Soul-destroyer, walk on
to Naindelinde, one of the highest peaks of the Kauvandra
mountains. Here the path to Mbulu ends abruptly at the
brink of a precipice, the base of which is said to be washed
by a deep lake. Beyond this precipice projects a large
steer-oar, which one tradition puts in the charge of
Ndengei himself, but another, more consistently, in the keeping of an old man and his son, who act under the direction
of the god. These accost the coming spirit thus: "Under
what circumstances do you come to us? How did you
conduct yourself in the other world?" If the ghost should
be one of rank, he answers, "I am a great Chief. I lived
as a Chief, and my conduct was that of a Chief. I had
great wealth, many wives, and ruled over a powerful
people. I have destroyed many towns, and slain many in
war." To this the reply is, "Good, good. Take a seat
on the broad part of this oar, and refresh yourself in the
cool breeze." No sooner is he seated, than they lift the
handle of the oar, which lies inland, and he is thus thrown
down headlong into the deep waters below, through which

he passes to Murimuria. Such as have gained the special favour of Ndengei are warned not to go out on the oar, but to sit near those who hold it, and, after a short repose, are sent back to the place whence they came, to be deified.

Murimuria seems to be a district of inferior happiness in Mbulu, which is divided into distinct parts, and punishment and enjoyment awarded to its inmates, but not for offence or merit of a moral kind. Mburotu is the Fijian Elysium, and in its description the most glowing language is used. Scented groves and pleasant glades, smiled upon by an unclouded sky, form the retreat of those who dwell in this blest region, where there is an abundance of all that a native deems most to be desired. Such are the delights of Mburotu, that the word is used proverbially to describe any uncommon joy.

In most parts of Mbulu the inhabitants plant, live in families, fight, and, in short, do much as people in this world. They are said, however, to be larger than when on earth. Mention is made in native traditions of first, second, and third heavens; but the terms do not appear to convey any definite idea. Various punishments are inflicted upon those who have not lived so as to please the gods. Some are laid in rows on their faces, and converted into taro beds. Those who have not had their ears bored are doomed to carry for ever on their shoulders the log of wood on which cloth is beaten, jeered at by all who see them. Women that are not tattooed are chased by their own sex, who tear and cut them with sharp shells, giving them no respite; or they are scraped up, and made into bread for the gods. Men who have not slain an enemy are sentenced to beat a heap of filth with a club, because they used that weapon so badly while in the body. A native regards this as the most degrading of all punishments.

It thus appears that, although the Fijians allow a spirit to almost everything, they dispose of them in such a way that few attain to immortality. The spirits of meats and drinks are consumed by the gods, who also eat the souls of all whose bodies are devoured by the people. The souls of animals, etc., are appropriated by Mbolembole. Lewa Levu gets a share of the best-looking ghosts, and those of the bachelors all fall to Nanggananga. Samu and his brothers consume a great number. Mbati-ndua roasts all that belong to, but do not obey, him; and a further deduction must be made for the souls which are killed by men. Thus few, comparatively, are left to inhabit the regions of Mbulu, and the immortality even of these is sometimes disputed. The belief in a future state is universal in Fiji; but their superstitious notions often border upon transmigration, and sometimes teach an eventual annihilation.

The existence of witchcraft has already been noticed; and of all their superstitions, this exerts the strongest influence on the minds of the people. Men who laugh at the pretensions of the priest tremble at the power of the wizard; and those who become Christians lose this fear last of all the relics of their heathenism. Professed practisers of witchcraft are dreaded by all classes, and, by destroying mutual confidence, shake y the security and comfort of society. Some of these persons, but not all, are priests. Any suggestion of malice or envy may become a cause for bewitching a person. Theft is detected and punished by the same agen y. The design of the charms used is to destroy life, and most persons who have a long illness ascribe it to witchcraft.

One mode of operating is to bury a cocoa-nut, with the eye upwards, beneath the temple-hearth, on which a fire is kept constantly burning; and as the life of the nut is destroyed, so the health of the person it represents will fail, till death ensues. At Matuku there is a grove sacred to the god Tokalau—the wind. The priest promises the destruction of any hated person in four days, if those who wish his death bring a portion of his hair, dress, or food which he has left. This priest keeps a fire burning, and approaches the place on his hands and knees. If the victim bathe before the fourth day, the spell is broken.

The most common method, however, is the *Vakadranikau*, or compounding of certain leaves supposed to possess a magical power, and which are wrapped in other leaves, or put into a small bamboo case, and buried in the garden of the person to be bewitched, or hidden in the thatch of his house. Processes of this kind are the most dreaded, and the people about Mbua are reputed to prepare the most potent compounds. The native imagination is so absolutely under the control of fear of these charms, that persons, hearing that they were the objects of such spells, have lain down on their mats, and died through fear.

Those who have reason to suspect others of plotting against them avoid eating in their presence, or are careful to leave no fragment of food behind; they also dispose their garment so that no part can be removed. Most natives, on cutting their hair, hide what is cut off in the thatch of their own homes. Some build themselves a small house and surround it with a moat, believing that a little water will neutralize the charms which are directed against them. Those who suppose themselves to be under the power of a wizard, make offerings to the gods, or use counter spells, or bring presents to the Chief in whose domain the magician is thought to reside.

The evil-working power of these men may be purchased, and generally the pay is high. Nearly all sudden deaths are ascribed to this cause. Persons detected in the act of burying these deadly charms are summarily dealt with; or if found out afterwards, their houses are burnt, and they themselves killed.

Sticks or reeds are sometimes placed in gardens so as to wound trespassers. Superstitious forms attend their preparation, and they may be had warranted to infect the wounded intruder with ulcers, or dropsy, or leprosy. A milder agency, called *tabu gasau*, is often used in gardens. Several reeds are thrust into the earth, and their tops brought together and inserted in a banana or nut. This is done to produce boils on any person who may rob the garden.

The *yalovaki* is an ordeal much dreaded in the windward islands. When the evidence is strong against persons suspected of some offence, and yet they refuse to confess, the Chief, who is judge, calls for a scarf, with which "to catch away the soul of the rogue." A threat of the rack could not be more effectual. The culprit generally confesses on the sight and even the mention of the light instrument: if not, it would be waved over his head until his soul was secured, and then carefully folded up and nailed to the small end of a Chief's canoe; and, for want of his soul, the suspected person would pine and die.

An innocent conceit is entertained by the Lakembans. Some distance from the chief town is a small hill, having a plot of short reeds on the top. Whenever I passed, many of these reeds were tied together at the top, which, I found, was done by travellers in order to prevent the sun from setting before they reached their journey's end. On the same island baskets of earth were hung on a branch or pole in the yam-gardens, to attract the notice of the birds and make them chirp, as the yam-sets are supposed to hasten to sprout at their call.

Belief in second-sighted persons, dread of a thing falling on them which they are about to carry, faith in dreams, praying for those who sneeze, and planting the giant arum close by the doorway, to keep out death and the devil, are several forms of superstition in its Fijian development.

Although the traditions of Fiji constitute, for the most part, a series of wild and contradictory absurdities, yet some demand attention, shadowing forth, as they do, some of the great facts in the history of mankind, of which the Bible contains the exact and standard records.

A few specimens of the absurdities of native belief may be given first. The god Roko Mouta formerly took a walk along the coast of Viti Levu; and wherever his train touched, there all irregularities were swept away, and sandy beach left. But where he cast his train over his shoulder, the coast remained rocky.

Ndelai Loa, the highest hill on Ono, is said to be the top

of Korothau, a mountain in Viti Levu, a hundred and eighty miles distant. Two goddesses, wishing to add to the importance of Ono, stole away the top of this mountain in the night, but, being surprised by day-break, cast down their load about two miles short of the place they intended. In a very similar way the position of two rocks, Landotangane and Landoyalewa, between Ovalau and Moturiki, is accounted for, they having been intended to block up the Moturiki passage.

The substance of their traditionary account of the creation of man was thus stated by a Chief from the Kauvandra district. A small kind of hawk built its nest near the dwelling of Ndengei; and when it had laid two eggs, the god was so pleased with their appearance that he resolved to hatch them himself, and in due time, as the result of his incubation, there were produced two human infants, a boy and a girl. He removed them carefully to the foot of a large vesi tree, and placed one on either side of it, where they remained until they had attained to the size of children six years old. The boy then looked round the tree and discovered his companion, to whom he said, "Ndengei has made us two that we may people the earth." As they became hungry, Ndengei caused bananas, yams, and taro to grow round them. The bananas they tasted and approved; but the yams and taro they could not eat until the god had taught them the use of fire for cooking. In this manner they dwelt, and, becoming man and wife, had a numerous offspring, which, in process of time, peopled the world.

Another tradition describes Ndengei as giving life to the inferior animals, but not to man. Another represents him as more directly engaged in man's creation, but as having, like Brahma, made several clumsy failures in his first attempts. He was particularly unfortunate in framing the woman; so much so as to provoke the censure of a god named Roko Matu, who happened to meet the first specimen of womanhood, and at whose suggestion she was altered to her present form.

Ove is known in some parts of Fiji as a kind of continuous creator, on whom is laid the blame of all monsters
and malformations.   But the natives in other parts ascribe
the origin of these to different deities.

They speak of a deluge which, according to some of their
accounts, was partial, but in others is stated to have been
universal.   The cause of this great flood was the killing of
Turukawa—a favourite bird belonging to Ndengei—by two
mischievous lads, the grandsons of the god.   These, instead
of apologizing for their offence, added insolent language to
the outrage, and, fortifying, with the assistance of their
friends, the town in which they lived, defied Ndengei to do
his worst.   It is said that, although the angry god took
three months to collect his forces, he was unable to subdue
the rebels, and, disbanding his army, resolved on more efficient revenge.   At his command the dark clouds gathered
and burst, pouring streams on the devoted earth.   Towns,
hills, mountains were successively submerged; but the rebels,
secure in the superior height of their own dwelling-place,
looked on without concern.   But when, at last, the terrible
surges invaded their fortress, they cried for direction to a
god, who, according to one account, instructed them to
form a float of the fruit of the shaddock; according to
another, sent two canoes for their use; or, says a third,
taught them how to build a canoe, and thus secure their
own safety.   All agree that the highest places were covered,
and the remnant of the human race saved in some kind of
vessel, which was at last left by the subsiding waters on
Mbengga: hence the Mbenggans draw their claim to stand
first in Fijian rank.   The number saved—eight—exactly
accords with the "few" of the Scripture record.   By this
flood, it is said, two tribes of the human family became
extinct.   One consisted entirely of women, and the other
were distinguished by the appendage of a tail like that of
a dog.

The highest point of the island of Koro is associated with
the history of the flood.   Its name is Ngginggi-tangithi-Koro,
which conveys the idea of a little bird sitting there and

lamenting the drowned island. In this bird the Christians recognise Noah's dove on its second flight from the ark. I have heard a native, after listening to the incident as given by Moses, chant, " *Na qiqi sa tagici Koro ni yali:*" "The Qiqi laments over Koro, because it is lost."

SAVU FALLS.

Near Na Savu, Vanua Levu, the natives point out the site where, in former ages, men built a vast tower, being eager for astronomic information, and especially anxious to decide the difficult question as to whether the moon was inhabited. To effect their purpose, they cast up a high mound, and erected thereon a great building of timber. The tower had already risen far skyward, and the ambitious hopes of its industrious builders seemed near fulfilment, when the lower fastenings suddenly broke asunder, and scattered the workmen over every part of Fiji. It is remarkable that the people of Ono, the most distant island, say that they originally belonged to this locality; and it is still more remarkable that there exists a dialectic similarity between these extremes; and the inhabitants of each are *tauvu,* worshippers of the same god; and, in virtue of this, may take from each other what they like, and swear at each other without risk of giving offence.

Namosimalua, on hearing of the translation of Enoch and Elijah, at once named Kerukeru, a woman of Yaro, who was very good, but unkindly treated by her husband; so the gods, in consideration of her high character, removed her from this world without permitting her to die.

CHAPTER VIII.

LANGUAGE AND LITERATURE.

THE Fijian is not an isolated tongue like the old Etruscan, or the modern Chinese or Basque. It is a member of that wide-spread family of languages known as the Oceanic or Malayo-Polynesian type of human speech. From Formosa and Hawaii in the North Pacific as far south as to New Zealand, and from Easter Island below the tropic of Capricorn in longitude 109° west, across the South Pacific and Indian Oceans to Madagascar in 45° east longitude, languages are found to obtain, which less or more nearly resemble one another in their elementary sounds, their laws of syllabication, their vocabularies, and all their leading grammatical principles and processes. The language of the Malays and the Sumatrans is structurally that of the Malagasses ; and the Maori of the New Zealander is, to some extent, intelligible between three and four thousand miles away among the inhabitants of the Sandwich Islands. The principal features of the Malayo-Polynesian tongues may be exhibited in few words. Their alphabets exclude, for the most part, guttural and hissing sounds, and show a strong partiality for vowels, nasals, and liquids. Their syllables commonly consist either of a vowel alone, or of a single consonant followed by a vowel. The last syllable but one in a word is that upon which the accent is usually made to fall. The roots of these languages are generally dissyllabic, and the practice of reduplicating words has great favour with them. A dual as well as a plural number is recognised. Nouns rarely undergo any change to express the ideas of gender, number, or case ; and verbs have no inflexions properly so called. As in the Hotten-

tot tongue, the first personal and possessive pronoun, **when**
not in the singular, assumes different forms, according **as**
the "we," "us," or "our" is to be taken in what is **called**
an inclusive or an exclusive sense. The English **expres-**
sion, "Let us go," addressed by one individual to **another**
in the presence of a third, is equivocal. It may **either**
mean, "Let you and me go," shutting out the third **party,**
or, "Let us all three go together." No such **ambiguity**
can attach to the words in the mouth of a Polynesian.
In the former case, a Tongan, for example, would **say**
ke ta o, in the latter *ke tau o;* and other languages **of**
the Oceanic class make a similar distinction. In **regard**
to their syntax, the Malayo-Polynesian tongues **have**
little of the width, the elaborateness, or the symmetry **of**
the group of languages to which the English belongs.   At
the same time they are equally removed from the **chaotic,**
cramped, and ill-proportioned style of the Tartar, **the**
Chinese, and other leading tongues of Central and **Eastern**
Asia.   The expression of thought in Malayo-Polynesian **is**
simple, inartificial, flowing, and vigorous; and, as a **vehicle**
of Christian truth, whether by word of mouth or by **writing,**
the languages of this family will admit of **comparison**
with the capabilities of much more polished tongues.
    The characters, which have now been enumerated **as**
belonging to Malayo-Polynesian speech at large, are **all**
shared by the Fijian, of which a more minute account **will**
be acceptable to the students of language, and may not **be**
without its interest for the general reader.   It will **be**
necessary to premise, that Fijian is not a single **language,**
like that of the Friendly Islands, but is spoken in as **many**
as fifteen, probably in more than fifteen, dialects.   The **dis-**
tinction between some of these dialects is slight.   **Others**
of them are as unlike one another as the European
Spanish and Portuguese, or as the Bengali and **Mahratta**
of Northern India.   Not seldom their vocabularies **are**
quite dissimilar, the same ideas being represented by **terms**
differing in root as well as in form; and, in certain **cases,**
one or more of the elementary sounds of the language **are**

wanting; or, on the other hand, sounds obtain, which the bulk of the dialects do not acknowledge. The sound of the English *j*, for instance, is heard at Lakemba and in some of the neighbouring islands; while the Somosomo dialect has no *k*, and that of Rakiraki and other parts excludes *t*. The Missionaries are acquainted, more or less, with about seven dialects, and books have been printed in four of them, namely, in those of Mbau, Rewa, Somosomo, and Lakemba. Mbau, however, is at once the Athens and the Rome of Fiji; and it is the language as spoken there, into which the Scriptures have been translated, and of which the following statements are mostly designed to be illustrative.

The simple vowel sounds, both long and short, which are found in the Italian and other European tongues, are those which obtain in Fijian, though with a less open expression in the case of one or two of them. The compound vowels are *ai, au, ei, eu, oi, ou,* and *iu,* the separate elements in each being distinctly uttered. The consonantal part of the language excludes the sounds of the English aspirate, the *ch* of "chink," "churl," and the like, the soft *g* or *j*,* the *th* as heard in "thistle," "thought," and "truth," and the composites *x* and *z*. The letter *c* is used to represent the sound of *th* in "though," "that," which is of constant occurrence in Fijian; *g* answers to the *ng* in "ring," "swing," etc.; *k* is occasionally read as *g* in "guest;" thus Rakiraki, mentioned above, is pronounced *Ragiragi;* and *q* answers either to the English *nk* in "banker," or, which is much more commonly the case, to the *ng* in such words as "linger" and "mangle." The sounds of *d* and *b*, even though standing, where they continually stand, at the beginning of a word, are never enunciated without a nasal before them, *n* being heard before *d*,

* The last two, however, are both found in the Lakemba dialect, as, for instance, the *j* in the name *Fiji,* which is the designation of the group to windward. The presence of these sounds in this dialect may perhaps be traced to the fact, that Lakemba is the chief island of the group nearest to Tonga, and the one which has always had the most intercourse with the Tongans. The *F* sound in the name *Fiji* is to be accounted for in the same way.

m before *b*. Thus Doi, one of the islands, is pronounced Ndoi, and Bau, Mbau. *P* is only used in the Mbau dialect in foreign words, or in such as have been introduced from other dialects. *F* too is an exotic. Fijian stands almost alone among its fellows in possessing the sound of *s*. It is doubtful whether any Polynesian people employ this sound, with the exception of the Samoans and the Fijians; and it is much more frequent in the tongue of the latter than in that of the former. The general law of the Polynesian syllable, as already laid down, is strictly observed in the Fijian language, subject only to the qualifications, which the invariable use of the nasal before *d* and *b*, and the occurrence of the sounds represented by *q*, may be thought to require; together with the further fact, that *r* is not uncommonly employed after *d*, as in *dra*, "blood," *drodro*, "a current."

Fijian, like the Maori and others of the Polynesian languages, is rich in articles; *ko* or *o*, and *koi* or *oi*, answering under fixed rules to the English "the;" and *a* or *ai*, *na* or *nai*, being used, both before singular and non-singular nouns, when the meaning is indefinite.

The noun is either primitive or derived. Very many words are employed, at the will of the speaker, either as nouns or verbs. Many nouns expressing habit, character, mode of life, and the like, are formed by prefixing a frequentative particle *dau* to a verbal term. For example, from *vosa*, "to talk," comes *dauvosa*, "one who talks incessantly," "a chatter-box." Diminutives are made by reduplication; thus *vale* is a "house," *valevale*, a "little house," a "canoe house;" and so *vesivesi* is a "little spear," from *vesi*, a "spear."

Artificial gender is unknown to the language. When it is necessary to distinguish the sexes, *tagane*, "male," and *alewa*, "female," are put after nouns. Thus, while *gone* is "child," *a gone tagane* is "a boy," *a gone alewa*, "a girl." Number is not indicated by any change in the termination of a noun. Sometimes the personal pronouns corresponding to the English "he" and "they" are used to express the singular and the dual or plural respectively. In other cases the singular is denoted by the numeral *dua,* " one," and the particle *vei,* either with or without reduplication of the noun, is put before it for the purpose of giving it a plural meaning.

It is a remarkable feature of the language, though not limited to Fijian, that it has certain nouns which convey the idea of a specific number of things, such number being chiefly ten. Thus *sole* means " ten bread-fruits," *sasa,* " ten mats," *rara,* " ten pigs," *bure,* "ten clubs," while *bola* is " a hundred canoes," and *selavo,* " a thousand cocoa-nuts." All these words take numerals with them, like other nouns. *Sasa,* for example, with *tolu,* " three," before it, denotes three times ten, or thirty mats, and so of the rest.

The cases of nouns, so far as the language acknowledges them, are made by prefix particles. The nominative and objective are often alike. The possessive is indicated, with several nice distinctions, by the signs *ni* and *i,* or by the use of possessive pronouns. In such compound terms as " a basket of fish," " a bottle of water," where " of " is employed in the sense of "containing," the Fijian never uses a sign of possession, but always puts them as if they were written, " a basket fish," " a bottle water."

Many adjectives are primitive words. Derivatives are formed partly by the reduplication of nouns and verbs, partly by prefixing to substantives and other words the dissyllable *vaka,* which has the force of the English *ly* in " lovely," or else conveys the idea of possession. *Vakawere,* for instance, is " garden-having," and *vakatamata* is " manlike," from *were,* " garden," and *tamata,* " man ;" and such forms as *vulavula,* " white," *dredre,* " difficult," *lialia,* " silly," are of perpetual occurrence. Besides the derivative adjectives there are likewise compounds, which may be compared with such expressions as the English " sin-stained," "wind-swept," and others. The language has no special signs for representing the higher or lower degrees of the quality expressed by an adjective. In the absence of

such signs it either employs intensifying or depreciating
particles for the purpose of comparison, or it uses the posi-
tive in such a way as to answer the same object, or, yet
again, it gives the qualification it desires by adopting a particular arrangement of words in a sentence.

The pronominal system of the language is full of interest.
The circumstance that its demonstratives and interrogatives
are few and simple, is one which has its parallel in many
tongues. Nor is it very surprising that it dispenses with
the use of a specific form for the relative. The personal and
possessive pronouns, in Fijian, however, are a linguistic
raree-show. Most languages are content to use their pronouns of these classes in two numbers. The Fijian is not
satisfied with fewer than four; for it adds a dual and a triad
to the ordinary singular and plural forms. Thus the " our"
of the English may be represented now by *a nodaru*, now
by *a nodatou*, now by *a noda*, according as it refers to two
persons, or to three, or to many. The triad number is also
employed when a few are intended. The use of inclusive
and exclusive forms of the first personal and possessive
pronoun has been already named as a feature of Malayo-
Polynesian language in general. This distinction in Fijian
is carried through the dual, triad, and plural numbers alike,
so that, for example, there are as many as six separate
words in the language answering to the one English " we."
In addition to these characters, which the language shares
with the Tongan and some other Oceanic tongues, Fijian
has the further peculiarity—and in this perhaps it is
unique—that it varies the form of the possessives according as the nouns with which they are connected are names
of eatables, drinkables, or things of neither of these classes.
Let the Englishman who wishes to say, " My house, my
cheese, and my cider," be required by the laws of his
language to use a separate form of the " my " in each of
these three combinations, because cider is something to be
drunk, cheese something to be eaten, and house neither the
one nor the other; he will express himself with the nicety
on which the Fijian insists in this respect.

The correspondence between the numerals of the language and those of even the most distant members of the Malayo-Polynesian family of tongues is truly surprising. *Dua, rua, tolu, va, lima, ono, vitu, walu, ciwa,* and *tini,* the Fijian cardinals from one to ten, are forms to which the Malayan, the Hawaiian, the Maori, the Malagasse, and all their fellows present striking resemblances ; nor are they wanting in a family likeness, which connects them with languages belonging to others of the great groups into which the universal speech of mankind may be distributed. Ordinals are made in Fijian by prefixing *ka* to the cardinals. Like the Latin *bini, trini,* etc., it has also distributives, which it forms from the cardinals by putting before them *ya* or *tauya ;* thus *yalima* or *tauyalima* is "five a-piece," "five each," and so on. Beside these the language contains a distinct series of numerals which have a collective or defi-nite sense, "the one" or "one only," "the two" or "two only," etc. ; something like the Greek *monas, duas,* and their compeers. The definites or collectives are the cardinals wholly or partially reduplicated. Finally, by the use of the prefix *vaka* with the cardinals, Fijian furnishes itself with numeral adverbs equivalent to the English "once," twice," "thrice," and that with a completness and a consistency, which neither the Latin, nor the Greek, nor the Sanscrit itself can rival.

The doctrine of the verb in Fijian is large and complex. Its root form is always either monosyllabic or dissyllabic. The sources from which the derived verbs spring, as in other languages, are various. Substantives and adjectives, however, are the classes of words, which yield the bulk of them. Some are formed by adding *na* to a noun; thus, from *buka,* "fuel," comes *bukana,* "to add fuel." Others, like *cata,* "to hate," are made from adjectives, by append-ing the syllable *ta,* or, which is more common, by at once prefixing *vaka* and adding *taka.* What is most observable, however, in the Fijian verb is the peculiar manner in which it sets forth to the eye and ear the different ideas ex-pressed by words of this class, whether considered in them-

selves, or in their syntactical relations to other words. The
notions which the English expresses by such terms as
"lie," "sleep," "rest," on the one hand, and by such as
"consider," "strive," "walk," on the other, are essentially
unlike; yet the language makes no external distinction
between the two classes. It is otherwise in Fijian; for
verbs of the latter order, which imply voluntary action,
though to the exclusion of an object, are usually reduplicate
in form, while those of the former are for the most part
simple roots. Again, it is sometimes the case in English
that neuter verbs are used with a substantive after them;
thus, we say, "He sits his horse well," making "sit" to
govern "horse," though naturally incapable of exercising
such a power. With few exceptions, however, when we
wish to indicate any relation between a verb of this sort
and an object noun, we employ a preposition. The Fijian
does not commonly adopt the latter method. On the other
hand, it can give all its unreduplicated neuters a transitive
force by appending to them certain formative particles. On
this principle *mocera* is "to sleep upon," from *moce*, "to
sleep;" *qalova* is "to swim to," from *qalo*, "to swim;"
and *drotaki* is "to flee from," from *dro*, "to flee." Further,
a distinction in the use of verbs transitive prevails in Fijian,
which is perhaps without a parallel in any other tongue.
In their simple form they require that the nouns they
govern shall stand immediately after them without the intervention of an article or other word, and they represent
actions in an indeterminate and general manner; thus, *me
vau waqa* is "to fasten canoe," *me voli ka* is "to purchase
things." But if the object of such a verb in the mind of
the speaker be definite, if, for example, he wishes to speak
of fastening "a canoe," or "the canoe," the governed
noun, whether it precedes the verb or follows it, must have
an article, and the verb receives one of a series of affixes
used for the purpose, the chief of these being *a, ka, ta, ca,
na, va*, and *ya*, with the dissyllables *taka, raka*, and *vaka*.
The affix which any particular verb receives is determined
by laws that have not as yet been very accurately traced.
The Mbau dialect not unfrequently accents the last syllable

of verbs ending in *a*, instead of appending to them a particle of definition. The Fijian passive is made in various ways. Sometimes the simple form of the verb is employed, the meaning being fixed by the context. Sometimes the definite affixes just named are used for this purpose, their final *a* being changed to *i*. In other cases certain particles, *ka, ta, ra,* etc., prefixed to the verb, convey the passive sense. The last method is resorted to when a thing has come of itself, or when either the person who did it is unknown, or it is not thought well to mention him. *Dau* put before a verb either intensifies the idea of it, or denotes the frequent repetition of the state or action expressed by the verb. In like manner *vaka* before verbs has a causative power, and *vei* carries with it the notion of what is reciprocal or customary.

Tense and mood are represented in Fijian by certain independent words, which the language puts before the verbal form. Thus, *sa, ka* or *a,* and *na,* with certain equivalents, answer in general to the present, past, and future respectively; and *me* or *mo* makes a verb imperative, conditional, or infinitive.

In regard to the subordinate parts of the language, which have not as yet passed under review, the adverb, preposition, and conjunction, little needs to be said. The language is poor in the last two classes of words, and, for the first, it either makes use of separate terms like *eke*, " here," and *sega,* " not," or it creates forms from adjectives by prefixing *vaka,* the equivalent of the German adverbial ending *lich,* and the English *ly.* The expletives of the language, or, as they are called by the natives, "the ornaments of speech," are singularly numerous, and it is a piece of Fijian affectation to crowd as many of them as possible into sentences. Greek itself is often out-Greeked by these dainty word-worshippers of the Southern Sea.

The general character of the Malayo-Polynesian syntax was explained in the outset, and it is not necessary that many details should be given with respect to this feature of the. Fijian. Adjectives are put after their nouns when they are used attributively, before them when they stand as the predicates of propositions. The English expression, " the good man," appears in Fijian, " the man good; " the sentence, " The man is good," would be written, " Good is the man." The possessive pronoun precedes the noun with which it is joined, unless such noun imply relationship, or be the name of a member of the body, or of a part of any- thing, in which case the pronoun is put after it. Demon- strative pronouns follow their nouns. Verbs usually have their nominatives after them. When the nominative takes the lead, it is used absolutely. Personal pronouns, how- ever, do not come under this law; for they always go before their verbs. Adverbs follow the words they qualify.

Once more, it is interesting to find the language distin- guishing between the so called genitive of subject and genitive of object in the use of its noun. The term, " the Gospel of God," is equivocal in English. I may mean either " the Gospel of which God is the author," that is to say, the " of God " may be the genitive of subject; or it may mean, " the Gospel which has reference to God," where the " of God " is the genitive of object. In the latter case the Fijian uses the particle *ni* before the governed word, to express the objective meaning.

What the number of radical words in Fijian may be, it is difficult to conjecture. Its vocabulary is probably richer than that of many other Oceanic tongues. For relation- ships, for the smaller divisions of time, for metals, colours, etc., the language has few terms; but this is not the case with most other classes of ideas and objects. Whatever belongs to their religion, their political constitution, their wars, their social and domestic habits, their occupations and handicrafts, their amusements, and a multitude of par- ticulars besides relating either to themselves or to the sphere of their personal and national life, they not only express with propriety and ease, but in many instances with a minuteness of representation and a nicety of colouring, which it is hard to reproduce in a foreign language. Thus the Fijian can express by different words the motion of a snake and that of a caterpillar, with the clapping of the hands lengthwise, crosswise, or in almost any other way; it has three words for " a bunch," five for " a pair," six for " cocoa-nut oil," and seven for " a handle ; " for " the being close together " and for " the end " it has five terms each, for " fatigue " and " thin " seven each, with no fewer than eleven for " dirty ; " for the verb " to thank " it has two words, for " to pluck " four ; for " to carry, command, entice, lie, raise," it has five each ; for " to creep, return, pierce, see, squeeze," six each ; for " to care, draw, roll," seven each ; for " to make, place, push, turn," eight each ; for " to seize and split," nine each ; with four- teen for " to cut," and sixteen for " to strike." One other illustration of the copiousness of the language is worth mention. The Greek and other cultivated tongues have different words for " to wash," according as the operation has reference to the body, or to clothes and the like ; and, where the body is spoken of, their synonyms will some- times define the limb or part which is the subject of the action. The Fijian leaves these languages far behind ; for it can avail itself of separate terms to express the washing process, according as it may happen to affect the head, face, hands, feet, and body of an individual, or his apparel, his dishes, or his floor.

Fijian literature is in its cradle, but its infancy gives promise of a vigorous and energetic manhood. The New Testament and other parts of Scripture are printed in the language, and the Missionaries have published some useful books besides. These last, as the case of the people has affectingly required, have been, as yet, taken up for the most part with religious and moral subjects. As soon as possible, elementary works on various branches of general knowledge will be supplied for the use of the Mission schools.

In the year 1850, two literary productions of great merit issued from the Wesleyan Mission press at Viwa : the one a Grammar of the language, the other a Fijian-English and English-Fijian Dictionary, both by the late laborious and excellent Missionary—who did so much towards preparing the way for the forthcoming Fijian translation of the Old Tes- tament,—the Rev. David Hazlewood. This is a name which

s 5

ought not to die. Mr. Hazlewood's predecessors and contemporaries had studied the language; they had represented it by an alphabet, which all philologists will confess to be at once appropriate, simple, and scientific; they had collected vocabularies, and lists of phrases and idioms; they had printed numerous translations and original compositions in Fijian; they had provided themselves with manuscript illustrations of its system of sounds, of its general structure, and of its leading peculiarities: it was reserved for him to draw up and publish the first Grammar and Dictionary of the language properly so called. Mr. Hazlewood's Grammar is a book upon which the Bopps and Grimms of Germany will look with respect, for its philosophical accuracy and completeness, at the same time that they eagerly drink up its precious philology. In point of simplicity, comprehensiveness, and scholarly handling of its subject, it is a worthy associate of a Grammar of the Kafir tongue, which a Wesleyan Missionary in South Africa, the Rev. John W. Appleyard, published in the same year, and which is one of the most valuable contributions to linguistic science, that the world has received for many years past. Mr. Hazlewood's Dictionary is a work of great pains, and both the selection and the arrangement of his materials are such as might be looked for from the author of the Fijian Grammar. Appended to the Dictionary are two important tracts; the one being a list of the Fiji Islands, with their bearings and distances from either Mbau or Lakemba, so far as they are known; the other containing the names of the leading objects belonging to the natural history of the country, as plants, fishes, insects, and the like.

With a language such as has now been described, and with the blessing of God upon the continued labours of Christian Missionaries among a people so strong-minded, so enterprising, and so versatile as are the subjects of this volume, there is no reason why Fijian literature should not by and by take rank with the noblest cultures, to which the Gospel is at present shaping the genius and heart of so many heathen populations of our globe.

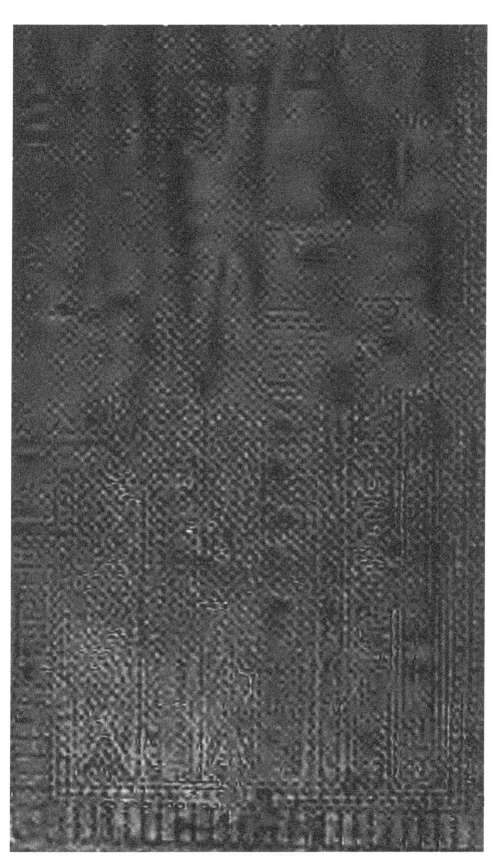

CPSIA information can be obtained
at www.ICGtesting.com
Printed in the USA
LVHW02s1255281017
554131LV00024B/80/P